**The Great Bibliographers Series
edited by Norman Horrocks**

1. *Ronald Brunlees McKerrow,* by John Philip Immroth. 1974.
2. *Alfred William Pollard,* by Fred W. Roper. 1976.
3. *Thomas Frognall Dibdin,* by Victor E. Neuburg. 1978.
4. *Douglas C. McMurtrie,* by Scott Bruntjen and Melissa L. Young. 1979.
5. *Michael Sadleir,* by Roy Stokes. 1980.
6. *Henry Bradshaw,* by Roy Stokes. 1984.

Henry Bradshaw
1831–1886

Roy Stokes

The Great Bibliographers Series, No. 6

The Scarecrow Press, Inc.
Metuchen, N.J. and London
1984

Library of Congress Cataloging in Publication Data

Stokes, Roy Bishop, 1915-
   Henry Bradshaw, 1831-1886.

   (The Great bibliographers series ; no. 6)
   "Checklist of the writings of Henry Bradshaw": p.
   Includes index.
   1. Bradshaw, Henry, 1831-1886. 2. Bradshaw, Henry,
1831-1886--Bibliography. 3. Librarians--England--
Biography. 4. Bibliographers--England--Biography.
I. Bradshaw, Henry, 1831-1886. II. Title. III. Series.
Z720.B8S78 1984   010'.92'4   [B]   83-20445
ISBN 0-8108-1679-2

Copyright © 1984 by Roy Stokes
Manufactured in the United States of America

CONTENTS

I. Commentary 1

II. Checklist of the Writings of Henry Bradshaw 41

III. Excerpts from the Works of Henry Bradshaw 75
  1. On the recovery of the long lost Waldensian manuscripts 77
  2. Letter on the Codex Sinaiticus 95
  3. Letter on the Oriental Manuscripts in the Library of King's College, Cambridge 99
  4. Letter on the Lambeth Library 103
  5. The Printer of the Historia S. Albani 106
  6. Ancient Greek Manuscript of the Gospels 127
  7. List of the Founts of Type and Woodcut Devices Used by Printers in Holland in the 15th Century 132
  8. Francis Thynne's Animadversions ... 160
  9. Notice of a Fragment of the Fifteen Oes and Other Prayers Printed at Westminster by W. Caxton about 1490-91 164
  10. The Irish Monastic Missal at Oxford 174
  11. Letter on the Ovid Manuscript in the Bodleian 180
  12. Note on Mediaeval Service Books 182
  13. Godfried van der Haghen (G.H.), the Publisher of Tindale's Own Last Edition of the New Testament in 1534-35 188
  14. A Word on Size-Notation as distinguished from Form-Notation 208
  15. Query concerning "The Toyes of an Idle Head" 213

16.	Discovery of a St. Albans Book	216
17.	The Early Collection of Canons commonly known as the Hibernensis ...	221
18.	A Half-Century of Notes on the Day-Book of John Dorne ...	234
IV.	Index	267

SERIES EDITOR'S FOREWORD

This is the second volume in The Great Bibliographers Series to be prepared by Professor Roy Stokes. His earlier compilation dealt with Michael Sadleir whose expertise in nineteenth-century bibliography came from his background in publishing. Henry Bradshaw, the subject on the present volume, was a scholar and librarian, whose bibliographical interests were in a much earlier period than Sadleir's. Bradshaw's significant contributions to our knowledge of early writings are well brought out in Professor Stokes's biographical introduction which precedes a selection from Bradshaw's writings.

                              Norman Horrocks
                              Dalhousie University
                              Halifax, Nova Scotia
                              Canada

PART I

COMMENTARY

"By the death of Henry Bradshaw, Cambridge has lost one of the rarest of her scholars, Europe her first scientific bibliographer, and a narrower circle of personal friends one of the truest and purest characters. The loss is so unexpected, so irreparable, that we cannot yet realize its magnitude. To many Cambridge can never mean again what it has meant in the past; the centre of scholarly influence, the source of inspiration for earnest work and genuine research, has been taken from amongst us. We have the memory of his aims and of his method, but the master is no more."[1]

Obituary notices, especially nineteenth-century ones, are often fulsome in their praise and singularly lacking in objectivity. The anonymous columnist quoted here was expressing a genuinely and widely held regard which the passage of a hundred years has done nothing to diminish.

Bradshaw was born in London on 3rd February, 1831. His father was a banker and belonged to the Irish branch of an old English family which had long been settled in Cheshire and Derbyshire. Joseph Hoare Bradshaw, Henry's father, was a member of the banking firm of Barnett, Hoare and Co., with which he was connected through his mother, whose maiden name he bore. He was known as a scrupulously honest business man and was for many years a member of the Society of Friends, a practice which he ceased on his marriage to Catherine Stewart of

County Antrim, after which he brought up his family as members of the Church of England.

From the age of eight Henry was at school at the Temple Grove School at East Sheen where he stayed until 1843. It was a school which was destined to have two bibliographical connections within a short space of time because Montague Rhodes James was a student there from 1873 to 1876. In 1843 Bradshaw passed from Temple Grove to Eton and thence to King's College, Cambridge in 1850. By the time of his birthday in 1853 Bradshaw was qualified, by virtue of his three years of probation, to be elected as a Fellow of King's. He was also entitled to claim the old privilege of Kingsmen of obtaining the B.A. degree without examination. The cessation of this immunity was one of the hard-fought reformations at Cambridge in the middle of the nineteenth century. Examination became compulsory in 1856, but Bradshaw was one of those in an interim period when exemption could be claimed or the examination could be taken. He was one of the first of those who, approving strongly of the reforms, elected to sit the examination and in 1854 he was granted his degree.

By this time, when he was 23, several of Bradshaw's life-time interests had been clearly determined. His father had amassed a large library, including an important collection of Irish books which, on his death in 1845, were bequeathed to Henry. The son's tastes were similar to the father's and this collection formed the basis of his bibliographical studies. The books which he inherited from his father, together with those which he added over the years in the same fields of interest, formed the backbone of his own personal collection.

Once, and once only, did he consider, and take action on, selling some of his books. In 1862 he sent off to Sotheby's "twenty large cases containing rather more than two thousand volumes.... I have not sent off a stick of what my father left me, but only the best and choicest of those I have bought myself."[2] The results of the sale were a profound disappointment to him and when, many years later, it was suggested that he should sell some of his collection, he replied, "As for realizing money, I have had enough of selling books. I never did it but once, and I got just sixpence a volume for every pound that I gave, sometimes less. This was a sufficient dose."[3]

Later on, he had no doubts what to do in the dispersal of his own collection. His devotion to Cambridge University, and to its Library, took a pre-eminent position over virtually any other consideration. In 1867 he presented the library with twelve volumes of Sanskrit works printed in Bombay; in 1868 he gave fifty-eight incunabula, mostly printed by Ulrich Zel and other Cologne printers, the remainder being mainly Dutch, Flemish and French books. In 1869, several books including the first Prayer-book of Edward VI were donated and in 1870, another collection of incunabula.

The greatest gift of Bradshaw's was undoubtedly his second donation of 1870 when he presented the University Library with the whole of his Irish collection. The Library Report described it as "a collection of books and papers, pamphlets and broadsides, either (1) printed in Ireland, or (2) written by Irish authors, or (3) relating generally to Irish affairs, about 5,000 in number."[4] In the letter, dated March 30, 1870, which Bradshaw addressed to the Vice-Chancellor respecting this gift, he wrote, "literary men used to come to my father's house to work at these books when engaged in writing upon Irish affairs, and from the time that I was a child, they have had a particular interest for me. Although I have been able to give but little attention to them for some years past, yet I have by me a mass of bibliographical notes on the subject, collected during the last twenty years; and if I could feel that these books and papers were deposited in some more permanent resting-place than my own library, I should more readily try to put my notes in order so as to turn them to some practical use."[5]

It is quite clear in which direction Bradshaw's interests were tending even "from the time that I was a child." There are other indications which suggest concerns of similar importance which were later to be grafted on this central stem. It is a cliché to say of many people in a variety of scholarly fields that they were avid readers in their youth; perhaps it is even regarded as a prerequisite to that kind of life-time devotion. In Bradshaw's case there is documentary evidence of the reality of this claim. The books which were in his father's house were not simply a background to his youth; they led him to surround himself with books which were necessary for his daily living. "He brought up with him from Eton a library which both in size and character was unusual for a young man of his age. Among his papers I have found a complete catalogue of it, written out carefully in his neat, small hand. It numbered nearly five hundred volumes. About one-fifth of these were Latin and Greek books, or books connected with classical history and literature. Divinity, ecclesiastical history, and devotional works made up another fifth. The greater portion of the library consisted of English literature."[6] There was nothing unusual in the authors who made up his wide-ranging reading program, which was so discursive that it seems almost inappropriate to apply the idea of a "program" to it. One author, however, was to be of more than average interest to him when the mainstream of his life's work developed. In Prothero's words, "He studied Chaucer and read him aloud to one of his friends, showing as he did so that he had found out already how to read him and how to pronounce his rhyme-endings."[7] This attraction was to remain for him for many years to come.

The devotional works which formed a significant part of his Eton to King's library were, also, something more than a formal mid-nineteenth-century concession to popular taste. His interest was more in the church itself, its history, its architecture, and its ritual, rather than in theology. In the words of one contemporary friend, "His religious views were at that time those of what would then have been called a moderate High Churchman. He had no doubts or misgivings, and fully intended to take orders."[8] Out of this came another of his abiding preoccupations, various aspects of church history and, above all, his tremendous knowledge of the liturgy.

With deeply rooted interests in areas such as these it is difficult to predict exactly what a student might do immediately upon graduation. As things fell out, Bradshaw went in a direction which seemed to encompass several of his enthusiasms. He accepted an appointment as assistant-master at St. Columba's College, near Dublin. It had been founded in 1843 as a college of the High-Church movement to educate the clergy in divinity and the Irish language and also to act as a public school very much on the English model. Bradshaw had every intention at the time of his going to St. Columba's of entering holy orders. Gradually, with no loss of his faith, he abandoned this idea and he also discovered that he had no taste for teaching. He gave up the appointment in April 1856 and very soon afterwards entered upon the work which was to occupy him for the rest of his life.

In November 1856 Bradshaw was appointed as assistant librarian to Cambridge University Library, a position from which he resigned in October 1858. His reason for this action was clear. He had hoped that the appointment would permit him to follow more effectively his own lines of research and was disappointed when conditions proved unsuited to this objective. The release from the official position gave him the required leisure and he devoted himself to a thorough examination of the outstanding books in the library's collections. Before long a move was made by several of his friends to harness his activities more directly to the needs of the library. The Syndicate reported to the University Senate that "the department of manuscripts and early printed books stood in need of a thorough overhauling; that the bindings of the manuscripts should be properly repaired and re-lettered, and the manuscripts themselves re-arranged." They proposed "that authority be given to Mr. Bradshaw, of King's College, to carry into effect the above-mentioned suggestions, under the direction of the Library Syndicate, and to perform similar duties in regard to rare and early printed books."[9] The report was accepted in June 1859 and Bradshaw commenced work.

Bradshaw's life and career was, from this moment onwards, inextricably entwined with the University Library until his death. It was a career which was remarkably cohesive from the standpoint both of the areas of his interest and of the level at which he conducted his research. At an early stage of his life he demonstrated quite clearly which subjects were of interest to him and he was always conscious of the relationship between them. There was never truly a stage at which it would be possible to say that he had lost interest in any one area or that he ceased to work within it. It is equally true to say that the level of excellence which is normally thought of as being of Bradshaw quality was apparent from the outset. Although he gained in experience and added continually to the vast range of examples which he could cite with reference to any specific point, there are no examples of what seem to be specifically apprentice work. His mastery of the material was demonstrated very early on in his career and the quality never deteriorated. A chronological assessment of his work, consequently, is less indicative of his work as a whole than a consideration of it field by field.

Although Bradshaw always maintained that he was not a liturgist in the strict sense of the word, he had an acute understanding of the liturgy of the Church as conveyed in the medieval service books. These had always held a great fascination for him and he returned to a study of them time after time. It is clear, and not at all surprising, that his interest in the service books of the Church grew out of his own religious convictions. The study of the liturgy was for him a concern with something which was alive and vibrant, even though it was the books of the medieval period to which he devoted his attentions. He saw the connections between his own observances and the objects of his historical and bibliographical research. When he was in Venice in 1865, he wrote, "Yesterday evening [Maundy Thursday] we went to a service at St. Mark's, and it was with some difficulty we made out what the service was. Cornish has an 'Officium Septimanae Sacrae,' but we were long puzzled, until I noticed that after every one thing a candle on the great stand was put out, and by that means was able to calculate that it must be a certain psalm in Mattins for Good Friday, said over-night; and on turning to that part of the office, sure enough there they were. I must try and make out the services, for if there is one thing more uncomfortable to me than another, it is going to church and being obliged to stand like a dissenter in King's Chapel, wondering and not knowing in the least what is going on."[10]

Much of this work was based on the large collection of liturgical books which he had available at Cambridge, but his peripatetic nature was an assurance that he would not be limited to this. His clearest survey of the whole range of the service book was the contribution which he made in March 1881 to a work on the chronicles of the Collegiate Church in Derby.[11] The piece provides a good example of two things which are important in considering all of Bradshaw's work. He had a complete mastery of the complex details of the work upon which he was engaged and the ability to record his facts simply and clearly. It also exemplifies the necessity, in bibliographical work, of understanding the background to the material which is being studied. This was as true for Bradshaw with his service books as it was for Sadleir with his nineteenth-century novels. The society, or segment of society, which produced the material is an important field of investigation if the books themselves are to be understood. The study of books, if pursued beyond the surface level of simple enumerative bibliography, is frequently a key to the unraveling of the events for which they were designed.

The complex interrelationship between service books and the services in which they were used is one of the most practical of examples in the whole field of bibliography. The long entry under "Liturgies" in the revised Short-Title Catalogue provides a vivid reminder of the complexities in this field, although it deals with books of much later date than those with which Bradshaw was here concerned.[12] Even though nearly a century passed between the publication of Bradshaw's work and Katherine Pantzer's note in the revised S.T.C., his work was still of sufficient importance to have reference made to it.

Bradshaw wrote at a period which had witnessed a great deal of concern on liturgical matters and his innate historical sense, which touched everything which he did, is patently evident. For example, in the letter which he wrote for the Cox and Hope book, he treats of each category of service book against its developing usage within the history of the Church. When he writes of the processional, he explains very simply the historical background of the appropriate part of the service. "The Procession Services were contained in the Processionale or Processionarium. It will be remembered that the rubric in our 'Prayer-Book' concerning the Anthem ('In Quires and places where they sing, here followeth the Anthem') is indicative rather than imperative, and that it was first added in 1662. It states a fact; and, no doubt, when processions were abolished, with the altars to which they were made, cathedral choirs would have found themselves in considerable danger of being swept away also, had they not made a stand, and been content to sing the Processional Anthem without moving from their position in the choir. This alone sufficed to carry on the tradition; and looked upon in this way the modern Anthem Book of our Cathedral and Collegiate Churches, and the Hymn Book of our parish churches, are the only legitimate successors of the old Processionale."[13]

    One service book occupied his attention and bulks larger in his published writings than any other, the Sarum Breviary. The service books of the early church exhibited a considerable degree of uniformity, as had been enjoined by the Council of Braga in 561. In Britain, the Council of Clofeshoh (a place not yet firmly identified) in 747 required conformity with the model received from the Church in Rome. When the three great cathedrals of the active building period of the Norman Church from 1090-1092 were established, York, Salisbury (Sarum) and Lincoln, they each began to formulate a measure of individuality. Initially, the influence of each was strongest in its own geographical area but gradually each "usage" established itself in a wide variety of areas. A few smaller and more purely localized ones grew up but none challenged the three. With the passage of time the strongest prevailed and the advent of printing tended to increase the movement towards uniformity in this respect as in so many others.

    The Sarum Usage became the most widely used of all until the Tudors, like the Popes, desired to bring about a conformity of service. The Preface to the 1549 Book of Common Prayer had acknowledged this, "Where heretofore, there hath been great diversitie in saying and synging in churches within this realme:

some folowyng Salisbury use, some Herford use, some the use of Bangor, some of Yorke, and some of Lincolne: Now from henceforth, all the whole realme shall have but one use." The Injunction of Edward VI of 14th February, 1549/50 went further and required that "all antiphoners, missales, grayles, processionalles, manuelles, legendes, pies, portasses, jornalles, and ordinalles after the use of Sarum, Lincoln, Yorke, or any other private use, and all other bokes of service" which varied from the new book should be "defaced and abolyshed." The work, therefore, to which Bradshaw devoted so much attention was one of outstanding importance within the English liturgy.

Work on the Sarum Breviary was one of the main occupations during the last seven or eight years of his life. His contribution was designed not as independent work but, as was so often the case, to provide details of a bibliographical nature for somebody else's work. Christopher Wordsworth and Francis Procter had already begun work on an edition of the Breviary when Bradshaw began to assist them in 1878. The work was designed to be based on the Paris folio of 1531 published by Chevallon and Regnault. It was finally published in three fascicules by the Cambridge University Press between 1879 and 1886.[14] Bradshaw's contribution was largely contained in the third part with his listing of all the printed editions of the breviary and other service books of the Sarum usage. His listing ordered the books under nine headings: breviaries (of which three classes are distinguished), special services for particular feast-days, antiphoners or anthem books, psalters, hymnals, etc. Bradshaw's foundation for this study lay in his life-time study of the service books which gave him great fluency in all matters related to them. Christopher Wordsworth recorded an occasion on which Bradshaw had, without warning, written from memory a full and accurate list of the seven Sarum Breviaries printed in Queen Mary's reign with dates, names of printers and other details.[15] For the purposes of the listing in the Wordsworth-Procter work, however, he went far beyond anything which he had covered previously. He examined 210 out of the 277 volumes or fragments of the book which were then known to exist, in addition to 58 volumes of other choir service books of the same usage.

He anticipated by a long time the tenets of modern bibliographical work in collating and comparing a number of copies of the same printing. Whenever he had reason to suspect that any copy contained any kind of variation he made every effort to see it. He spared himself not at all in pursuit of such material. In October 1879, he wrote to Christopher Wordsworth from Dublin, "Here I am, after three days' work, and crammed full of breviary collations. When I wrote to you from London, I hardly knew where the next hour would start me for--whether to Paris, to master the 1483 edition; to Antwerp, to see for the first time the long-lost Louvain edition of 1499; to Edinburgh, to examine for myself the Great Breviary of 1496...; or, finally, here to master the editions of 1494 and 1516, as well as the Roman edition of 1556."[16]

It was around this same time that he was completing the only other substantial piece of publication related to service books. For an edition of a Breviary of the York Usage, he compiled a list of editions similar to that which he had done for the Sarum Breviary.[17] Bradshaw's York listing was neither as extensive nor as complex as that for Salisbury, but it was as detailed as the circumstances required. It was equally an outcome of his long years of study of this form and it was a contribution to liturgical studies that probably nobody other than Bradshaw could have made at this time.

In one of his lectures, Sir Arthur Quiller-Couch said "that literature cannot be divorced from life: that (for example) you cannot understand Chaucer aright, unless you have the background, unless you know the kind of men for whom Chaucer wrote and the kind of men whom he made speak."[18] Precisely the same is true of bibliography: the study is only fully effective when it is conducted against a background of deep understanding. It draws heavily and importantly upon a knowledge of the period and the circumstances in which the books were written, and in due course it makes a contribution in its turn to the field of inquiry. Bradshaw's knowledge of liturgical books enabled him to produce important findings, the recordings of which have played a significant part in the furthering of bibliographical work on late medieval service books. Bradshaw's personal published contribution was regrettably more limited than the knowledge which he had amassed, but his death was not the end of his influence. As a memorial to him and as a means of furthering his work, the "Henry Bradshaw Society" was founded in 1890 with the expressed purpose of forwarding "the editing of rare liturgical texts."[19]

One area of background study which had a very direct bearing on his bibliographical work, and a field in which he also published, was the various antiquarian aspects of church history. He was greatly interested in ecclesiastical architecture and made drawings of window-moldings and traceries. The relationship between these interests and his bibliographical work is precisely of the same nature as M. R. James's. In each case, it was all one piece and neither man was ever conscious of donning another hat.

The most extensive piece of research which Bradshaw conducted in this area was his work on the Statues of Lincoln Cathedral. This work was still incomplete by his death but it was edited by Christopher Wordsworth and issued in three parts between 1892 and 1897.[20] When Dr. Wordsworth was enthroned as Bishop of Lincoln in 1869 he promised, in accordance with custom, to observe all the statutes, customs and ordinances contained in the "New Registry" and in the "Laudum" or award of Bishop Alnwick. Because these documents existed in manuscript only, Bishop Wordsworth decided that it would be of general interest to have them printed and they appeared in 1873.

Bradshaw visited Lincoln in September 1880 in order to examine some documents in the muniment room and so began the investigations which led him to consider the problems relating to the statutes of the Cathedral. The chief documents with which he was concerned were the "Liber Niger," which dated from the early thirteenth century, and the "Laudum" of 1439. The latter became of great importance because of a major dispute regarding jurisdictions which arose between Dean Mackworth and his chapter. This was one only of a number of problems which had surfaced between 1412 and 1452 due to the disputatious and dictatorial manners of the then Dean. The issue was decided by Bishop Alnwick and promulgated in his award of 1439. The third important statute, the "Novum Registrum," was brought about because, not unnaturally, Bishop Alnwick hoped to prevent similar disagreements in the future by embodying the statutes in a "new registry" which should have general acceptance. After long and acrimonious debate, enlivened by the opposition of Dean Mackworth, the bishop's proposal failed to be accepted and so did not achieve the necessary authority.

It is frequently to be regretted that such a high percentage of texts which appear to yield to bibliographical investigation are purely literary in interest and doubt is sometimes cast on the effectiveness of such methodology in other circumstances. In letters which Bradshaw wrote to Bishop Wordsworth in 1882, enclosing an analysis of "The Bishop's Statute-Book," he wrote of his work in this instance in precisely the same terms as he was to use in many other less documentary cases. "My only wish has been to collect facts, in order that others may form a judgment upon them.... Only a few months ago Canon Robertson brought me an undoubted autograph signature of Remigius, the founder of the see of Lincoln, to examine; and I confess that to one like myself, whose life is spent in the care of books, the very sight of such a document is enough to stir me to do my best to clear the ground for those who want a knowledge of the historical facts, in order to form a just judgment on what is put before them.... How far the continuous acceptance of a body of statutes (which were first acted upon two hundred and fifty years after date, under an erroneous conviction that they had been ratified at the time of their composition) is a tenable form of acceptance, is a <u>legal</u> difficulty upon which, of course, it does not concern me even to offer a suggestion. But having a very great love for anatomising books, and for working out what I may call the <u>bibliographical</u> elements of a problem of this kind, so as to ensure to those who wish to form an opinion a sound basis on which to form it, I have been unable to resist the temptation to work out the results of my various searches."[21]

Bradshaw was here making an important distinction, one which, if it were widely understood at that time, was rarely expressed so cogently. The insistence upon the bibliographical elements of a problem and the elucidation of the facts which will provide a sound basis on which to form opinions embodies a theme to which Bradshaw returned constantly. It has within it the germ of Greg's later and most forthright statement that bibliography "has nothing to do with the subject matter of books, but only with their formal aspect." The division was observed easily in relation to medieval ecclesiastical legal documents and bibliographical work rarely raises contentious issues when applied to fields such as this. Problems of demarcation more frequently arise in relation to purely, or primarily, literary texts of a nature such as that of one of Bradshaw's other life-time concerns.

Chaucer had long been one of his special interests but it was not until 1864 that there is evidence that he began to direct much serious attention to the study. In Bradshaw's day the only reliable text of Chaucer's main work was the edition of <u>The Canterbury Tales</u> which had been edited by Thomas Tyrwhitt and published in 1775-1778. It was of this text that A. W. Pollard wrote: "As is well known, the early editions of Chaucer from Caxton to Urry's [1721] are full of errors, so serious as to have completely obscured the poet's oral mastery of his art-- only a percentage of the lines being susceptible of scansion and the sense being frequently destroyed. From the discredit thus cast on him, Chaucer was at last rescued by the edition of the <u>Canterbury Tales</u> brought out by Thomas Tyrwhitt, in 1775. Though with only second-rate manuscripts to work from, Tyrwhitt, by virtue of his true literary feeling, produced a text which went far towards vindicating Chaucer's reputation as a master of poetry, while the majority of his annotations are so excellent that they form the basis of all subsequent work."[22] Although editions of Chaucer continued to multiply over the next century, including several reprints of Tyrwhitt, little substantial progress was recorded. The only real advance was in the edition edited by Thomas Wright and published by the Percy Society between 1847 and 1851. Wright's method had been to select the manuscript which seemed to him to be the nearest to Chaucer's own time and most free from clerical error. This brought him to the Harleian MS. No. 7334 in the British Museum and he made this the basis of his edition. In view of much more modern discussions on the use of a copy-text, it is interesting to observe Wright's method of operation. He did not follow his chosen text uncritically but collated it with another, the next in his opinion in age and value, No. 851 in the Lansdowne collection, and also, so far as The Wife of Bath's Tale, with two in the Cambridge University Library.

It was against this background of textual work that Bradshaw openly turned his attention to Chaucer in the early 1860 period. In 1864 the Clarendon Press invited W. Aldis Wright, Professor Earle and Henry Bradshaw to edit a standard library edition of Chaucer. In spite of several years of preparatory work this edition never appeared in the form as originally intended, but Bradshaw's areas of work can be traced in a number of ways. In 1866 "he projected a treatise, which he entitled, 'An attempt to ascertain the state of Chaucer's Works as they were left at his death, with some notices of their subsequent history.' The introductory pages of this treatise, which are all that I have been able to find among his papers, state the author's intention of examining what works were attributed to Chaucer by himself or his contemporaries; what works, not yet recognized as his, may reasonably be assigned to him. This being done, he proposed further to give some account of the history of the text of each work, dividing them into five groups according to their metre, the prose works being in a sixth group. Unfortunately, he appears to have gone no further with this plan."[23]

The substance of Bradshaw's work, however, appeared in his Memorandum No. 4.[24] Bradshaw introduced the crux of the problem as follows: "The critics have unfortunately looked upon Chaucer's great work as simply a collection of twenty-four tales each preceded by a prologue introducing the next narrator. Until this notion is thoroughly uprooted, the poem must remain an inextricable mass of confusion. On the other hand, as soon as we perceive that the author composed the work piecemeal with the intention of finally working all his pieces into one harmonious whole, this confusion disappears. Every one allows that this finishing process was never reached by the author, so that it remains for us to make the best of the several fragments as they have come down to us. We must look upon these fragments as so many portions of the story of the Canterbury pilgrimage into which the tales are introduced; the so-called prologues then become the main line of the action of the poem; and in each fragment we shall see that the story is taken up at one point and dropped at another without a clear reference to what has gone before or what is to follow."[25]

Bradshaw went back to the manuscripts and "having found between fifty and sixty copies of the Canterbury Tales, and having further noticed that very few of them have the contents in the same order, I have been able, after a minute examination of a good number, so far to break the work up into what I have been led to believe were the fragments as left by the author, that it is now comparatively easy to describe, on finding any particular manuscript, in what order or disorder the contents are placed."[26] The scribes of the extant manuscripts had made individual efforts to straighten the sequence of tales, shifting the links from place to place, omitting them entirely or contributing links of their own imagination.

Following his analysis and collation of the manuscripts Bradshaw divided the whole work into twelve fragments or groups of tales. The groups varied considerably in size, some containing as many as five or six tales, some only one. Bradshaw classified and organized the manuscripts into three families, described the characteristics of each family and tabulated the fragments including a listing of the "gaps" for which there were no suitable and appropriate links. Although Tyrwhitt and Wright among the earlier editors had given serious attention to the manuscript sources, none before Bradshaw had subjected them to a detailed scrutiny. He provided a new basis for the study of Chaucer's text and several of the substantive editions which followed accepted the premises which he had established.

In his work on Chaucer's minor poems Bradshaw mixed bibliographical and literary evidence. Bradshaw was the first scholar in England to apply the rhyme-test to Chaucer's work. He argued persuasively that the pattern of rhyme was one of the most reliable guides as to the authenticity of a work. This evidence was never used in isolation because Bradshaw invariably allied it to his study of the manuscripts. Textual, linguistic and bibliographical indications were made to mesh together in a manner which has still not become commonplace a century later.

It is also salutary to study the phraseology in which Bradshaw wrote of his conclusions. He did not specifically deny Chaucer's authorship of some of the minor poems, but wrote of "the total want of trustworthy evidence in favour of attributing to Chaucer any of the following pieces: 'The Romaunt of the Rose,' 'The Court of Love,' 'The Flower and the Leaf,' 'The Cuckow and the Nightingale,' 'Chaucer's Dream,' 'The Testament of Love,' 'The Complaint of the Black Night,' and other smaller pieces, both from an external and an internal examination of them...."[27] He urged his ideas upon all the scholars with whom he was in contact, but always in the same terms: "The fact is, you want me to lay down the law dogmatically, and I don't wish to do anything of the kind. I give my reason for accepting certain pieces until they are proved to be not his, and I also give my reasons for not accepting certain things which are proved not to be his. But in no case do I lay down as a certainty either that the one set of things are his, or the other not his...."[28]

Typically, the results of Bradshaw's work showed more in other people's work than in his own, and in many instances the debt was far more than the matter most immediately to hand. Bradshaw wrote to W. W. Skeat congratulating him on his election to the Professorship of Anglo-Saxon in 1878. In his reply Skeat wrote of his indebtedness to Bradshaw: "... it is for me to know what you have been for me and what you have done for me. In my beginning to study, I was, with the best of intentions, all abroad. I could not read a manuscript; I did not know what a manuscript was. I wanted to read books, but did not know what books. I wanted to understand Chaucer's rhymes (or rimes) and his grammar, and his ways in general, and I had none but vague ideas. And in hundreds of ways I wanted to know (and I still want to know) all sorts of things more or less connected with manuscripts or literature. Well, it is the merest truth that it is, practically, to you that I owe all my best ideas. You have set me thinking where I was before thoughtless; you have helped me to read manuscripts; you have told me of this or that book or edition, over and over again, and thrown out hints (so thankfully received), and told me of points and, in fact, helped me, in and out, in hundreds of ways and thousands of times. Your remarks have always been treasured; some have seemed wrong to me at first, but they generally came right, and I can only say that I never remember a remark of yours that was not received with profound thankfulness and with a determination to follow it out."[29]

A large part of Bradshaw's career was devoted to the study of manuscripts and especially to their historical development. When he began work with them in 1859, Bradshaw knew very little about manuscripts and years later he could still, with complete honesty, say that "he was very ignorant of palaeography. By this he meant that there were lacunae in his knowledge, as there must always be in the case of a man who refuses to take things at second-hand."[30] Yet it was recorded that Mommsen, upon whom Bradshaw had made a great impression, had written. "I told Mr. Bradshaw of a contraction I had seen in a manuscript of the British Museum, which, with all my experience of Pandect manuscripts, I had never seen before. The British Museum people, who have also great knowledge, had not seen it either. When I told it to Mr. Bradshaw, he said nothing, but presently brought me a manuscript and showed me the very thing."[31] Professor Robertson Smith expressed a widely held opinion when he said, "In everything that relates to the history of manuscripts he was facile princeps. As to English manuscripts, he could often tell by the writing alone in what monastery they had been written. But he knew all about his manuscripts. I learned from him, for example, a very simple mark, characteristic of Arabic manuscripts written in India, which I don't think any orientalist was aware of till he discovered it."[32]

A tribute somewhat similar to this could be paid to many bibliographers who have worked with manuscripts but they were remarkably few in Bradshaw's day. The phrases do, nevertheless, call to mind M. R. James, who was influenced by Bradshaw and eventually typified the same kind of interest in manuscripts. In his reminiscences M. R. James wrote of Bradshaw: "Would that I had made a practice of going oftener to his rooms than I did! I think I was deterred by so seldom getting at Bradshaw himself. All sorts of dons and undergraduates might be there: some of them, like Chawner, simply sat there whole evenings and said nothing at all: others monopolised Bradshaw: whereat, as I was bursting with questions I wanted to ask him, I was discontented. It did sometimes happen, though, that one stayed late and got him almost alone. That was delightful."[33]

As with Bradshaw, James's friends were amazed at the breadth and the depth of the knowledge which he brought to bear upon his work; history of libraries and their collections, mediaeval art, apocryphal literature, church architecture and decoration--all these and much besides formed part of his armory. "Monty's memory at any rate swept everything into its net. All the results of his vast reading, immense variety of interests and constant observation were stored there, fresh and ready for use; so that in the cataloguing of mediaeval MSS his knowledge of handwritings, bindings, pagination and so on enabled him to get through his work at a pace which would have been impossible for anyone who had to be constantly referring to notebooks."[34] James could, however, still say with complete honesty, as Bradshaw had done, that he was not, in the strictest sense, a palaeographer. "I have had to handle so many collections of quite miscellaneous volumes that I have been distracted from specializing on any one class or period, and though I imagine myself able to date most books correctly enough, I cannot and never could cultivate the sort of brain and eye, such as Jenkinson possessed in a marvellous degree, which carries in it the special form of the letter g (say) and can tell you with certainty that it does not occur after the year 850."[35]

It is impossible to assess the number of manuscripts with which Bradshaw was occupied during his lifetime because so much of it was unrecorded work done in conjunction with visiting scholars in the University Library. There are, however, several manuscripts of outstanding importance with which Bradshaw was very closely associated. In 1857 he discovered in the University Library the ninth-century manuscript of the Book of Deer. It is an unfinished manuscript of the four Gospels, with the Apostles' Creed, written by a scribe whose vernacular was Gaelic, in which the glosses and the closing subscription were written. Bradshaw transcribed the Gaelic portions of the manuscript, which were his major interest, and prepared to edit the work for publication. He became involved with other work and could not settle a number of points to his own satisfaction; the result was that, despite the urging of the Spalding Club, which hoped to issue it, it remained unpublished for a number of years. He eventually handed the work over to a Scottish antiquary, John Stuart, who completed Bradshaw's work for publication in 1869.

Among the problems which exercised Bradshaw's attention during this same period were the manuscripts which led to the publication of his paper "On the recovery of the long lost Waldensian manuscripts."[36] Because they involved some rather out-of-the-way episodes of ecclesiastical history they had an especial appeal to him. Bradshaw's paper described the origin of these documents. "It will be known to all who have interested themselves in the history of the Vaudois, that Morland, the envoy from the Protector Cromwell to the Duke of Savoy on their behalf in 1655, wrote on his return in 1658 what he calls a History of the Evangelical Churches in Piedmont, based not only upon previous writers but upon authentic documents which he brought home and deposited in the Public Library of this University."[37] It was these "six books or volumes" which had unaccountably disappeared. Their importance lay in the light which they could shed upon the doctrines of the sects concerned.

The manuscripts were "all written in the old Vaudois dialect, and to which Morland assigned very early dates, ranging from the 10th to the 13th century. The copies were so old, says Morland, and the writings probably much older. It was a point of considerable importance that the Cambridge manuscripts should be examined; for not only Morland and his Vaudois friends, but also their advocates in our own time, agreed in maintaining the claim of this community to have held the pure Genevan doctrines long before the time of Calvin. The historians of the 17th century, knowing that in the 13th the followers of Peter Waldo had been separated from the Roman communion, and knowing that their descendants in the 17th held the doctrines of Geneva, were illogical enough to conclude that therefore their ancestors in the 13th had anticipated Calvin's views by three centuries."[38]

Bradshaw found the documents--"the only wonder is how they could ever have been lost sight of." One of Bradshaw's footnotes to this paper draws attention once again to what he rightly regarded as the "bibliographical" aspect of the search. "It must be borne in mind that ever since the death of William Moore (in 1659), under whom every part of the library seems to have been thoroughly explored, all the librarians and their assistants have uniformly, though unaccountably, declined to make themselves in any way acquainted with the manuscripts under their charge. So, when fresh catalogues were required, both Mr. Nasmith and, more recently, the laborious compilers of the printed catalogue, were employed at a large cost to the University, as being supposed to know a good deal of the subjects of the works existing in MS., but a knowledge of the history of the individual volumes was not to be expected from them. These facts afford the only possible explanation of the reputed loss of the Waldensian MSS."[39] Bradshaw's examination of the documents resulted in his ascribing dates to them, the earliest at the close of the 14th century and the latest to 1519-20. His brief paper makes the whole investigation appear disarmingly simple, as was his wont, but it was, nevertheless, a major piece of bibliographical rehabilitation.

Few manuscripts, if any, have exercised a greater hold on the popular imagination than the Codex Sinaiticus. It had been discovered in 1844 by Constantine Tischendorf in the monastery of St. Catherine at Mount Sinai. Written in the first half of the fourth century, one of the oldest extant biblical manuscripts, its authenticity and importance have hardly been called into question since its first discovery. The one important occasion when its antiquity was challenged brought Bradshaw into one of his very few public statements. Shortly after Tischendorf's discovery, a Greek named Constantine Simonides claimed that he had written the codex. He was already well known as a forger of manuscripts, including such choice specimens as a copy of Saint Matthew's Gospel written only fifteen years after the Ascension and other portions of the New Testament dating from the first century. Tischendorf, in his capacity as the most distinguished European palaeographer, had played a leading role in exposing these as forgeries. Simonides' revenge on Tischendorf was simple. He maintained that all those works of which he had been accused were genuine but that he would admit to one forgery, the Codex Sinaiticus. There is always difficulty in proving a forgery for what it is, even in these days of much more sophisticated techniques. There was, for example, a wide acceptance of the Vinland map in 1965 before its subsequent exposure.[40] In the mid-nineteenth century decisions had to be made on evidence which was much more debatable.

Bradshaw entered the discussion. Simonides had written a letter to the Guardian on January 21st, 1863 saying that, in order to prove his capability of writing the Codex, he had sent a letter to Bradshaw in uncial characters. Colleagues and friends of Bradshaw had attempted to involve him in the controversy earlier but he had been reluctant. Faced with the letter of Simonides, he had little choice. He wrote a letter which appeared in the <u>Guardian</u> on January 28th, 1863.[41]

In the light of other discussions related to Simonides, it is interesting to note the tenor of Bradshaw's reply. He admitted the difficulties in determining the genuineness of a manuscript: that "it was really difficult to define; that it seemed to be more a kind of instinct than anything else." He made no attempt to dispute the fact that Simonides might have written a Bible, it was simply that the Bible which Simonides had described as having written could not, on bibliographical grounds, have been the Codex Sinaiticus. Prior to Bradshaw nobody had drawn attention to the unusual construction of the book itself. "I had been anxious to know whether it was written in even continuous quaternions throughout, like the Codex Bezae, or in a series of fasciculi each ending with a quire of varying size, as the Codex Alexandrinus, and I found the latter to be the case. This, by-the-by, is of itself sufficient to prove that it cannot be the volume which Dr. Simonides speaks of having written at Mount Athos." Simonides had a few supporters but all responsible opinion was against him and his claim very soon ceased to have any support.

The same kind of evidence from the construction of the book was used by Bradshaw in connection with another of the famous biblical codices. The <u>Codex Alexandrinus</u> is now, in a modern rebinding, arranged in gatherings of six leaves. Bradshaw suspected the rightness of this and showed that the manuscript had originally been gathered in eight leaves. At the time of a rebinding in the early nineteenth century the conjugate leaves were divided into halves, remounted and bound in gatherings of sixes. In each case of these codices Bradshaw was ahead of his time in using the physical make-up of the book as bibliographical evidence.

Much of Bradshaw's work stemmed from the period of his second appointment on the staff of the University Library in 1859. The initial requirement of his position was that he should bring some order to the manuscripts which, according to Dr. Luard's report to the Library Syndicate, "have in all probability not been dusted for centuries, certainly not since George I gave them to the university."[42] Following the completion of this labor, virtually a labor of love since he was paid only £20 a year, Bradshaw was "to perform similar duties in regard to rare and early printed books."[43] It was in this field that Bradshaw was to make his most significant contributions to bibliographical scholarship in general.

Although much of Bradshaw's work was communicated directly to those who sought his advice in the library, his voluminous correspondence records, in massive detail, the work on which he was engaged. Two sets of his letters to different correspondents indicate the detail which was embraced by these exchanges and the growth of bibliographical understanding.

William Blades (1824-1890) was another key figure in the development of bibliography in the mid-nineteenth century and he corresponded with Bradshaw for several years regarding their enthusiasms and problems with early printing. Blades was apprenticed to his father's printing establishment and grew up learning at first hand the intricacies of the printing trade. From these beginnings it was an easy transition which led him to investigate the problems of early English printing and of Caxton in particular. Bradshaw and Blades corresponded for about twenty-five years from 1857 onwards, and each contributed to the other's solution of difficulties. Blades understood the practical problems of the trade while Bradshaw had at his disposal the vast resources of the university library. It was a fruitful friendship and it certainly influenced Bradshaw's development starting, as it did, when he was only twenty-six years old. Although Bradshaw was six years younger than Blades and although he learned much from him, it was by no means a senior-junior relationship. Bradshaw gave Blades an immense amount of information about the books of the early period, a fact which Blades acknowledged in May 1861 in the first volume of his The life and typography of William Caxton: "Your acceptance of the accompanying volume will give me sincere pleasure, and afford me another opportunity of thanking you for the very great assistance you have afforded me in my researches."[44]

The second important group of Bradshaw's correspondence is one which has only become readily available in recent years: the letters which passed between him and J. W. Holtrop, the librarian of the Royal Library at The Hague, and also with his successor, M.F.A.G. Campbell.[45] The correspondence begins with a letter from Bradshaw to Holtrop dated 5th January 1864 and continues until Holtrop's death in 1870; it then switches to Campbell until Bradshaw's death. It is a body of material which is of major importance in a study of Bradshaw, his work and his relationship with other bibliographers. It was an association which Bradshaw valued highly.

On one occasion, having received news of Holtrop's illness, Bradshaw wrote, "I always look upon you and speak of you as the chief of my department--the département des incunables--for indeed there is no one connected either with any English library, still less in Paris, who has the leisure and inclination to study our subject scientifically, and a merely dilettante employment upon it is of all things the most pernicious and contemptible."[46] A few years later, on writing to Campbell following Holtrop's death, Bradshaw wrote again in the same vein: "I cannot help feeling a sort of loyalty to him as my chief in these things, in a way that I feel to no one at all in England or elsewhere--because there is no one, except yourself, to whom I can look for the least help and sympathy in these studies in the way that they really demand."[47]

It was within this context, one which was entirely congenial to him, that Bradshaw was able to immerse himself to the full in the discussion of his bibliographical problems and pursuits. Apart from Bradshaw's regular initial apologies for his dilatoriness, "my own grievous habit of not answering letters," his letters are solely concerned with bibliography. Very little deals with personal matters but with what Campbell described as "almost always consisted in exchanging ideas and descriptions relating to exact bibliography."[48] The exchanges covered the verification of collations, detailed discussions of typographical evidence, initial letters, book sales and their catalogues, the history and provenance of copies, the work of other bibliographers, make-up of copies, woodcuts--in fact, there is little within the range of bibliographical evidence which was not either covered or at least substantially referred to.

When Bradshaw commented on the few people working on early printed books "in this way" there was no implied exclusiveness or superiority in the remark. It was a frank recognition that he and a very few others, such as Holtrop and Campbell, were viewing the products of the press in a manner which was new. Earlier bibliographers, bibliophiles and book collectors for the most part, had viewed the book as an isolated item for study or admiration. Bradshaw began to study it as we now regard it one hundred years later. It is both the product of a particular series of technical processes and also an artifact of a society at one special moment in history. His was an attempt to discover, through the evidence of the book itself, the circumstances which brought it into existence.

Professor C. H. Pearson, in an obituary notice of Bradshaw, wrote, "Bibliography and palaeography were but the means to a greater end: the study of history, of folk-development. 'I want to see the printer at work,' he would say. 'I want to understand why he printed this particular book, and what guided the form of his production.' Thus his bibliography and palaeography were geographical and historical. 'The watershed,' he would say, in his quiet, half-paradoxical way, 'is as important for books as for trade.' His great hope was that some day the German incunabula and the German woodcuts would be worked out by grouping towns together geographically; thus the intellectual life of each district, and its influence upon its neighbours, would become, for the first time, manifest.... In books which the mere bibliographer described as reprints, he would find the local colouring, the peculiar prejudice or the special glory of a district, introduced by some slight change. What for us had been at first merely twenty editions of the same book, he would show were all variations. He would trace the development from one prototype, and he would point out the local or temporal value of each phase of growth. As he handled the pages of some early folio, and described how two presses had been employed, one working away at this point, the other at that; how the first stock of paper had been exhausted here, and the second there; how at this point the printer had thought to improve on his original, or had bought somebody else's cuts, or chopped up his own--the auditor felt himself carried back centuries, and saw the men of the past at their work. Not improbably, Bradshaw would conclude with the remark: 'I wish I could find out anything about that book.'"[49]

The work of this small group of men--Bradshaw, Holtrop, Blades and Campbell--was the first visible sign of this new development in bibliographical work. It is not an entirely happy idea to apply the term "scientific bibliography" to the pursuit which they so largely inaugurated; there would be too great an implied limitation. The phrase can, however, be useful in that it suggests a correspondence with the equally unhappily named "scientific historians" of the same period. It was, in the words of R. G. Collingwood, "the period of Stubbs and Maitland, the period when English historians first mastered the objectively scientific critical methods of the great Germans, and learnt to study facts in all their detail with a proper apparatus of scholarship."[50]

The nineteenth century had witnessed an important evolution in attitudes to evidence in a number of studies. Historical studies in Europe were reshaped at that time by the creation or opening up of state archives. In England, the opening of the Public Records Office in 1851, following the initial legislation in 1838, had created completely new conditions, and the development of the Historical Manuscripts Commission from 1869 onwards was another manifestation of the same idea. German

historians were advanced by the archives in Berlin which provided them with an outstanding service, and the incomparable archives of the Vatican were officially opened to scholars in 1882 by Pope Leo XIII, who declared, "the Church needs nothing but the truth." The German philological movement of the early part of the nineteenth century had its counterpart in England in Archbishop Trench's preliminary work for the <u>Oxford English Dictionary</u>. The insistence upon the historical record of words rather than their literary acceptability stressed a similar concern for the accuracy of the basic elements of communication.
The process was carried to its logical conclusion in Bradshaw's day in the work of bodies such as the Early English Text Society with its desired achievement of certainty in textual studies. All of these movements, in their respective fields, emphasized the importance which was being attached to original source material, whether historical record, linguistic or literary. It is important to see all this as a related background to the work of Bradshaw and his colleagues. They were concerned to investigate the reliability of the evidence of the material means for the transmission of the text. If that bibliographical record could be shown to be true or to be false, then obvious conclusions could be made with respect to the text which the material conveyed.

If Bradshaw's work with early printing is seen as a continuation of his work with manuscripts, then his concentration on typographical evidence is the natural corollary to palaeography. His correspondence, as well as his published writings, bear witness to the keenness of his observation and his phenomenal memory. On one occasion Bradshaw visited a library in Orleans accompanied by an old friend and they were being conducted around by M. Bimbenet, president of a learned society in the city. "M. Bimbenet showed Bradshaw an early printed Bible. 'How nice!' he exclaimed at once; 'printed at Paris in' such and such a year. M. Bimbenet looked up astonished. 'You will find the imprint at the end,' he continued, and the date was as he said. M. Bimbenet then brought him a second Bible, and then a third, and Bradshaw, without hesitation, gave the place and date of each. When asked how he could know them so accurately, he replied, looking at his friend, 'Just as I know _him_. I know every line of his face, and could never mistake him for anybody else'; and then, placing the Bibles side by side, he pointed out the minute variations in the form of the letters which sufficed to enable him to distinguish them at a glance."[51]

Time and again it is clear that the spirit of the collector, the librarian, was as strong as the bibliographer in many of his actions. In 1860, he wrote to Blades, "You must remember that all my inferences are drawn from the incomplete collection in our own library, and therefore are liable to be corrected by the inferences you draw from having so much fuller collections to go to. My grand object is to render our collection just so complete that a person may be able to see at a glance all the early varieties of our English type."[52] He was able to travel some way along this road, notably at the sale of the Enschedé collection at Haarlem in December 1867, but the "grand object" still eluded him. Even at the now unbelievable book prices of Bradshaw's day, the amount of money allowed to him for such purchases was too small to admit of purchase on a grand scale. In fact the greatest accession to the University Library at this time came with Bradshaw's presentation of fifty-eight incunables from his own private collection. More than half of these were from the presses of Ulrich Zel and other Cologne printers, the others being Dutch, Flemish and French books.

It has often been urged, sometimes with great force, that one of the demerits of modern bibliographical work has been its avoidance of any interest or concern with the topics with which the books deal. Bradshaw would have escaped some of the bitterest denunciations because of his work with Chaucer and also because of his special concentration upon Irish books and printing. His father's collection of Irish literature had been one of the earliest influences on his life and his notice of the Celtic glosses in a manuscript of Juvencus at Cambridge had constituted one of his first important antiquarian or bibliographical discoveries. During the last ten years or so of his life he turned again to this early love of his.

One instance provides a splendid example of the background which Bradshaw brought to one of his searches, in this case for the Echternach Martyrology. He wrote to M. Vanderhaeghen, of the Library of the University of Ghent, in November 1875, "I am very much interested in the Plantin Library, from many points of view.... One thing especially I am anxious about. Herbert Rosweyd was engaged upon a facsimile reproduction (engraved on copper) of an eighth-century manuscript 'Martyrologium,' borrowed by Bollandus from the Abbey of Echternach. On Rosweyd's death the work must have been suspended, when it had proceeded as far as July. D'Achery obtained (about 1662) from Moretus a copy of the facsimile sheets as far as July from the unpublished stock at Antwerp, and Bollandus sent him a transcript of the remainder from the original manuscript, which was still in his keeping. The original manuscript did not go back to Echternach and with the rest of that collection to Luxemburg, and it is now probably lying buried in some library.... The manuscript was the earliest known copy of the 'Martyrology,' and must have come from Ireland, as is clear both from the handwriting (which is to be seen in the 'Acta Sanctorum'), and from the mention of Irish saints otherwise unknown."[53] Early in the following year he went to Paris in pursuit of another book which contained Breton glosses and, while in the Bibliothèque Nationale, discovered the Echternach Martyrology which he had been seeking.

Even when the mind thinks that it has become accustomed to the quantity of Bradshaw's work, there is still a measure of surprise in hearing him list his recent activities, as in September 1876 when he wrote, "I give an account of all my harvesting up to now, including all my Breton discoveries made in March and April. Besides the new Bodleian Cornish glosses, and the new Bodleian and Corpus manuscripts with Breton glosses, I have got two Paris manuscripts, one ninth to tenth, the other eleventh century, with Breton glosses; also one in the British Museum with ditto. Also I have been to Rennes and seen the cartulary of Redon, and been to Quimper and seen the 'Book of Landevennech.'"[54] In the following spring, in the space of just over a week while on yet another search for glosses which he transcribed, he visited Cambrai, Amiens, Orleans, Tours and Paris. The detailed preparation for journeys of this kind, the painstaking amassing of all relevant evidence, the deductions which Bradshaw's experience allowed him to make from all this information at hand--none of this could ensure success but it certainly led him to spectacular results. Events which might have seemed to be the results of pure chance or, at best, happy serendipity were usually a tribute to his immense knowledge and skills.

The range of Bradshaw's work and interests is formidable and would, of itself, have created a splendid example for all who followed him. But this alone would not have accounted for the position which he holds in bibliographical studies. Sir Stephen Gaselee said that Bradshaw developed bibliography "by a change of direction almost comparable to the work of Darwin or Mendel."[55] Such a ranking derives from more than a vast range of work well done. Bradshaw's "change of direction" was a direct result of his methods. There can be no doubt that he began with a deep regard, even an old-fashioned love, for books. It was fed by his father's large library and expanded by his experience at St. Columba's College. Crone's book on Bradshaw noted that William Tuckwell (later known in England as "The Radical Parson") recalled "with what skill and completeness Bradshaw catalogued the school library. It was a treat to see him handle a rare volume. First, the caressing clasp of the closed book in his two broad hands; then the rapid estimate of lettering, tooling, gilding; then the critical glance at type and margin, the survey of title-page and colophon, and the bit of erudition or instructive anecdote in illustration of his judgement."[56]

Bradshaw propounded no elaborate theories regarding his work, but equally he left no doubt as to the direction in which his methods tended. Prothero recorded a letter which Bradshaw wrote to F. J. Furnivall on 7th August 1868 in which he said, "As for the originality, I, of course, never laid claims to any new facts. My only point is my method, which I always insist on in anything in bibliography--arrange your facts vigorously and get them plainly before you, and let them speak for themselves, which they will always do."[57] A few months earlier, on 5th April, Bradshaw had written in similar terms to J. W. Holtrop: "There are so very few bibliographers who will be content to sift, sort, and arrange their FACTS so that they may speak for themselves. When they have got their facts, let them speculate of course, because it is only by such happy suggestions that the further truth is elucidated from the facts."[58] It was Bradshaw's arrangement of facts which was to be one of the most influential aspects of his method. His friend, G. R. Crotch of St. John's, was an enthusiastic entomologist and Bradshaw said that Crotch's methods of dealing with his insects helped him with his bibliographical studies and that his own methods developed closely on the lines of natural science. It is interesting that Bradshaw's friend and successor, Francis Jenkinson, was another gifted entomologist and carried on further with Bradshaw's work.

In the light of Bradshaw's towering reputation in bibliography and his importance in the development of the study, it comes almost as a shock to discover how small is the corpus of his published work. Much of it, because it was done within the boundaries of his official duties within the University Library, must be sought within the accomplishments of the Library during the period in which he directed it. But there is another and more potent cause for this limitation.

Few people in the history of scholarship have been more unrestrained in the lavish manner in which they have given help to others, even when this gift could only be to the detriment of their own work. This was certainly so with Bradshaw. His correspondence on bibliographical matters was enormous. A wide variety of people turned to him for advice and seldom did they do so in vain. The even tenor of his own work was often interrupted by visitors bringing him problems. They rarely received any delay other than a request to allow him to finish the sentence upon which he was currently engaged. "Then he would perhaps only point with his pen to a chair, and work on, till at last he would shut his book with a bang and come to you with both hands stretched out, to say, 'How d'you do?' properly."[59]

One of the few public expressions of this attitude which Bradshaw ever uttered was in his Presidential Address to the Library Association at its meeting in Cambridge in 1884. He spoke of a librarian as "one who earns his living by attending to the wants of those for whose use the library under his charge exists, his primary duty being, in the widest possible sense of the phrase, to save the time of those who seek his services."[60] Bradshaw interpreted this idea widely and generously. He told a young student on one occasion that the most delightful thing in the world was to have people come for help, and it is clear from many of the letters which he received and from comments in other peoples' writings that no one could doubt the sincerity of this remark.

In view of his own clearly established areas of interest it is not surprising that many of the inquiries were on bibliographical matters and especially so concerned with copies within the University Library. When W. M. Conway was beginning his life's work on the development of engraving and wood-cutting he was introduced to Bradshaw, who "went to the shelves and took down book after book, and showed me the same cut turning up now in the possession of one printer, now in the possession of another. He showed me the wanderings and developments of founts of type; he showed me the structure of books, and I know not what besides. For three hours I followed him like a dazed person into a new world--a world of what I had before thought to be dry and dusty things, but which his illuminating speech showed to be a very kingdom of romance and surprise."[61] A short time afterwards, in order to help Conway to further his researches abroad, Bradshaw offered him "out of his own pocket fifteen pounds a quarter, as an earnest to my friends that what I was doing was really work which some one thought it worth while to pay for." Bradshaw's explanation to Conway was typical and simple. "The library had given him some kind of endowment-of-research post when he was younger, and he had always stated that the fact that he had been able to do the bibliographical work he did was due to that appointment. The library, he said, could no longer afford to do for another as it had done for him, so he felt it a pleasure to step in personally in its place and do what he should like to see it do if he could."[62]

His prodigious memory allowed him to perform quite extraordinary feats even when far from both his notebooks and his collections. He could, quickly and without apparent effort, list early printed books for an enquirer, complete with press-numbers, which were never inaccurate. On one occasion at least he was able to provide a similar service to a friend in a field with which he does not usually seem familiar. "While in my house, he found the original edition of the Waverley novels, in a rather neglected condition. He gathered them all together, all but one (since found), which he noted as missing, and wrote off a catalogue of them for me, then and there, in a few minutes, seeming to have all their titles and the order of their publication in his head."[63] Yet, in another sense, many varied subjects came within his orbit. His work constantly stressed the relationship and the connections between the main areas of his research and he moved easily among them without any realization that he was, in any way, changing channels.

J. W. Clark, in the preface to his Architectural History of the University of Cambridge, spoke for a wide circle when he recorded his own personal debt: "No language that I can think of can adequately express what I owe to our late librarian, Henry Bradshaw. From the outset of my work, he took it, so to speak, into his hands, and treated it as if it had been his own. Notwithstanding the incessant demands upon his time, he always found leisure to help me, to teach me to read difficult mediaeval handwriting, or to dictate to me some document which I had reason to copy. On one occasion, I remember, he took the trouble to travel from Cambridge to Eton in order to settle the signification of a single contraction in one of the building-rolls, on which a good deal depended, and about which I could not feel quite sure.... --he insisted on reading all the proof-sheets, not merely for the purpose of detecting clerical errors, but that he might copiously annotate them, and show me how difficult points in history and archaeology might be set in the best light."[64]

Much of the work which Bradshaw did on glosses was passed on to Whitley Stokes, who wrote in the preface to his edition of them, "The following old Breton glosses were found in 1877 by the late Mr. Henry Bradshaw.... When I was leaving England for India in 1880, he presented me with a copy in his own hand, not only of the glosses, but of the context of most of the Latin words glossed; and I seize this occasion to express my gratitude for a generosity as rare as it is precious. In 1881 I printed them privately in Calcutta, with a commentary, and in 1882 Mr. Bradshaw recollated them with the manuscript.... There are 322 glosses, but of these no less than 109 are only portions of words intended by the glosser.... These 109 abbreviations do not, of course, add much to our knowledge of Old Breton, but the remaining 213 glosses are of great value, not only from the point of view of the lexicographer, but also from that of the grammarian."[65]

Lavish assistance of this kind to so many enquiries must assuredly have limited the amount of time which Bradshaw could devote to his own studies. A high percentage of the results of his work appeared in other people's writings, and this is how he wished it to be. His influence was exerted much more in a personal and direct manner than through the medium of his published work. He was constantly available for consultation and his reputation for erudition and insight was widely known. In Prothero's words, "Had he known less he would undoubtedly have written more."[66] There is small wonder that he was one of the most beloved scholars of his time, an understandable result of so much learning, so lightly borne and so freely given with what one friend termed "a courtesy of thought, quite beyond and surpassing that of manner."

Notes

1. The Athenaeum, No. 3043, February 20, 1886, p. 262.
2. Prothero, G. W. A Memoir of Henry Bradshaw. London: Kegan Paul, Trench & Co., 1888, p. 82.
3. Ibid., p. 83.
4. Ibid., p. 171.
5. Ibid., p. 172.
6. Ibid., p. 25.
7. Ibid., p. 23.
8. Sir Arthur Gordon, quoted by Prothero, ibid., p. 27.
9. Ibid., pp. 66-67.
10. Ibid., p. 125.
11. Cox, J. Charles and Hope, W. H. St. John. The Chronicles of the Collegiate Church or Free Chapel of All Saints, Derby. London and Derby: Bemrose and Sons, 1881.
12. A Short-title Catalogue of Books Printed in England, Scotland, & Ireland and of English Books Printed Abroad, 1475-1640. First compiled by A. W. Pollard and G. R. Redgrave. Second edition, revised & enlarged by W. A. Jackson and F. S. Ferguson, completed by Katherine F. Pantzer. Volume 2, I-Z. London: The Bibliographical Society, 1976, pp. 68-107.
13. Cox, J. Charles and Hope, W. H. St. John. op. cit., p. 424.
14. Fascicule i, contained the Kalendarium and Temporale, 1882; Fascicule ii, contained the Psalterium and Commune, with Officia Missalia, 1879; Fascicule iii, contained the Sanctorale and Accentuarius, with the bibliographical and critical apparatus, 1886.
15. Ibid., Fascicule iii, p. xlii, note.
16. Prothero, op. cit., pp. 269-270.
17. Lawley, Stephen W. Breviarium ad usum insignis ecclesie Eboracensis. Surtees Society Publications, 1880, lxxi.
18. Quiller-Couch, Sir Arthur. Lecture No. VI. "On a school of English," On the Art of Reading, 1920.
19. The Henry Bradshaw Society was founded in memory

of Bradshaw "for the purpose of printing liturgical MSS. and rare editions of service books and illustrative documents, on an historical and scientific basis, preference being given to those which bear upon the history of the Book of Common Prayer or of the Church of England."

20. *Statutes of Lincoln Cathedral*, arranged by Henry Bradshaw, with illustrative documents, edited by Christopher Wordsworth. 3 parts. Cambridge: University Press, 1892-1897.
21. Prothero, *op. cit.*, pp. 279-280.
22. Pollard, A. W. ed. *Chaucer's Canterbury Tales*. 2 vols. London: Macmillan & Co., 1894, v. 1, p. vii.
23. Prothero, *op. cit.*, p. 347.
24. *The Skeleton of Chaucer's Canterbury Tales*. Printed in 1868, published in November 1871. Reprinted, Bradshaw's *Collected Papers*, 1889, pp. 102-148.
25. *Ibid.*, p. 114.
26. *Ibid.*, p. 102.
27. Letter to John Payne Collier, dated April 23, 1867, quoted in Prothero's *Memoir*, p. 355.
28. *Ibid.*, pp. 353-354.
29. *Ibid.*, p. 358.
30. *Ibid.*, p. 333, quoting Professor Robertson Smith.
31. *Ibid.*, pp. 333-334.
32. *Ibid.*, p. 334.
33. James, M. R. *Eton and King's, Recollections, Mostly Trivial, 1875-1925*. London: Williams & Norgate, Ltd., 1926, p. 110.
34. Lubbock, S. G. *A Memoir of Montague Rhodes James*. Cambridge: University Press, 1939, p. 22.
35. James, *op. cit.*, p. 199.
36. Bradshaw, Henry. *Collected Papers*. Cambridge: University Press, 1889, pp. 1-15.
37. *Ibid.*, p. 1.
38. *Ibid.*, p. 2.
39. *Ibid.*, p. 3n.
40. The existence of the map was known from about 1957, but I am dating it from the appearance of the full account: Skelton, R. A., Marston, Thomas E. and Painter, George D. *The Vinland*

Map and the Tarter Relation. New Haven and London: Yale University Press, 1965.
41. This letter is printed in full in the Excerpts.
42. Prothero, op. cit., p. 66.
43. Ibid., pp. 66-67.
44. Ibid., p. 75.
45. Henry Bradshaw's Correspondence on Incunabula with J. W. Holtrop and M.F.A.G. Campbell, edited by Wytze and Lotte Hellinga. Amsterdam: Menno Hertzberger & Co., 1966-1978. 2 vols.
46. Ibid., letter No. 16, 10th May, 1866.
47. Ibid., letter No. 32, 25th April, 1870.
48. Ibid., letter No. 100, 27th April, 1886, to G. W. Prothero.
49. The Academy, No. 721, 27th February, 1886, pp. 147-149.
50. Collingwood, R. G. The Idea of History. London: Oxford University Press, 1946, Part IV, Section i (iii).
51. Prothero, op. cit., pp. 239-240.
52. Ibid., p. 74.
53. Ibid., p. 227.
54. Ibid., p. 229-230.
55. The Library, 4th S. (1932-1933), XIII:228.
56. Crone, J. S. Henry Bradshaw, His Life and Work. Dublin: Sign of the Three Candles, 1931.
57. Prothero, op. cit., p. 349.
58. Henry Bradshaw's Correspondence, op. cit., p. 134.
59. Prothero, op. cit., p. 387.
60. Ibid., pp. 378-379.
61. Ibid., p. 246.
62. Ibid., pp. 247-248.
63. Ibid., p. 312.
64. Willis, Robert. Architectural History of the University of Cambridge ..., edited, with large additions and brought up to the present time by J. W. Clark. Cambridge, University Press, 1886. 4 vols.
65. Stokes, Whitley. The Breton Glosses at Orleans. Calcutta, 1880.
66. Prothero, op. cit., p. 325.

Reference to and Works about Henry Bradshaw

The Globe, 11 February 1886.
Pall Mall, 12 February 1886 (anon. but Lionel Cust).
The Times, 12 February 1886, 16 February 1886 (funeral service).
Cambridge Express, 13 February 1886, 20 February 1886 (funeral service).
Cambridge Independent, 13 February 1886 (result of inquest); 20 February 1886 (funeral service).
The Cambridge Review: "Henry Bradshaw" by G. W. Prothero. Three articles: 17 February 1886, 24 February 1886, 3 March 1886.
Nature, 18 February 1886, by A. N.(ewton).
Cambridge Chronicle and University Journal, 19 February 1886 (account of the funeral service, including mention of a special anthem composed for the occasion by Mr. C. V. Stanford).
The Academy, 20 February 1886, by J. H. Hessels.
The Athenaeum, 20 February 1886.
Saturday Review, 20 February 1886: "Henry Bradshaw" (anon. but J. W. Clark). Reprinted: Old Friends at Cambridge and Elsewhere by J. W. Clark. London: Macmillan, 1900, pp. 292-301.
The Guardian, 24 February 1886 (signed 'R.J.S.').
The Academy, 27 February 1886: (i) anon., (ii) by F. E. Warren.
The Athenaeum, 27 February 1886, by W. P. Bennett.
Daily Telegraph, 6 March 1886.
The Printers' Register, 6 March 1886: "In Memoriam" by William Blades.
The Tablet, 6 March 1886.
Cambridge University Reporter, 23 March 1886 (recording a meeting on Tuesday 16 March regarding the setting up of a memorial to H.B.).
The Athenaeum, 27 March 1886: (i) Letter by Henry N. Stevens on "The Coverdale Bible of 1535" mentions H.B.; (ii) Letter from Professor Mahaffy on H.B.'s Irish connections.
The Library Chronicle, March 1886: "In memoriam; Henry Bradshaw" by C. E. Grant. reprinted (1886) by Dryden Press, London. J. Davy & Sons, 137, Long Acre.

The Library Journal, March 1886.
Paper & Printing Trades Journal, March 1886.
Walford's Antiquarian: A Magazine & Bibliographical Review, March 1886.
Book-lore: A monthly magazine of bibliography, April 1886: "Henry Bradshaw--in memoriam" by C. W. Sutton.
Macmillan's Magazine, April 1886: "Henry Bradshaw" by A. C. Benson. Reprinted, under the same title but with several interesting changes in the text, in Benson's Essays (Heinemann, 1896).
The Library Journal, November 1886: "Memories among English librarians" by R. R. Bowker, contains section on H.B.
Englische Studien, Vol. X. (1886), by Karl Breul (at Cambridge).
Prothero, G. W. A Memoir of Henry Bradshaw. Fellow of King's College, Cambridge, and University Librarian. London: Kegan Paul, Trench & Co., 1888.

Reviews:
    The World, December 12, 1888.
    Daily News, December 14, 1888.
    Leeds Mercury, December 15, 1888.
    Manchester Guardian, December 17, 1888.
    Scottish Leader, December 20, 1888.
    Saturday Review, December 22, 1888.
    Birmingham Daily Post, December 28, 1888 (by S. Timmins).
    The Athenaeum, January 12, 1889.
    Aberdeen Free Press, January 28, 1889.
    Journal of Education, February 1, 1889.
    The Academy, February 2, 1889 (signed 'X').
    Scots Observer, February 9, 1889.
    The Guardian, February 13, 1889.
    The Library, February, 1889.
    The Spectator, July 6, 1889.
    The Bookworm, Vol. 2. (1889), pp. 221-224.
    The Church Quarterly Review, Vol. XXVIII (1889), pp. 94-112.
    The Library Chronicle, Vol. V, No. 58, 1889, pp. 179-188, by Ernest C. Thomas.
    Journal of the Friends' Historical Society, Vol.

XVIII (1921), p. 39.

The Dictionary of National Biography, ed. Sir Leslie Stephen and Sir Sidney Lee. Vol. XXII, Supplement, 1901 (article by G. W. Prothero).

Library Association of Australia Proceedings, 1901. South Australia: C. E. Bristow, Government Printer, North Terrace, Adelaide. "A Scholar-librarian." A paper read at the Adelaide Conference of the Library Association of Australasia on Friday, October 12, 1900 by Dr. Alexander Leeper, Warden of Trinity College, Melbourne; President of the Victoria Branch of the Library Association of Australasia.

The Library Journal, August 1904: "Henry Bradshaw: librarian and scholar" by Ewald Flügel.

The Library Association Record, August 1905: "Some aspects of the work of Henry Bradshaw" by C. F. Newcombe. Reprinted 'for private use', 1905, by James Price, 1 B, Havil Street, Camberwell, London S.E.

The Cornhill Magazine, N.S. XXX:Jan.-June 1911, pp. 814-825: "The leaves of the tree. No. IX.--Henry Bradshaw" by A. C. Benson. This is a completely different essay from that which Benson published in 1886 and 1896.

Crone, John Smyth. Henry Bradshaw, His Life and Work. Read before the Bibliographical Society of Ireland on 23rd February 1931. Printed at the Sign of the Three Candles, Fleet Street, Dublin (1931).

Leslie, Sir Shane. "Henry Bradshaw: Prince of bibliographers," in To Dr. R. Essays here collected and published in honor of the seventieth birthday of Dr. A. S. W. Rosenbach. July 22, 1946. Philadelphia, 1946. Reprinted in: The Collected Catalogues of Dr. A. S. W. Rosenbach, 1904-1951. Vol. IX, pp. 124-135. McGraw-Hill, 1967. 10 vols.

Oates, J. C. T. "Young Mr. Bradshaw," in: Essays in Honour of Victor Scholderer, ed. Dennis E. Rhodes. Mainz: Karl Pressler, 1970, pp. 276-283.

PART II

CHECKLIST OF THE WRITINGS
OF HENRY BRADSHAW

1862

"On the recovery of the long lost Waldensian Manuscripts." Read 10 March 1862. <u>Antiquarian communications: being papers presented at the meetings of the Cambridge Antiquarian Society</u>. Cambridge. Vol. II. 1864, pp. 203-218. Reprinted in the <u>Collected papers</u>. 1889, pp. 1-15.
 This paper was reprinted as an appendix to the following volume to which "the Author has added to this reprint one or two additional notes, which are marked with his initials."
 Todd, James Henthorn. <u>The Waldensian manuscripts preserved in the library of Trinity College, Dublin</u>. Macmillan and Co., London and Cambridge; Hodges, Smith and Co., Dublin. 1865.
 The C.U.L. copy (Hib. 7. 865.3) has a few manuscript notes by Bradshaw.

"Two lists of books in the University Library." Read 17 November 1862. <u>Antiquarian communications: being papers presented at the meetings of the Cambridge Antiquarian Society</u>. Cambridge. Vol. II. 1864, pp. 239-278. Reprinted in the <u>Collected papers</u>. 1889, pp. 16-54.

1863

Letter, dated from Cambridge, 24 January 1863, referring to "The Codex Sinaiticus." The Guardian (Supplement), 28 January 1863, p. 85.

"An early University Statute concerning hostels." Read 11 May 1863. Antiquarian communications: being papers presented at the meetings of the Cambridge Antiquarian Society. Cambridge. Vol. II. 1864, pp. 279-281. Reprinted in the Collected papers. 1889, pp. 55-57.

"Catalogue des livres de la Bibliothèque de l'Université, à Cambridge, imprimés entièrement ou en partie sur velin." Le Bibliophile, Illustré par J. Ph. Berjeau. Londres: E. Rascol, Libraire-Editeur, 4, Brydges Street, Covent Garden. Vol. II (Nos. XIII-XXV), 1 September 1863, pp. 105-108; 1 November 1863, pp. 123-127.

"The English block-printed broadside." Le Bibliophile, Illustré. Vol. II (Nos. XIII-XXV), 1 December 1863, pp. 141-142.
    Refers back to an article in Le Bibliophile, 1 May 1863, pp. 53-56, "Une xylographie anglaise.--Moral Play dans la collection de M. T.-O. Weigel."

1864-1867

Chaucer, Geoffrey. Poems by Chaucer and others, mostly in MSS. in the University Library, Cambridge. Twelve specimens printed between 24 June 1864 and 27 July 1867 in connection with a proposed edition of Chaucer's Works.
    In 1864 Professor Earle, W. Aldis Wright and Henry Bradshaw agreed to edit an edition of Chaucer for the Clarendon Press. In due course each editor dropped out because of lack of time. In 1864 Bradshaw also had a proposal from Alexander Macmillan to edit Chaucer for the Globe series. Although Bradshaw worked on Chaucerian problems for many years these specimens are virtually all that remain in print of these ventures.

Checklist of Writings / 43

1. Incipit legenda Cleopatrie regina
    a Ftyr the deth of tholome the kyng ... to I
    preye god, let oure hedys neuere ake. Amen.
   Explicit Cliopat'.
   (From MS. Gg. 4.27 in C.U.L.)
   Cambridge. University Press. 24 June 1864.

2. A Thousent sythis haue I herd men telle ... to
   And ryght thus on myn legende gan I make.
   Explicit prohemium.
   (From MS. Gg. 4.27. in C.U.L.)
   Cambridge. University Press. 30 June 1864.

3. Incipit ....
    a T babiloyne whylom fyl it thus ... to
    A woman dare and can as wel as he.
   (From MS. Gg. 4.27. in C.U.L.)
   Cambridge. University Press. 30 June 1864.

4. De Amico ad Amicam and Responcio.
   (From MS. Gg. 4.27. in C.U.L.)
   Cambridge. University Press. 11 July 1864.

5. In may whan euery herte is lyzt ... to
   En dieu maffie sanz departer Amen.
   (From MS. Gg. 4.27. in C.U.L.)
   Cambridge. University Press. 11 July 1864.

6. There nys so high comfort to my plesaunce ... to
   Of Graunson floure of hem that make in Fraunce.
   (From MS. Ff. 1.6. in C.U.L.)
   Cambridge. University Press. 26 August 1864.

7. Somtyme the world so stedfast was and stable
    ... to
   And wedde thy folke ayen to stedfastnesse
   Explicit.
   (From first collected edition of Chaucer's works, edited by William Thynne, London, Thomas Godfray, 1532) Cambridge. University Press. 26 August 1864.

8. The first stok, fader of gentilnesse ... to

44 / Henry Bradshaw

    Al were he crowne mytor or diademe.
    (From volume printed by Caxton about 1477 marked
    AB. 8.48.6. in the University Library at Cambridge.
    It there occurs as a quotation in Skogan's address
    to the young princes)
    Cambridge. University Press. 26 August 1864.

9.   The compleint of chaucer vnto his empty purse.
    (Taken from a volume printed by Caxton about
    1477 and marked AB. 8.48.6. in the University
    Library at Cambridge)
    Cambridge. University Press. 26 August 1864.

10. Balade of the vilage without peynting.
    (Taken from a volume printed by Caxton about
    1477 and marked AB. 8.48.6. in the University
    Library at Cambridge. It contains the Parlement
    of Foules, Skogan's address to the young princes,
    and some small pieces by Chaucer.)
    Cambridge. University Press. 26 August 1864.

11. Litera directa de Scogon per G.C.
    (From MS. Gg. 4.27. in the University Library
    at Cambridge)
    Cambridge. University Press. 18 July 1867.

12. Lenvoy de Chaucer a Bukton.
    (Taken from the Fairfax MS. as represented by
    Mr. R. Morris in his edition, the spelling only
    in most cases corrected by H.B.)
    Cambridge. University Press, 18 July 1867.

13. Cap^m lv^m And thanne of the clowde a scripture
    she kaste me ... shrewede paas.
    Cap^m lvi^m Now I tell yow the scripture I vndide.
    ... if it be neede.
    Cap^m lvij^m Incipit carmen secundum ordinem literarum alphabeti.
        Al mihty and al merciable queene ... to
        To penitentes that ben to merci able. Amen.
          Explicit carmen.
    Cap^m lviij^m When thus I hadde ... goodshipe rauhte
    it me.

This is an extract from a copy of <u>The Pilgrimage of the lyfe of the manhode</u>, marked Ff. 5.30. among the MSS. in the University Library at Cambridge. This prose translation of the first of Guillaume de Deguileville's three Pilgrimages is divided into four parts, containing respectively 153, 152, 65, and 65 chapters. The poem occurs in the third part. The italics denote the original corrections. H.B.
Cambridge. University Press. 27 July 1867.

<u>1865</u>

"On the possible connection between Bunyan's 'Pilgrim's Progress' and the 'Pèlerinage' of Guillaume de Deguilleville." <u>Le Bibliophile, Illustré</u>, January, pp. 11-12, under heading "Variétés."

Bradshaw's note read: "About the 'Pèlegrinage' de Guillaume de Deguilleville (not Guilleville). There is a book called 'The Pilgrim,' which is supposed to be an English translation of the 'Pilgrimage of Man,' printed by Pynson, in 4to., of which the only known copy is in the library of Queen's College, Oxford. But I have never seen it, and I doubt it accordingly. The copies which you saw here, formerly belonged to Bishop Moore, who died in 1714, and not to Dr. Barlow. The one at Oxford belonged to Archbishop Laud, who died in 1644. The copy in St. John's College Library here belonged to the Earl of Southampton, who gave it to the College in the time of James I; and the copy at Magdalene College is in Pepys' library. I have never been able to trace any other English copies in any library, though there must be two lurking somewhere in private libraries. Two of those that I mention are modern versions of the story made in the time of Charles I, and transcribed between 1630 and 1660, and the two missing ones are like these. Every one of them Bunyan may have seen and read with ease, but the old one of course he could not read. When Mr. Offor how-

> ever says so triumphantly that Bunyan could not have read the book because of the old handwriting, he was not aware that modern copies were going about in Bunyan's time. It is a matter which such an admirer of Bunyan ought to have examined and sifted; but I believe his attention has never been drawn to these books. -- Henry Bradshaw."

"On a copy of the work entitled 'Fr. Antonii Andreae Scriptum super Logica,' printed at St. Albans in the fifteenth century, now in the Library of Jesus College, Cambridge." <u>Annales du Bibliophile Belge et Hollandais</u>. No. 10, August 1865, pp. 169-171.

> Bradshaw's letter on this subject was communicated by 'C.R.' who had written an article on "Un incunable anglais inconnu" which had appeared in No. 8 of the <u>Annales</u>, June 1865, pp. 146-148.

<u>Irish Literary Inquirer; or notes on authors, books, & printing in Ireland, biographical and bibliographical, notices of rare books, memoranda of printing in Ireland, biographical notes of Irish writers</u>, etc. Conducted by John Power. No. 2, September 23, 1865, p. 15.

A note from Bradshaw, described by the editor as "a gentleman at Cambridge, well known for his intimate knowledge of Irish books," relating to Burke's <u>Hibernia Dominicana</u>:

> I have never been able to trace the statement that the work was printed by Edmund Finn, of Kilkenny, farther back than to the notice of it in the Anthologia Hibernica, in 1793 or 1794, but when copies with the uncancelled title-page are to be seen, they ought to be described first, and the others put afterwards.
>
> I have never myself seen a copy of the original issue, but I believe Mr. Heber had one of the ordinary copies with the imprint of <u>Coloniae Agrippinae</u> on the title. Sale Catalogue VI, 1881, which was resold, VIII 1249. I don't know what price it brought. But in IV. 1180, is Pope Leo the Twelfth's

copy, with the true imprint, 'Kilkenniae, ex Typographia Jacobi Stokes, juxta Praetorium, 1762.' And in the title Burke is called 'Postea Episcopum Ossoriensem.' Where is this copy now? I fancy it sold for about £15, but I have not a marked catalogue.

"Description of a manuscript of Wyclif (B.16.2) in the Library of Trinity College, Cambridge." Shirley, Walter Waddington. A catalogue of the original works of John Wyclif. Oxford, Clarendon Press, 1865.
    Shirley states, "I subjoin Mr. Bradshaw's detailed description," pp. xiii-xvi.

1866

"On two hitherto unknown poems by John Barbour, author of the Brus." Read 30 April 1866. Antiquarian communications: being papers presented at the meetings of the Cambridge Antiquarian Society. Cambridge. Vol. III, 1879, pp. 111-117. Reprinted in the Collected Papers, 1889, pp. 58-68.

"A view of the state of the University in Queen Anne's reign. With a facsimile, "Handwriting of Dr. John Edwards. Cambr. Univ. Libr. MS. Add. 58." Read 3 December 1866. Antiquarian communications: being papers presented at the meetings of the Cambridge Antiquarian Society. Cambridge. Vol. III, 1879, pp. 119-134. Reprinted in the Collected papers, 1889, pp. 69-83.

Morris, R. ed. Poetical Works of Geoffrey Chaucer. London: Bell and Daldy. 6v.
    In his Preface (p. ix) Morris notes against "Aetas Prima" (from MS. Hh.4. 12. 2. [late MS. Moore 947] in the Public Library, Cambridge):
        I am indebted to Henry Bradshaw, Esq.,
        King's College, Cambridge, for the transcript
        of this little poem, and to the Rev. W. W.
        Skeat for the collation with the MS.

In his obituary notice of Bradshaw in Printers' Register,

6 March 1886, William Blades (following a list of H.B.'s writings) concludes:
> From this list it will be seen that No. 1 [of Memoranda] is dated 1868; yet another No. 1 was sent to the printer in 1866, which, however, never went beyond a few proofs. It was entitled "Memoranda. Belgium. Books of the First Printers at Bruges, 1475-1484," and was intended as the commencement of a series of issues upon the early presses of Holland, Belgium, and England, a design which unfortunately was never carried out.

1867

"On the earliest English engravings of the Indulgence known as the 'Image of Pity': (with a facsimile of the indulgence, printed at Westminster by W. Caxton)." Read 25 February 1867. <u>Antiquarian communications: being papers presented at the meetings of the Cambridge Antiquarian Society</u>. Cambridge. Vol. III, 1879, pp. 135-152. Reprinted in the <u>Collected Papers</u>, 1889, pp. 84-100.

<u>Catalogue of the Oriental Manuscripts in the Library of King's College</u>, Cambridge, by Edward Henry Palmer. Royal Asiatic Society's Publications, June 1867, pp. 1-3.
    Contains letter by Bradshaw to Palmer (of St. John's College, Cambridge) referring to the oriental manuscripts at King's College, Cambridge and Eton College, dated November 12, 1866.

Letter on the Archiepiscopal Library at Lambeth. <u>Times</u>, October 7, 1867.

1868

Memorandum No. 1. The printer of the Historia S. Albani. (with one photographed facsimile)." February 1868. Macmillan & Co., London.1/-. Reprinted in the <u>Collected Papers</u>, 1889, pp. 149-163.

"An inventory of the stuff in the College Chambers (King's College), 1598." Read 9 March 1868. <u>Antiquarian communications: being papers presented at the meetings of the Cambridge Antiquarian Society</u>. Cambridge. Vol. III, 1879, pp. 181-198. Reprinted in the <u>Collected Papers</u>, 1889, pp. 164-180.

Letter, dated from University Library Cambridge on 27 July, 1868, on "Greek MS. of the Gospels." Published in full in a letter from the Rev. Edmund Tew, <u>Notes and Queries</u>, 4th.S.ii, 15 August 1868, pp. 162-163.
    Referring to an enquiry from Tew, <u>Notes and Queries</u>, 4th. S, ii, 25 July 1868, p. 80, under heading "Ancient Greek Manuscript of the Gospels."

Furnivall, Frederick J. ed. <u>Early English meals and manners</u>. London: Early English Text Society. Original Series, No. 32.
    Contains section, "'Latin graces' (from the Balliol MS. 354, leaf 2' signed at end 'Henry Bradshaw.'"

1869

<u>The Pilgrimage of the lyf of the Manhode from the French of Guillaume de Deguileville</u>. Edited by William Aldis Wright, Librarian of Trinity College, Cambridge. Printed for the Roxburghe Club. London, J. B. Nichols and Sons, 25, Parliament Street.
    Bradshaw began editing this work and referred to it in a letter to F. J. Furnivall dated 22 February 1867. Later in 1867 H.B. handed it over to W. G. Clark. It was eventually finished in 1869 by William Aldis Wright. In the Preface (p. xii) Wright wrote: "I cannot conclude without expressing my obligations to Mr. Henry Bradshaw, University Librarian, Cambridge, for the valuable assistance he has rendered me whenever I have had occasion to consult him in the course of the work."

1870

Memorandum No. 2. A classified index of the Fifteenth Century books in the collection of M. J. de Meyer, which were sold at Ghent in November, 1869. April 1870. Macmillan & Co., London. 1/-. Reprinted in the Collected Papers, 1889, pp. 206-236.

"On the engraved device used by Nicholaus Gotz of Sletzstat, the Cologne printer, in 1474." Read 21 November 1870. Antiquarian communications: being papers presented at the meetings of the Cambridge Antiquarian Society. Cambridge. Vol. III, 1879, pp. 237-243, with "Note on a book printed at Cologne by Gotz in 1477, with two illustrations engraved on copper," pp. 244-246. Reprinted in the Collected Papers, 1889, pp. 237-246.

"On two engravings on copper, by G.M., a wandering Flemish artist of the XV-XVIth. century, with two notes." Read 21 November 1870. Antiquarian communications: being papers presented at the meetings of the Cambridge Antiquarian Society. Cambridge. Vol. III, 1879, pp. 247-254, with: Note A. On three engravings on copper, fastened into the Cambridge copy of the Utrecht Breviary of 1514, pp. 255-256. Note B. On the engravings fastened into the Lambeth copy of the Salisbury Primer, or Horae, printed by Wynkyn de Worde (about 1494), pp. 257-258. Reprinted in the Collected Papers, 1889, pp. 247-257.

1871

"An instrument relating to proceedings in the cause of King Henry VIII's divorce from Catherine of Aragon."
 Cambridge University Library has 11 sets of unbound proof sheets of an edition prepared by Bradshaw, but never published. (C.U.L. Adv.C.77.74).
 Proof consisted of 4 proof sheets which contained 64 pages and bear dates, on University Press stamps, of 8 March, 11 March, 14 March and 12 June 1871.
 Text obviously incomplete since it finished mid-

Checklist of Writings / 51

sentence at foot of page 64. Numerous marginalia and corrections by Bradshaw throughout.

Memorandum No. 3. List of the founts of type and woodcut devices used by printers in Holland in the Fifteenth Century (with four facsimiles). June 1871. Macmillan & Co., London. 1/-.
 Bradshaw's preface is dated June 1871, but date on verso of T/P is June 1870.

 Reprinted in the Collected papers, 1889, pp. 258-280.

"On the oldest written remains of the Welsh language." Read 20 November 1871. Antiquarian communications: being papers presented at the meetings of the Cambridge Antiquarian Society. Cambridge. Vol. III, 1879, pp. 263-267. Reprinted in the Collected Papers, 1889, pp. 281-285.
 (C.U.L. has proof-sheets of this work with many MS. corrections and notes). (C.U.L. Adv.C.77.67).

Memorandum No. 4. The skeleton of Chaucer's Canterbury Tales: an attempt to distinguish the several fragments of the work as left by the author. (Bradshaw's preface is dated 8 September 1867 and it was printed in 1868; but note at end [by H.B.] is dated November 23, 1871 and explains why it was not issued until then.) Macmillan & Co., London. 1/-. Reprinted in the Collected Papers, 1889, pp. 102-148.

1872

"On the collection of portraits belonging to the University before the Civil War." Read 3 June 1872. Antiquarian communications: being papers presented at the meetings of the Cambridge Antiquarian Society. Cambridge. Vol. III, 1879, pp. 275-286. Reprinted in the Collected Papers, 1889, pp. 286-296.

"List of the editions of Chaucer's works." A Treatise on the Astrolabe addressed to his son Lowys by Geoffrey Chaucer. A.D. 1391. Edited from the earliest MSS. by the Reverend Walter W. Skeat, M.A., late Fellow of Christ's College, Cambridge. Chaucer Society. First Series, XXIX. <u>also</u> Early English Text Society. Extra Series, XVI. p. xxvi in each issue. Issues identical except for title-page. Also printed in Skeat's preface to Bell's edition of Chaucer (Bohn series), v. 1, p. 3.

Skeat made no specific reference to Bradshaw's contribution in this regard; only general reference in footnotes to <u>Preface</u>.

> Prothero's <u>Memoir</u> (p. 356) has this comment: The bibliography of the poet was, it is almost needless to say, at his fingers' ends. 'I wrote to him one day,' says Professor Skeat, 'with a request for information as to the old black-letter editions of Chaucer, not reckoning the editions of separate works by Caxton and others. He at once took a pen, and there and then, without a pause, wrote out a complete list, with title, date, size, and other particulars of each edition.

1873-83

<u>Publications of the Palaeographical Society</u>, 1873-1883, Vol. ii.

H.B. provided descriptions to accompany the plates of: (a) the Cambridge manuscript of the <u>Historia Ecclesiastica</u> of Bede (C.U.L.Kk.v.16), plates numbered 139 and 140. (b) the <u>Book of Deer</u> (C.U.L. Ii.6.32), plates numbered 210 and 211.

1875

"Notes of the Episcopal Visitation of the Archdeaconry of Ely in 1685." Read 24 May 1875. <u>Antiquarian communications: being papers presented at the meetings of the Cambridge Antiquarian Society.</u> Cambridge. Vol. III, 1879, pp. 323-361. Reprinted in the <u>Collected Papers</u>, 1889, pp. 297-332.

"On the ABC as an authorised School-book in the Sixteenth Century." Read 24 May 1875. <u>Antiquarian communications: being papers presented at the meetings of the Cambridge Antiquarian Society.</u> Cambridge. Vol. III, 1879, pp. 363-370. Reprinted in the <u>Collected Papers</u>, 1889, pp. 333-340.

Animaduersions vppon the Annotacions and Corrections of some imperfections of impressiones of Chaucers workes (sett downe before tyme, and nowe) reprinted in the yere of oure lorde 1598 sett downe by Francis Thynne. Now newly edited ... by F. J. Furnivall, M.A. and a preface by G. H. Kingsley, M.D., F.L.S. Chaucer Society. Early English Text Society. Original Series, 9.

    It had originally appeared, edited by G. H. Kingsley, in 1865. The 1875 edition had several contributions by Bradshaw who was thanked by Furnivall "for his happy hits."

    Bradshaw's contributions were: p. xxvi, referring to Sir Bryan Tuke; p. 30, footnote to 'The Dethe of Blaunche the Duchesse'; pp. 75-76, referring to Thynne's edition of Chaucer; p. 101, note at beginning of the Plowmans Prologue.

1877

Memorandum No. 5. Notice of a fragment of the Fifteen Oes and other prayers printed at Westminster by W. Caxton about 1490-91, preserved in the Library of the Baptist College, Bristol. November 1877. Macmillan & Co., London. 1/-. Reprinted in the <u>Collected Papers</u>, 1889, pp. 341-349.

<u>Dictionary of Christian Biography, Literature, Sects and Doctrines, being a continuation of the Dictionary of the Bible.</u> Edited by William Smith and Henry Wace. London: John Murray. Vol. 1, A-D.

    Lives of: St. Abbanus (p. 1), St. Abel (p. 4), St. Abranus (p. 9), St. Achea (p. 17).

1878

"The Irish monastic missal at Oxford." A letter dated January 5, 1878. The Academy, 12 January 1878, Vol. XIII, pp. 34-35.

1879

"Note on the Light of St. Erasmus and on the various spellings of his name in the Churchwardens' accounts of Trinity Church, Cambridge, during the years 1504 to 1530." Read 17 November 1879. Read by the Rev. J. Barton, Vicar of the Parish of Holy Trinity, as a postscript to his communication, "Notes on the past history of the Church of Holy Trinity, Cambridge." Cambridge Antiquarian Communications: being papers presented at the meetings of the Cambridge Antiquarian Society. Cambridge. Vol. IV, 1881, pp. 327-331. (Barton's paper: pp. 313-335). Reprinted in the Collected Papers, 1889, pp. 350-353.

1880

Ellis, R. (of Oxford), "De Artis Amatoriae Ovidianae Codice Oxoniensi." Hermes. Vol. 15, 1880, pp. 425-432.
    Embodies a letter from Bradshaw regarding the Bodleian Manuscript, Auct.F.iv.32, pp. 425-427.

"A memorandum, into the history of the statute books of Lincoln Cathedral."
    Cambridge University Library has 7 sets of unbound proof sheets of an edition prepared by Bradshaw, but never published. (C.U.L.Adv.C.77.74)
    Proof consisted of 3 proof sheets which contained 48 pages which bear dates of 19 and 24 November 1880.
    Text incomplete, at foot of p. 48, reads: "It is of this newer and fuller Register, the Consuetudines of 1267, that I have next to speak."

1880-1883

<u>Breviarium ad usum insignis ecclesie Eboracensis</u>, edited by Stephen Willoughby Lawley. Surtees Society Publication. 2 vols. Vol. LXXI, 1880. Vol. LXXV, 1883.
    Vol. LXXI includes a "table of all the editions known and copies extant of the York Breviary, with the place and date of printing, and summary of contents" (p. xiii), with the editor's footnote, "This table has been drawn up by Mr. Bradshaw: to whose kindness I owe so much." (p. xiii).
    Vol. LXXV includes a "List of copies of the York Breviary" (p. xii), with the editor's note, "At the close of this Preface will be found a new Table of the Contents of all the copies of our Breviary. It is intended to take the place of the Table in the First Volume, which is less full and less exact. I owe this, and much more, to the kindness of Mr. Bradshaw." (p. ix).

1881

Unheaded note, correcting an error relating to a binding of the Mazarine Bible in an article by Francis St. John Thackeray on the Eton College Library. <u>Notes and Queries</u>. 6th.S.iii, 14 May 1881, p. 384.
    Thackeray had stated that on each side of the binding there were "four scrolls, with Joannes Fust decipherable on each of them." Bradshaw corrected this name to read "Johannes Fogel."

Memorandum No. 6. The University Library. Papers contributed to the "Cambridge University Gazette, 1869." November 1881. Macmillan and Bowes, Cambridge. 1/-. Had previously appeared in issues of <u>Cambridge University Gazette</u>, dated 3, 10, 17, 24 February and 3, 10, 17 March 1869. Reprinted in the <u>Collected Papers</u>, 1889, pp. 181-205.

Cox, J. Charles and Hope, W. H. St. John. <u>The chronicles of the Collegiate Church or Free Chapel of All Saints, Derby</u>. Bemrose & Sons, 23 Old Bailey,

London and Irongate, Derby.

To this work Bradshaw contributed two notes, both of which are acknowledged in footnotes: (i) Notes on "the bokes in our lady Chapell tyed with chenes y^t were gyffen to Alhaloes Church in Derby" (pp. 175-177); (ii) Note on the service books used in the old Church of England, with a list of those in the Church of All Saints from an inventory of 1466. Dated from Cambridge, March 17, 1881 (pp. 229-231).

1882

"Godfiied van der Haghen (G.H.), the publisher of Tindale's own last edition of the New Testament in 1534-35." Bibliographer, No. 1, January 1882, pp. 3-11. Privately reprinted by William Blades. 1886. Reprinted in the Collected Papers, 1889, pp. 354-370.

Memorandum No. 7. The President's Address at the opening of the Fifth Annual Meeting of the Library Association of the United Kingdom. Cambridge, Sept. 5, 1882. October 1882. Macmillan and Bowes, Cambridge. 1/-. Also published in the Transactions and Proceedings of the Library Association at the Fourth and Fifth Annual Meetings, 1882, pp. 107-115. Reprinted in the Collected Papers, 1889, pp. 371-409.

> Preceding the text Bradshaw appended a note:
> The details of the working of the University Library promised in the concluding paragraph of the following address were brought before the members of the Association when they visited the library on Friday afternoon, September 8, at the close of the meeting. They are here thrown into an appendix in a slightly fuller form. (pp. 385-404.)
>
> Two notes are added, on questions intimately connected with the proceedings of the Cambridge meeting. One forms the introduction to a paper relating to local libraries considered as museums of local authorship and printing (pp. 404-405), which was to have been brought forward in con-

nexion with Mr. W. H. K. Wright's paper on local bibliography. The other is a contribution to the vexed question of size notation, which formed the subject of a report presented to the Cambridge meeting by a Committee appointed a year ago. (pp. 406-409.)

The <u>Transactions ... of the Library Association</u>, 1882, printed: (a) "Some account of the organization of the Cambridge University Library." <u>Appendix</u>, pp. 229-237; (b) "On local libraries considered as museums of local authorship and printing." <u>Ibid.</u>, pp. 237-288; (c) "On size-notation as distinguished from form-notation." <u>Ibid.</u>, pp. 238-240.

1883

<u>Statutes for the University of Cambridge and for the Colleges within it, made, etc., under the universities of Oxford and Cambridge Act.</u> [Editor's preface signed H.B.]. At the University Press Cambridge.

1884

"Biographical notes on the University Printers from the commencement of printing in Cambridge to the present time." Communicated by Robert Bowes Esq., on 28 January 1884. <u>Cambridge Antiquarian Communications: being papers presented at the meetings of the Cambridge Antiquarian Society.</u> Cambridge. Vol. V, 1886, pp. 283-362.

At the end of the paper Bradshaw made some comments which were recorded in: <u>Report presented to the Cambridge Antiquarian Society at its forty-fourth Annual General Meeting</u>, May 26, 1884. Cambridge. 1886.

> "Mr. Bradshaw remarked upon the importance of carrying through the two wholly distinct processes of research, (1) examining the books, and (2) searching through all Registers which relate to the printers of them. Either, if carried on alone, often gave an erroneous idea to the worker. He suggested

that all the Parish Registers and such books might be searched, and copies made of everything that concerns the Cambridge printers, as had been done at Bruges by Mr. Weale, and that a systematic collection of Cambridge printed books should be made, as was being done to some extent at the Free Library, and as had been done for Oxford so thoroughly by Mr. F. Madan, of the Bodleian Library. Mr. Bowes' paper was likely to give just such an impetus to the investigation, that we might hope to incite others to contribute to the work on this as a satisfactory basis." p. cxxii.

"Mr. Mullinger brought under the attention of the meeting a volume (small quarto) from the library of St. John's College (Gg. 6. 41.) without date or either printer's name or author's name, which he submitted was probably a production of the Cambridge Press during Thomas's time, but anterior to any of the volumes of 1584 bearing his imprint....
Mr. Bradshaw pointed out the unusual character of the signatures in the book, which ran thus A, 2,3,4, and so on; an arrangement which ought to afford some help in tracing the printer. He also suggested that as the licence to print was given in May, 1583, and in the following month the sheets of Whitaker's work were actually seized in the press, no evidence is wanted to shew that 1583, not 1584, is the first year of the University Press. At the same time it would be most interesting to recover a specimen of work done in the earlier year." pp. cxxiii-cxxiv.

"The Toyes of an idle head." Notes and Queries. 6th.S. x, 6 September 1884, p. 187.

1885

"Discovery of a St. Albans book." A letter dated 8 January 1885, in continuation of a letter by E. Gordon Duff in the same issue relating to a copy of Antonii Andreae Questiones super Logica in the library of Wadham College, Oxford. The Academy, 17 January 1885, Vol. XXVII, pp. 45-46.

Report by H.B. on the wants of the University Library due to the constantly increasing pressure for accommodation. University Reporter, 1884-85, pp. 679-682. Report dated 6 May 1885. Publication dated 12 May 1885.

Bradshaw read a paper on "Early Bibles" at a meeting of the Library Association in London, May 1885. Never printed. See Prothero, pp. 306 and 369.

Memorandum No. 8. The early collection of canons, commonly known as the "Hibernensis." A letter addressed to Dr. F. W. H. Wasserschleben, Privy Councillor, Professor of Law in the University of Giessen. June 1885. Macmillan and Bowes. Cambridge. 1/-. Also printed by Dr. Wasserschleben in his Irische Kanonensammlung, 2nd. ed., 1885. Introduction, pp. lxiii-lxxvi. Reprinted in the Collected Papers, 1889, pp. 410-420.

1886

"A half-century of notes on the Day-Book of John Dorne as edited by F. Madan for the Oxford Historical Society. Reproduced at Cambridge in facsimile of Bradshaw's MS."
    Bradshaw's introductory letter to Madan dated 30 January 1886.
    Reprinted in the Collected Papers, 1889, pp. 421-451. Reprinted in Collectanea, 2nd. Series, edited by Montagu Burrows, published for the Oxford Historical Society at the Clarendon Press, 1890.

Catalogue of the valuable and important library of books

of the late Henry Bradshaw, Esq., M.A., Fellow of King's College and University Librarian. To be sold by auction, by John Swan & Son at their Rooms, 19, Sidney Street, Cambridge, on Tuesday, November 16, 1886, and 3 following days, Each day at 1 o'clock punctually, By order of the Executors.
 1330 items.

Godfried van der Haghen.... Printed by William Blades from the text in the Bibliographer, 1882, in a pamphlet, "30 copies, not for sale."

"Papyrii Gemini Eleatis Hermathena ... reproduced in exact facsimile from the copy in St. John's College Library. With an appendix taken from Mr. Bradshaw's notes." Printed by C. J. Clay, John Clay, & C. F. Clay for Alexander Macmillan and Robert Bowes.
 Publishers' Note:
  ... A bibliographical description of the book will be found in Mr. Bradshaw's introduction prefixed to Bullock's Oration.
  He there gives a general description of the three successive proofs or states in which the first sheet is found. The Appendix here printed contains a detailed account of the differences between them, taken from his notes....
 H.B.'s Appendix, pp. 1-6.

Bullock, Henry. Doctissimi Viri Henrici Bulloci theologiae doctoris, oratio habita Catabrigiae, ... Apud praeclarissimam academiam Cantabrigiensem. An. M. quingentesimovicesimoprimo. Reproduced in exact Facsimile from the copy in the Bodleian Library: with a bibliographical introduction by the late Henry Bradshaw ... Printed by C. J. Clay, John Clay & C. F. Clay for Alexander Macmillan and Robert Bowes.
 In the "Publishers' Note," it reads:
  The completion of Mr. Bradshaw's Bibliographical Introduction enables us to issue the three additional volumes of Siberch's books announced in 1881, and makes us the more desirous to complete the series of reproductions by the issue of the remaining

four books.

This <u>Introduction</u> was the last work on which Mr. Bradshaw was engaged when his health gave way in August 1885. On the 31st. of that month he wrote: 'I managed to go to London on Friday, and worked hard at <u>all</u> their Cambridge Siberch books, with satisfactory results.'

He intended to re-examine the Bodleian copies and then to finish the MS. for press, but he was never again able to resume his work upon it. But by the result of his 'honest and patient observation of facts' connected with these books for many years as given in the following pages he has added an important chapter to the history of printing in England.

The introduction as it now stands was compiled by Francis Jenkinson from Bradshaw's notes as Jenkinson makes very clear:

> The following introduction consists of two parts: first, a summary of what was known on the subject of Siberch's books by the successive bibliographers who have noticed them, followed by Mr. Bradshaw's own determination of the order in which the books were printed: and, secondly, a list of the books, with descriptions and remarks. The first part is exactly as Mr. Bradshaw left it and shows well his clear and methodical way of conducting such investigations. With regard to the second part, several years had elapsed since the list was written out; and he had begun to rewrite it in a somewhat altered form and had finished the account of the first book. I have therefore continued what he had begun, the necessary changes being merely changes of form, except in the case of the <u>Papyrius Geminus</u>. When Mr. Bradshaw wrote his account of this book, he was aware of only two different states or issues of the first sheet, which he described accordingly. Since then, however, he had the delight of securing, from the catalogue

of a German bookseller, a copy in a still earlier state, hitherto unknown: and this led him to make a minute study of the variations presented by the different copies. I have selected the most important particulars from his notes and incorporated them in the description on page 20.
Cambridge University Library possesses the original MS. and first proof of Jenkinson's article and it throws additional light on the relationship between the work of Bradshaw and Jenkinson. (C.U.L. Adv. bb. 110.1)

An interesting contemporary notice regarding the reprints of the Bullock and the "Hermathena" volumes is found in Notes and Queries, 7th. S. 111, January 15, 1887.

> Henrici Bulloci Oratio, 1521.--Fidelis Christiani Epistola, 1521.--Papyrii Gemini Eleatis. --Hermathena, 1522. Reproduced in exact Facsimile. With Appendixes, Illustrations, Bibliographical Introductions, &c. By the late Henry Bradshaw, University Librarian. (Cambridge, Macmillan & Bowes.)
> Six years have elapsed since Messrs. Macmillan & Bowes commenced to reprint in facsimile the few books, eight in all, known to belong to the press of John Siberch, the first Cambridge printer. Linacre's 'Galen De Temperamentis' was issued in 1881 to a limited number of subscribers. After a long but excusable delay the task has been resumed, and three works from the same press, constituting, with the previous volume, half Siberch's productions, have seen the light. The books now given to the world are all in Latin, and consist of the 'Oration of Henry Bullock' ("Bovillus," Erasmus styles him) to Cardinal Wolsey on the occasion of the visit of that dignitary to Cambridge in 1520; a volume containing a letter of wholesome admonition "ad christianos omnes," by a certain faithful Christian, and

St. Augustine's discourse, 'De Miseria ac Brevitate Huius Mortalis Uitae'; and 'Hermathena, seu de Eloquentiae Victoria' of Papyrius Geminus. These works are, as is to be expected, curious and rare rather than interesting or important, and two of them occupying, indeed, only a few pages. The 'Hermathena,' which is dedicated to Richard Pace, chief secretary to Henry VIII., is a fair specimen of the kind of allegory, which in prose and in verse, in Latin and in the vulgar tongue, was in high favour in the fifteenth and sixteenth centuries. The scene is laid in part in the Elysian fields, and Wisdom, with her daughter Eloquence, sails to Britain, where she is welcomed by that most illustrious prince Henry VIII., and is held in great reverence.

From the bibliographical standpoint the works are all rarities. Of Bullock's 'Oration' four copies are known: one in the British Museum, a second in the Bodleian, a third in the Archiepiscopal Library at Lambeth, a fourth in Archbishop Marsh's library, St. Patrick's, Dublin. Of the epistle a single copy is found in the Bodleian. Copies of the 'Hermathena' are in the library of the late Henry Bradshaw, in St. John's Coll., Camb., Archbishop Marsh's library, Lincoln Cathedral, and the British Museum. One on vellum is in the possession of the Duke of Devonshire. Besides these some fragments of another copy exist. What will probably most interest the reader is the admirably exact and conscientious manner in which Mr. Bradshaw, whose interest in these reprints was inexhaustible, ascertained the exact date of the various works and arranged them in their order. The result of his investigations is that Linacre's translation of Galen, which Cotton ('Typographical Gazetteer') mentions as the first book printed in Cambridge, is relegated to the sixth place, the first being taken by Bullock's afore-mentioned 'Oration.' In the case of the 'Hermathena' Mr. Bradshaw proves that the work exists in three states, and gives a minute detail of the differences. On the bibliographical introduction to these volumes Mr. Bradshaw was engaged when death arrested his labours. Concerning Siberch little that is definite has been traced, and the place whence he came for his brief residence of little over a year in Cambridge and that to which he betook himself remain conjectural. The supposition of the editor who has taken up Mr. Bradshaw's labours is that he may have come from Strasbourg. Why Cambridge should, in respect of printing, have come far behind Oxford is not easy to understand. Putting on one side the disputed 'Expositio S. Hieronymi,' which bears date 1468, Oxford can point to two works printed in 1479; while the earliest work of the sister university is forty-two years later. The printing of the facsimile is admirable.

Procter, Francis and Wordsworth, Christopher. <u>Breviarium ad usum insignis ecclesiae Sarum.</u> Fasciculus I, 1882; Fasciculus II, 1879; Fasciculus III, 1886.

Fasciculus III has "Appendix II": "Printed editions of Sarum Books: from the papers of Henry Bradshaw, M.A., late University Librarian and Fellow of King's College, Cambridge, with notes by the Editors." (pp. xli-cxxx.)

The authors' preface "To the Reader" says (p. xix):

"With grateful and tender memories we now print as a second Appendix to this Introduction the Lists of Editions of the Breviary and other Choir Service--books of the Church of Salisbury, which were first <u>sketched</u> for us by Mr. Henry Bradshaw six years ago. Three weeks before his death he was applying for the loan of two Sarum Breviaries, the only copies in England which yet required to be examined by him. To him are really due the 'notice of the printed books which contain the Breviary proper, or portions of it,' and the 'brief statement of the contents of the Sarum Breviary,' which will be found in the Introduction to our Fasciculus II, published in 1879."

Thanks are also offered to librarians as well as to private owners

"whose names appear in the columns of the bibliographical lists which follow, and which as we have already intimated are due to the labours of Mr. Henry Bradshaw, to whose sympathetic help and kind offices we have been indebted from first to last. His original draft was what anyone else would have considered perfect; but he made corrections in it up to the last. We have several precious letters from him, and it was our practice instinctively to make notes of our occasional conversations with him." (p. xxii.)

1889

Collected papers of Henry Bradshaw, late University Librarian: comprising 1. 'Memoranda'; 2. 'Communications' read before the Cambridge Antiquarian Society; together with an article contributed to the 'Bibliographer,' and two papers not previously published. Edited for the Syndics of the University Press. With thirteen plates. Cambridge. University Press.

Reviews: The Academy, December 7, 1889 (E. Gordon Duff); The Athenaeum, December 21, 1889; Saturday Review, January 11, 1890; Spectator, March 8, 1890 and March 22, 1890 (letter on 'The antiquity of the Waldenses').

1892-97

Statutes of Lincoln Cathedral arranged by the late Henry Bradshaw ... edited for the Syndics of the University Press by Chr. Wordsworth. Cambridge at the University Press. Part. I, containing the complete text of 'Liber Niger' with Mr. Bradshaw's Memorandums, 1892; Part. II, containing early Customs of Lincoln, Awards, Novum Registrum etc. with documents of Salisbury, York, Lichfield, Hereford and Truro, 1897.

In his "To the Reader" (Part I, pp. V-VIII) Wordsworth wrote:

> "The present volume contains the text of the 'Liber Niger,' or Black Book of Customs of the Cathedral Church of Lincoln, preceded by some papers which the late Mr. Henry Bradshaw prepared with reference to its contents and history.
>
> The Church of Lincoln possesses a fine collection of valuable records. Upon the second shelf of one of the presses in the Muniment-room are placed nine volumes which contain statutes or customs belonging to the Dean and Chapter. Among this collection the 'Black Book' is the one which has enjoyed the longest, and perhaps, if all circumstances be considered, the widest reputation....
>
> It required more than ordinary scholarship and more than ordinary antiquarian knowledge to ascertain the history of the Black Book, and to place it in its true relative position with regard to other collections of statutes. Also it needed patience and research, which no choice of laudatory epithets could describe beyond their due.
>
> Henry Bradshaw was able to bring the necessary qualifications to the task, and during the years 1879-1884 he gave much attention to the problem, and has left in writing, and in a few half-corrected proof-sheets, several sketches of his solution (or, more strictly speaking, of more than one solution) of it. The peculiar difficulties of the case, and the

ways in which he dealt with them, have been fully described in the ninth chapter of Mr. G. W. Prothero's "Memoir of Henry Bradshaw" (Kegan Paul, Trench & Co., 1888).

But Bradshaw had not health or leisure to work out the problem upon paper so perfectly as he had conceived it might be done. He was taken away from us (Feb. 10, 1886) before he had written out the main problem to his satisfaction. But he left piles of papers evidently intended for the press, and he prepared more than one table of contents or draft of the arrangement of his projected treatise. A few chapters or sections were completed, and some others had been just begun.

The proof-sheets to which I have referred extended only to forty-eight octavo pages. And, important as these are, they do not represent Bradshaw's latest conclusions. They had been composed before his personal visits to the Chapter Muniments at Lincoln in 1880, at a time when Mr. Wickenden's researches were preparing the field for him (as it proved) to work to greater advantage. The statement about the oaths taken by members of the Chapter on installation he fully re-investigated and re-wrote entirely in a different way, and he was of course enabled greatly to increase the list of books after he had been to Lincoln. He naturally felt dissatisfied with the old proof-sheets and cancelled them, but he retained a few copies and marked two of them so as to show what passages he had found to need revision.

I have accordingly been able to make use of the greater part of these earlier proofs in one chapter or another of the work which he sketched out afresh. That he intended to use portions of his own old material in this way is evident from the fact that he adopted some pages of it, and has made references by catch-words to certain portions of it in the opening chapters which he contrived to put on paper for his "Memoranda" in their later arrangement.

He thus expressed his own opinion of his own manner of working, and his difficulties, in Nov. 1883:--'I cannot turn out a piece of work clean with any rapidity.' His re-cast proofs accordingly never make any progress, but he wrote from time to time, and thus he has left sections in manuscript more valuable and more trustworthy than the most elaborate published work of many a student who has written more easily; for almost every line that came from his pen was in reality 'clean' work.

He left one all-important section of the contents of this volume completed in his own handwriting, namely the entire text of the Black Book. This he had deciphered, transcribed and re-arranged, placing each entry in the chronological order in which it had been registered in the original volume, which the kindness of Dean Blakesley and the Chapter allowed him to examine from 1881 to 1883."

Bradshaw's transcript of the text of the 'Liber Niger' occupies pp. 273-426 in this First Part. It is, in his own words, 'copied so as to show the gradual growth of the book during three centuries, 1300-1600,' and he records having completed it at '1.30 A.M. Jan. 29-30, 1882.'

Aside from this there is a Preface which Wordsworth "extracted from a long letter of Henry Bradshaw's to the present Archbishop of Canterbury," in which Bradshaw wrote, "I can truly say that I have never been engaged in such an intensely interesting piece of anatomical work."

There is also an introductory 'Memorandum,' giving the background to the documents, which Bradshaw wrote in May 1882 (pp. 3-10), followed by two further memoranda. The first is a Memorandum on the oaths, taken by members of the Chapter on installation, written by Bradshaw in 1880, but never published in that form and entirely recast in its present form some time before December 1883 (pp. 11-27). The second Memorandum is on the books, copied from time to time, in which the laws of the Chapter are contained and registered. This section was drafted and several parts written in 1880 and revised and recast between January and May 1882 (pp. 30-223).

    Reviews: Spectator: 69, 601-02. October 29, 1892; English Hist. Rev. 8 (1893):764; English Hist. Rev. 13 (1898):344.

1893

The early collection of canons known as the Hibernensis: two unfinished papers by the late Henry Bradshaw. Edited for the Syndics of the Press. Cambridge, at the University Press. Price Two Shillings and Sixpence.

    In his 'Preface' Jenkinson, who edited the work for publication, explains:

> "In a note prefixed to the Appendix which concluded the volume of Henry Bradshaw's Collected Papers, published in 1889, I mentioned the existence of a fragment of his more detailed work on the Hibernensis. Although I was familiar with it, having had it read to me by the author himself, I had not been able to find it among his papers; or it would have been included in that collection. As there seems little chance of making up another volume, and as several persons have expressed a desire to see his latest work on the subject in print, unfinished as it unfortunately remains, the Syndics of the Press have consented to publish it in the present form."

Jenkinson also writes in the same preface:

> "In the Academy for 1888 and 1889 will be found several letters relating more or less directly to the Hibernensis and to Mr. Bradshaw's work. In particular Dr. B. F. MacCarthy takes exception to the suggested identification of the compiler of the Hibernensis with Cummeanus, the author of the Penitential (see pp. 37, 38 of the present pamphlet). It would be presumptuous in

me to do more than ask students of the subject to consider his objections very carefully before they accept them. They do not appear to me to be conclusive."

The two unfinished papers in this work are: (i) A letter to Dr. Wasserschleben on the general problems and Bradshaw's conclusions regarding the work, dated from Cambridge, April 28, 1885; and (ii) Notes on the Chartres and Tours MSS. containing the Hibernensis. Dated about November 1885.

Review: English Hist. Rev. 9; 726-28, October 1894.

1904

Letters of Henry Bradshaw to officials of the British Museum. Introduced by A. W. Pollard. The Library (n.s.) V: 266-292 and 431-442.

1908

The Hisperica Famina, edited with a short introduction and index verborum by Francis John Henry Jenkinson, Fellow of Trinity College, Cambridge, University Librarian. With three facsimile plates. Cambridge: at the University Press.

Although this work is attributed to Jenkinson alone he makes reference in his "Introduction" to Bradshaw's contribution to this study in the following words:

"When Henry Bradshaw died, several investigations upon which he had been more or less constantly engaged as opportunity offered, perished with him. They had been so much a part of him that while he lived it seemed unnecessary to commit them to paper. He would pour out enchanting disquisitions upon them to sympathetic listeners, who however seldom knew enough of the matter to carry away a clear recollection of what had sounded so delightful and so convincing. He would write and re-write what may be called the documents of the subject; but the conclusions he drew from them were not often committed to paper.

It was so with the Hisperica Famina, upon which, as he told a friend a few months before his death, only a fortnight's work remained to be done.

Bradshaw died in February, 1886. Exactly a year afterwards, appeared J. M. Stowasser's edition of the Vatican (the only complete) text; we may be sure that if Bradshaw had heard that it was in preparation, he would have communicated the results of his own work to the editor; and so have preserved what it is now impossible to recover.

Such a text as he desired to see has not yet been printed. Every editor has been content to reproduce the work as prose; whereas Bradshaw points out its metrical character and arranges it in lines, with a colon or point to mark the middle of each line. He had written out the A-text and as much as was known to him of the B-text; and I have reproduced his arrangement, occasionally but very rarely introducing modifications of my own....

Further than this I have not dared to go. I do not feel that like Bradshaw I can construe the whole. And where the meaning of a word does not come home to me, I prefer to leave others to pursue the investigation without prejudice or infelicitous suggestion to lead them from the right way."

1909

Cambridge University Library Bulletin. (Extra Series). The Henry Bradshaw Irish Collection presented in 1870 and 1886. Cambridge. 1909.

"In March 1870, Henry Bradshaw, Librarian, presented to the Library his collection of Irish books and papers, about 5,000 in number. After his death in February 1886, his executors presented a second large accumulation of similar books, which he had brought together since 1870. These two collections have been incorporated together, and a few books have been added, chiefly by purchases made out of the residue of the Bradshaw Memorial Fund. A full catalogue of the whole collection is in preparation and will, it is hoped, be published at no distant date."--<u>Note</u>, dated June 21, 1909.

Published in parts in the <u>Bulletin</u> between December 1906 and February 1909.

<u>Fasciculus IOANNI WILLIS CLARK dicatus</u>. CANTABRIGIAE: typis academicis impressus, MDCCCCIX.

Eleven Letters from Henry Bradshaw to S. W. Lawley. Edited by Francis Jenkinson, M.A., Librarian of the University of Cambridge, from originals in the possession of H. F. Stewart, B.D., Fellow of St. John's College, Cambridge.

1913

<u>Athenae Cantabrigienses</u> by Charles Henry Cooper and Thompson Cooper. Vol. 3, 1609-1611. Cambridge. Bowes & Bowes.

"With additions and corrections to the previous volumes by Henry Bradshaw, Prof. John E. B. Mayor, John Gough Nichols, and others and from the University Grace Books, etc. and also a new and complete index to the whole work by George J. Gray."

Copies of the first two volumes belonging to Bradshaw, Mayor and Nichols with corrections and additions had come into the hands of the publishers and had been used for this purpose.

The second volume, covering 1586-1609, published in 1861, had recorded 'special thanks' to Bradshaw.

1916

<u>A catalogue of the Bradshaw collection of Irish books in</u>

the University Library Cambridge. v. I. Books printed in Dublin by known printers, 1602-1882; v. II. Others. (Without printers' names, provincial towns, Irish authors, books relating to Ireland.); V. III. Index.

"During the last years of his life Bradshaw made considerable purchases at the Drake (1883), Sunderland (1883) and Wodhull (1886) sales."--v. I. Preface, p. vi.

H.B.'s letter presenting the collection to the University, dated March 4, 1870, was printed in the Report of the Library Syndicate dated May 4, 1870, in the Preface to Vol. I of the catalogue and in Prothero's Memoir (pp. 172-174).

Review: Times Literary Supplement, December 7, 1916, p. 586, headed 'Henry Bradshaw.'

1966-1978

Hellinga, Wytze and Lotte, eds. Henry Bradshaw's correspondence on incunabula with J. W. Holtrop and M. F. A. G. Campbell. Vol. I. The correspondence, 1864-1884. Amsterdam: Menno Hertzberger, 1966. (The volume is dated 1966 but was actually published in 1968); Vol. II. Commentary. Amsterdam: A. L. Van Gendt & Co., 1978.

1972

Machiels, J. Henry Bradshaw's Correspondentie met Ferdinand Vander Haeghen. Archives et bibliothèques de Belgique, XLIII (1972), pp. 598-614. Letters between 29 January 1870 and 21 March 1884.

1980

McKitterick, David. "Henry Bradshaw and M. F. A. G. Campbell: some further correspondence" (five letters from Campbell to H.B., Jan.-July, 1883). Hellinga Festschrift. Forty-three Studies in Bibliography presented to Prof. Dr. Wytze Hellinga on the occasion of his retirement from the Chair of Neophilology in the

University of Amsterdam at the end of the year 1978. Ed. by A. R. A. Croiset van Uchelen. Nico Israel, Amsterdam.

    Although this and the following item consist of letters to Bradshaw they need to be considered in conjunction with his correspondence.

1981

McKitterick, David. "Henry Bradshaw and J. W. Holtrop: some further correspondence." Quaerendo, Vol. XI/2 (1981), pp. 128-164.

    Letters to H.B. from Holtrop, 1866-1870.

PART III

EXCERPTS FROM THE WORKS OF HENRY BRADSHAW

In 1889 Francis Jenkinson, Bradshaw's successor as University Librarian at Cambridge, published the Collected Papers of Henry Bradshaw. In his prefatory note, Jenkinson wrote:

> This volume consists chiefly, as will be seen, of matter which has already appeared in print. It may perhaps be thought that some of the papers were hardly worth reprinting, either because they were sufficiently accessible before, or because they have done their work. As to the latter point; most of them are valuable not only for their results, but as specimens of method: and in one subject at least, bibliography, such specimens are as much needed as ever. As to their accessibility, it is perhaps true that those who wanted them have been able to see them. But though the Memoranda were much appreciated by a few readers, not many copies were sold, while the illustrations referred to in several of them have long been quite unprocurable. Again, no. xvii of the Cambridge Antiquarian Communications, in which seven of Bradshaw's papers appeared, is rarely to be met with. So there is some reason to hope that in the present form they may have a wider range of usefulness.

Now--nearly a century later--the same conditions make this further reprinting a highly desirable event. The Collected Papers of 1889 is a work which, while not rare, can not be consulted by students with the ease and frequency which would benefit them. Many of the conclusions at which Bradshaw arrived have now been assimilated into the corpus of bibliographical work. Later bibliographers have built on his foundations, few if any of which have proved unsound. It is not the outcome of Bradshaw's researches, therefore, which provides the chief reason for studying his papers. It is the breadth of his knowledge and his interests, his ability to record and marshal an intricate pattern of facts, the authority of the positions which he established: these are the essence of his importance as a pioneer worker in the field. Bibliography provides no better example of the fact that bibliography in a narrow sense is not sufficient for the bibliographer. It is a field of study which must have constantly expanding horizons and can not fruitfully be delimited. Bradshaw's knowledge of pure bibliography was unsurpassed in his own day, and justifiably he is regarded as one of the creators of the study as we now know it.

These excerpts are arranged in chronological order of their appearance.

1. ON THE RECOVERY OF THE LONG LOST
   WALDENSIAN MANUSCRIPTS

Read before the Cambridge Antiquarian Society, March 10, 1862. Reprinted in <u>Collected Papers</u>, 1889, pp. 1-15.

    This paper has a special interest in that it is the first work of Bradshaw's to be published. He was only a month past the age of 31 when he read the paper before the Society and it demonstrates clearly the knowledge and experience which he had already acquired. The bibliographical details are conveyed with great clarity following a close examination, typical of the minute attention to detail which was to be the hall-mark of his work.
    Bradshaw's interest in and knowledge of the history of library collections, the development of religion and church history, proclaim themselves and, more importantly, link themselves as essential elements in his bibliographical work. His footnote regarding his "ignorance of the language" is indicative of the crucial importance which he attached to the study of languages in relation to bibliography.

    It will be known to all who have interested themselves in the history of the Vaudois, that Morland, the envoy from the Protector Cromwell to the Duke of Savoy on their behalf in 1655, wrote on his return in 1658 what he calls a History of the Evangelical Churches in Piedmont, based not only upon previous writers but upon authentic documents which he brought home and deposited in the Public Library of this University.

He tells us that it was Abp Ussher who stirred him up to lose no opportunity of securing any old books or papers which could throw light upon the early history and religious opinions of the Vaudois; and the results of his efforts may be appreciated by any one who will read the detailed catalogue of his books and papers which is prefixed to his History.

At the close of last century, Mr. Nasmith, who was employed to make a fresh Catalogue of the Manuscripts in the Library, and under whose eye every single volume must have passed, stated that the papers were almost all safe, but that the six books or volumes mentioned by Morland had unaccountably disappeared. During the last forty years much has been written on the subject, and infinite trouble has been taken by Dr. Maitland, Dr. Todd, Dr. Gilly, and other writers at home and abroad after them, both to search out any existing remains of the early Vaudois literature, and to account for the mysterious disappearance of these treasures from Cambridge. Their loss, it was justly alleged, was the more provoking, because they contained copies of portions of the Bible, of religious treatises, and specimens of poetry, all written in the old Vaudois dialect, and to which Morland assigned very early dates, ranging from the 10th to the 13th century. The copies were so old, says Morland, and the writings probably much older.

It was a point of considerable importance that the Cambridge manuscripts should be examined; for not only Morland and his Vaudois friends, but also their advocates in our own time, agreed in maintaining the claim of this community to have held the pure Genevan doctrines long before the time of Calvin. The historians of the 17th century, knowing that in the 13th the followers of Peter Waldo had been separated from the Roman communion, and knowing that their descendants in the 17th held the doctrines of Geneva, were illogical enough to conclude that therefore their ancestors in the 13th had anticipated Calvin's views by three centuries.

A long controversy was carried on in the British Magazine about twenty years since. Amongst the good results of this, it elicited from Dr. Todd a most minute and careful description of the whole of the Ussher Collection of Waldensian MSS. in the Dublin University Library: and from this it appears that all the books there were written from 1520 to 1530, or at any rate in the 16th century. A volume at Geneva was also described, which was attributed by the librarian there to the 12th century, but which from the writing Dr. Todd and other judges assigned without hesitation to the middle or latter half of the 15th.

One poem in particular, the Noble Lesson, was the subject of much discussion. Near the beginning occur the two lines which Morland prints and translates thus:--

>Ben ha mil e cent an compli entierament,
>Que fo scripta lora, Car son al derier temp.

>There are already a thousand and one hundred years fully accomplished, Since it was written thus, For we are in the last time.

The Geneva and Dublin copies both appear to agree with Morland's representation of the Cambridge copy, as far as the date goes, and all parties were accordingly at a loss for an explanation of the appearance of a clearly Waldensian poem before the days of Peter Waldo. It even afforded to the followers of Leger and Morland an additional argument for the derivation of the name from Vallenses, or Churches of the Valleys, rather than from the name of the founder of the sect.

It will be readily believed, therefore, that it was with some pleasure and some surprise that I laid my hand upon the whole of these volumes a few weeks ago. In the same binding as the rest of the documents --three of them with Morland's and the donors' names and the date on the first page,--all six with the reference-letters ABCDEF clearly written inside the cover,--and all standing on the shelves as near to the "documents" as the difference of size would allow,--the only wonder is how they could ever have been lost sight of.

The insinuation in the British Magazine that the collection was placed here but a few weeks before Cromwell's death, and that, on that event, these books were removed to some safer stronghold of the Genevan views with the connivance of the Puritan Librarian of the day, I had long since felt to be groundless. Not only was the place then held by the model librarian and devoted loyalist William Moore,[1] of Caius College, but I some time since found a cancelled receipt (dated 1689) for four of these very volumes, in the handwriting of Peter Allix, who seems to have examined them for his Remarks on the Ecclesiastical History of the Ancient Churches of Piedmont, published in 1690.

It will be sufficient for the present purpose to give but a brief description of these six diminutive volumes; for, though undoubtedly the oldest extant relics of Vaudois literature, even when brought down from the 10th, 12th, and 13th centuries (to which Morland ascribes them) to the 15th; yet it cannot be doubted that, when they are once brought into due notice, which it is the object of this paper to procure, they will engage the attention of some scholar who is able to use them. To take them in the probable order of age:

F is a parchment volume measuring $5\frac{1}{2}$ by $4\frac{1}{4}$ inches, and written, I should say, at the close of the 14th century. It contains the greater part of the New Testament, and certain chapters of Proverbs and Wisdom, in the following order: St. Matthew (beginning gone), no St. Mark, of St. Luke only i. 1--iii. 6, followed at once by St. John, no Romans, 1st (no 2nd) Corinthians, Galatians, Ephesians, Philippians, no Colossians, of 1st Thessalonians only the first few words, and that clearly by mistake, and without heading, no 2nd Thessalonians, 1st and 2nd Timothy, Titus, no Philemon, of Hebrews only ch. xi. followed at once by Proverbs ch. vi. and Wisdom ch. v. and vi., Acts, James, 1st and 2nd Peter, followed possibly by the

Epistles and Revelation of St. John, but all after f. 158, 2 Pet. ii. 5, is wanting. There are leaves missing in several places, but in no case (except at the end) so as to prevent our knowing what the contents originally were.

B is a parchment volume measuring $4\frac{1}{4}$ by $3\frac{1}{4}$ inches, and written probably in the first half of the 15th century. It consists of three portions, but the handwriting is uniform. The first portion (ff. 1-124) contains (1) the seven penitential psalms, and (2) the In principio from St. John, in Latin; (3) Glosa Pater noster, partly printed from this by Morland (History, p. 133), (4) Treçenas, (5) Doctor, (6) Penas, (7) Li goy de paradis, (8) La pistola di li amic, and the poems, (9) Novel confort, (10) Lo novel sermon, (11) La nobla leyçon, printed from this by Morland (History, p. 99), (12) Payre eternal, and (13) La barca. The second portion (ff. 125-241) consists of a long treatise on the (1) ten commandments, (2) twelve articles of the faith, (3) seven deadly sins, (4) seven gifts of the Holy Ghost, (5) theological virtues, (6) cardinal virtues, (7) De li ben de fortuna e de natura e de gracia, (8) De seys cosas que son mot honorivol en aquest mont; and the remaining nine pages are occupied by two sermons and a paragraph De las abusions. The third portion (ff. 242-271) is imperfect at both ends, but now contains seven sermons.

C is on paper, measuring 3 3/8 by $2\frac{1}{2}$ inches, and written about the middle of the 15th century. It consists of three portions, all in one handwriting. The first (ff. 1-24) contains two sermons (1) De la confession, and (2) De la temor del segnor, the latter printed from this by Morland (History, p. 119). The second (ff. 25-32) contains one sermon; and the third portion (ff. 33-112, &c.) consists of (1) a sermon headed Tribulacions, (2) 7F. that is, a translation of 2 Macc. vii. from the Vulgate, (3) Job, a translation of Job i. ii. iii. and xlii. from the Vulgate, (4) Tobia, a translation of the whole book of Tobit from the Vulgate, (5) La nobla leyçon, which breaks off abruptly at the beginning of the fourteenth verse, the rest of the volume being lost.

A is on paper and parchment, measuring 3 7/8 by 2 7/8 inches, and written in the latter half of the 15th century. It consists of six different portions, all in one handwriting, except perhaps the last. Part I. (ff. 2-99) contains (1) <u>Genesis</u>, a translation of Gen. i.-x. from the Vulgate, (2) a Treatise on the nature of different animals, (3) <u>Lo tracta de li pecca</u>, (4) a sermon <u>De la parolla di dio</u>. Part II. (f. 100) is in Latin, and contains instructions to the clergy, headed <u>Sequitur de imposicione penitencie</u>. Part III. (f. 136) is a discourse beginning <u>Alcuns volon ligar la parolla de Dio segont la lor volunta</u>, on the <u>quatre manieras de trametament</u>, that is, of God, of God and man, of man alone, and of usurping preachers. Part IV. (f. 172) is a treatise entitled <u>Herman</u>. Part V. (f. 180) is a collection of Latin pieces. Part VI. (f. 232) contains, after three short paragraphs, a small historical passage on the voluntary poverty of the Church, unfortunately imperfect at the end, but of peculiar interest.

D is on parchment, measuring $3\frac{1}{2}$ by $2\frac{1}{2}$ inches, and written also in the latter half of the 15th century. It is imperfect at both ends, but now contains (1) a collection of medical recipes (beginning gone); (2) a discourse on tribulations, headed <u>Ayci comença sant ysidori</u>; (3) a sermon on the seven deadly sins and their remedies, on the text <u>Donca vos mesquins perque tarçen de ben far</u>, &c.; (4) a sermon on almsgiving, on the text <u>O vos tuit li qual lavora</u>, &c.; (5) three short pieces beginning <u>Dio bat li ome en .5. modo</u>..., <u>Nota che la son quatre cosas que nos apellan</u>..., <u>Nos vehen esser na .3. perilh en aquisti temp</u>...; (6) several short moral paragraphs; (7) a short Discourse on the twelve joys of paradise, on the text <u>Voç dalegreça e de salu es en li tabernacle di li iust</u>; (8) a general but brief exposition of Christian doctrine, commencing <u>A tuit li fidel karissimes christians sia salu en yh^u xp^t lo nostre redemptor Amen</u>..., and arranged under eight heads, but unfortunately breaking off in the middle of the third.

E is on paper, measuring $4\frac{1}{4}$ by 3 3/8 inches,

Excerpts from the Works / 83

and consists of four parts, the handwriting not uniform throughout, but agreeing well with the dates 1519, 1521, which are found in the book. Parts I. and II. are parts of a Latin grammar. (1) De interrogationibus, De participiis, De casu genitivo locali, De comparativis, De gerundivis, with some Flores legum on one of the blank leaves at the end; (2) De verbis, with the translation of the verbs in the Vaudois dialect. In rubric at the beginning is: Anno domini millesimo q :1521: dies :9: mensis Januarii. Part III. contains Latin abstracts of (1) Proverbs, (2) Ecclesiastes, (3) Ecclesiasticus, followed by (4) some sentences from St. Gregory; (5) a poem of 24 lines beginning:

Tout ce que la terre nourist;

(6) a poem of 282 lines headed: Sequuntur mettra ceneche (or ceueche) and beginning:

Commensament de tout ben es
Temer diou soubre tout quant es;

(7) a piece, contained on one leaf, headed: Sequitur liber Arithmetti[cus] extratus a Johannono Albi filio mgri Johannis Albi notarii de Fenestrellis sub Anno domini .1519. et die .22. mensis Augusty, and beginning, Per ben entendre lart... Part IV. contains (1) Albertani moralissimi opus de loquendi ac tacendi modo, an abridgment only; (2) liber primus de amore et dilectione dei et proximi et de forma vite, ejusdem domini Albertani, also an abridgment; (3) versus morales, beginning:

Est caro nostra cinis,
modo principium modo finis;

(4) Exortation de bien vivre et bien mourir, in 100 lines, beginning:

Qui a bien vivre veult entendre;

(5) Optima consilia; (6) Sentences headed Philosophus, with translations in verse; (7) 42 versus morales, beginning:

Au jorn duy qui se auausse trop,

with which the volume concludes.

Judging from Dr. Gilly's edition of St. John, the text and dialect of our New Testament closely resemble the Grenoble, Zurich, and Dublin copies; and, but for the alleged antiquity of the Grenoble and Zurich copies, the incompleteness of this one might suggest the inference[2] that at this date the entire New Testament was not yet in circulation among the Vaudois. Those parts which were read as Epistles and Gospels in Church would naturally be the first translated, and we find these in MS. B; and, were this suggestion confirmed, we should have no proof of the existence of a regular translation of the New Testament earlier than the period which produced the Wycliffite versions in our own country.

In B the most noticeable pieces are the Treçenas and the Nobla Leyçon. The four treçenas are the four quarters of the year, each containing thirteen Sundays, and the Epistles and Gospels are headed 1st, 2nd, 3rd ... Sunday of the 1st, 2nd ... treçena, without any further distinctive name derived from the season. On a minute comparison, however, with the unreformed Roman, as well as other missals, they appear to be precisely the same, with only such small variations as are found to exist between the uses of different Churches at the same time; and this is particularly interesting, as so very few relics of the early Vaudois ritual are still in existence. The copy of the Nobla leyçon in this volume is the one which has created all the discussion, by the expression which I have quoted before, 'Ben ha mil e cent an,' &c. It is, therefore, highly satisfactory to notice that the line runs in this copy:

Ben ha mil e * cent an compli entierament,

with an erasure before cent, where, by the aid of a glass, the Arabic numeral 4 is visible, of the same shape as those frequently used in this volume. The only thing which could be needed to prove the certainty of this reading, is that in MS. C there is the commencement of another copy of this same poem, which, as it is but a short fragment, and has escaped the attention of Leger and Morland altogether, I shall give entire. It is written continuously, the divisions being marked by points and coloured initial letters. It runs as follows:[3]

AYCI COMEṈCA / LA NOBLA LEYÇON. /

O frayres enteṉde u/na nobla leyçon. /
Sovent deven velhar e/istar eṉnauracion.
Caṟ nos / ven aqṵest moṉt esseṟ pres / del
  chauon.
Mot curios / deoran esseṟ de bonas obras /
  far.
Caṟ nos ven aqṵest moṉt // a la fin apṟopiar.
Ben ha / mil e .cccc. anz compli eṉ/tieramenṯ.
Que fo scṟita lo/ra ara sen al derier temps. /
Pauc daurian cubitaṟ / caṟ sen al romanent. /
Tot / iorn ven las ensegnas / venir a com-
  plimeṉt.
Acre/ysameṉt de mal e amerma/ment de bens.
Ayço soṉ / li perilh que lescṟitura di. /
Li auangeliṉ o recoytaṉ / e saiṉt paul atresy.
Caṟ / neun home qṵe viva noṉ / po saber sa
  fin.
Peṟço//... [The leaves which should follow are wanting.]

There can be no doubt that the Geneva and Dublin copies are both later than our two; and, however we may explain the omission from them, it is at least the evidence of two earlier against two later copies, and this, added to the great difficulty of giving a reasonable explanation of the lines, seems enough to satisfy the most strenuous advocates of the antiquity of the poem.

A is the volume which, at the end of the sermon De la parolla de dio, contains the supposed date of transcription, 1230. The conclusion of the sermon is as follows:

Da 4ª. endurczis enayci fay aliome la

parolla dedio &c.
1530.

I can see nothing in the second figure but a badly made 5, though I confess it is difficult to explain the meaning of it. It seems to be in the original ink, and beyond any suspicion of tampering, but the handwriting and figures are clearly not those of the year 1530, nor indeed of 1430; while 1230, as the date of transcription, even apart from palaeographical considerations, is out of the question. In Part V. the collection of Latin pieces, the Doctor Evangelicus (Wyclif) is cited. And further, in the historical passage at the close of the volume, after speaking of Piero de Vaudia and his excommunication, mention is made of the success of his followers until, two hundred years (dui cent an) after his time, a persecution arose, which continued even to the times of the writer. This brings the date of the composition to the beginning of the 15th century at the earliest. It is true that dui has been partly erased, but even cent an would bring the piece down much later than 1230; while it must be allowed that it is somewhat suspicious, that Morland has taken no notice in his catalogue either of this piece or of the fragment of the Nobla leyçon containing the true date, even though his list in many cases deals with the most insignificant details.

The passage on the voluntary poverty of the church is as follows:[4]

[f. 236] Mas aço que la gleysa de li
eyleyt istes en sancta religion regla e orde
en sanct regiment, lo segnor ordene en ley
meseyme gouernadors e iuies speritals resplandent de celestial sapiencia, e que li
maior mostresan a li menor vita de sanctita
e eysemple de salu; Mas li menor dovesan
devota obediencia a li lor maior sotmettament e reverencia. De li regidor testimoniia
S. Paul en li At de li apostol, diçent:
Atende a vos e a tot lo greç al cal lo Sant
Sperit pause vos vescos a regir la gleysa

de Dio la cal el aquiste cum lo sio sanc. Mas
el dis enayci a li sotmes: Obede a li vostre
derant pausa, e sotmete vos a lor. Ac' Dio
pause alcuns en la gleysa prumierament li
apostol, li 2. li propheta, li 3. li doctor. E
Peyre apostol amonesta tant li derant pausa
coma li sotmes: Tuit demostrant humilita
entre vos. Car Dio contrasta a li superbi,
mas el dona gracia a li humil. Mas el despensa
aquesta degneta a li seo karissime quilh
luçessan de maior sanctita cum veraya pavreta,
e fossan liora a maior tribulacion, que
enapres ayço li eyleves de maior gloria, e
plus ample honor e enriqueça. Li eyleva
de le stercora de terrenals riqueças, e lor
done celestials consolacions. E aquilh que
foron plus char amic de lui suffriron maiors
e plus greos repropis. E sença dubi nos
cresen lor esser eyleva de maior degneta e
gloria. Mas aquesta sancta gleysa ac' al
temp de li appostol creyse en moti milhiers
e en sant orde per la redondeça de la terra,
e permas per moti temp en verdor de
sancta religion; e li regidor de la gleysa
permaseron en pavreta e en humilita, segont
las antiquas storias, encerque trey cent
anç, ço es entro a Costantin emperi cessar;
mas, regnant Costantin lebros, un regidor
era en la gleysa lo cal era apella Silvestre
[f. 237] roman. Aquest istava al mont de
seraphio iosta Roma, enayma es legi, per
cayson de perseguecion, e menava vita de
pavres cum li seo. Mas Costantin receopu
respost en li soyme, enayma e reconta, Anne
a Silvestre, e fo babteia de lui al nom de
y^u x^i, e fo monda de la lebrosia. Mas
Costantin vesent se sana al nom de x de
tanta miseriosa enfermeta, pense honrar
lui lo cal lavia monda, e liore a lui la corona
e la degneta del emperi. Mas el la
receop, mas lo compagnon, enayma ay anni
recontar, se departic de lui e non consentic
en aquestas cosas, mas tenc la via de pav-

reta. Mas Costantin se departic cum mooreça de romans en las part dautra lo mar, e aqui hedifique Constantinopoli enayma es e apelle ley del sio nom. Donca daquel temp la resiarcha monte en honore e en degneta, e li mal foron multiplica sobre la terra. Nos non cressen alpostot que la gleysa de dio sia departia maçament de la via de verita dal tot, mas una partia cagit, e la maior part, enayma es usança, trabuche en mal. Mas la part permasa permas per moti temp en aquela verita la cal ilh avia receopu. Enayci la sanctita de la gleysa manque poc a poc; mas enapres 8 cent ang de Costantin se leve un lo propi nom del cal era Piero, enayma yo auvic, mas el era duna region dicta Vaudia. Mas aquest, enayma dion li nostre derant anador, era ric e savi e bon fortment. Donca o el legent, o auvent de li autre, receop las parollas del evangeli, e vende aquellas cosas las el avia e las departic a li pavre e pres la via de pavreta, e prediche e fe deciples, e intre en la cipta de Roma e desputa derant [f. 238] la resiarcha de la fe e de la religion. Mas en aquel temp era aqui un cardenal de Pulha, lo cal era amic de lui e lauvava la via de lui e la parolla, e amava lui. A la perfin receop respost en la cort que la gleysa romana non poya portar la parolla de lui, ni non volia habandonar la via acomença. E dona a si sentencia fo fayt fora la sinagoga. Nent de ment el meseyme predicant en la cipta fey plusors deciples. E facent camin per las regions da Ytalia fe aiostament enayci que en plusors parç niutreron moti en la lor conversacion, tant el meseyme cant li sucessor de lui, e foron forment multiplica; car lo poble auvia lor volentier, emperço que la parolla de verita fossa en la boca de lor, e demostresan via de salu. E multipliqueron tant que sovendierament saiostesan en li lor conselh alcuna veç 8 cent, alcuna veç mil, alcuna veç mot poc. Dio obrava merevilhas per lor, enayma nos aven de plusors li cal parlan volentie verita; mas aquestas obras fructuosas dureron per lespaçi de (dui)* cent an, enayma es demostra per li velh. A la perfin, levant se lenvidia del satanaç e la maligneta de li fellon, perseguecion non peta es va entre li serf de Dio, e degiteron lor de region en region; e la crudelleta de lor persevera entro ara contra nos. E cum aquestas cosas seayan enaysi, consideren li temp li cal trapasseron devant lavenament de X^i. Car ilh foron umbra e figura daquisti temp, lo cal [f. 239] durare de X^i entro a la fin del segle. Nos non troben en las scripturas del velh testament que de Abram entro a X^i la luçerna de verita e de sanctita sia unca daltot en alcun temp alpostot steynta; mas permaseron totavia o poc o pro en sancta vita. Ni non legen quilh nenguesan unca a defalhir deltot. Enaysi ac' pense que del temp de X^i entro ara sia entre nengu enaquel meseyme modo. E enaysi cresen que sia avenir entro a la fin. Que del temp al cal la gleysa fo fonça entro a la fin del segle, la gleysa de Dio non defalhire enaysi del tot que la non sia totavia alcun de li sant, o en las terras, o en alcunas regions de la terra. Car lo son de lor issic en tota la terra. E la maior part de la gleysa de Dio crec al començament en las regions dautra lo mar. Dont es desser stima en alcuna maniera que otra lo mar e de aquesta partia del mar la lucerna de li sant sia nengua alpostot auniet per alcun temp. Car li nostre frayre en li temp antic cum ilh aguessan trapassa lo mar per una perseguecion atroberon li frayre en una region; mas car ilh mesconoysian lo lengaie daquela region, non pogron aver compagnia cum lor ni demostrar fermeça entre lor,

---

*This word has been partly erased.

enayma ilh agran fait volentier, e se departiron dentre lor. Entre aquestas cosas pensen la prophecia de Jeremia: Baron de li prever de levetienc meos menistres non perire de la mia facia, lo cal uffra holocaust e embrase sacrafici e aucia vedeoç per tuit li dia. Aquesta promession de Dio es dicta sobre la sancta gleysa. Car li dit de li propheta expiravan a X^i e a la gleysa. Donca veian calcosas dia, que de X^i entro a la [f. 240] fin del segle baron non perire, menistre de X^i, lo cal uffra holocaust e vedeoç e sacrifici per tuit li dia. Que calque cal son, membre del sobeyran prever per sanctita de vita, uffron hostias speritals a Dio sobre lautar de la fe entro en cuey. E se ilh non son moti, emperço la prophecia non ment; car el non di: Barons non periren, mas: Di baron de li prever non perire de la mia facia, lo cal faça aquestas cosas en aquelas. O karissime, considera; car la luna ja sia ço quilh sia iusta venir amenç de la soa pleneta, mas emperço totavia es luna. E silh es scurçia per alcunas tenebras e non apereysa a li olh de liome, emperço ilh es totavia luna; en la soa substancia, enayma nos cressen, dautra maniera Dio faria luna per chascun mes. Mas lescriptura de que Dio cree aquesta luna del començament. Donca pensen lo dit de David: El fey luna en temp, ço es en mermament e en renovellament. E la luna a figura sovendierament la gleysa, la cal regna alcun veç en moteça de sant en aquest mont; e alcuna veç es iusta a mancament. Donca si la gleysa es casi defalhia, enayma la luna, que se part per lenvidia del septanaç e per la superbia de li fellon e per la negligencia de plusors, e mootas greos tribullacions e perseguecions, si mays que non cressan ley en alcunas regions del mont totavia esser, permasa en la pavreta de li sant, e en bona vita e sancta conversacion. Car Salomon parlla per sperit de prophecia diçent: Cant li fellon multi-

pliqueren se levaren, e li iust sere scondren;
e cum ilh seren peri, e li iust multipliqueren.
Nos pensen a....

Here the text breaks off, and ff. 241-243 are wanting to complete the sheet.

D contains no indication of a date, as far as I have examined, but the headings of the eight divisions of the Exposition of Christian Doctrine are worth noticing, though, from the mutilation of the volume, only three chapters now remain. The prologue enumerates these divisions thus:

Donca prumierament nos diren breoment coma la ley del veray Dio e veray home Yh[u] X[i] per si sola es suficient a la salu de tota la generacion humana, E es plus breo e plus comuna e plus legiera a complir, e es ley de perfeita liberta, a la qual non besogna aiogner ni mermar alcuna cosa, E non es alcuna cosa de ben la qual non sia suficientment enclusa en aquella meseyma soa ley. Segondariament diren de la sancta fe catholica, la qual se conten en li article e en li sacrament e en li comandament de Dio. 3[a]ment diren de la vera e de la falsa penitencia e de la vera confession e de la satisfacion. La 4[a] diren alcuna cosa del vero purgatori e segur e de la falseta e meçonia se me[a] sobre lui. La 5a diren de la envocacion de li sant e de li herror sobre seme[a]. La 6[a] diren de la auctorita pastoral dona de Dio a li sacerdot de X[i]. La 7[a] diren de las clavs apostolicas donas de Yh[u] X[i] a sant Peyre e a li autre seo veray successor. La 8[a] diren de las veras endulgencias. fol. 81.

In Ch. 2, the sacraments are enumerated thus:

Sept son li sacrament de la sancta gleysa. Lo prumier es lo batisme lo qual es dona a nos en remesion de pecca. Lo .2. es la penitencia. Lo .3. es la comunion del cors e del sanc de Xp^t. Lo .4. es lo matrimoni ordena de Dio. Lo .5. es loli sant. Lo .6. es lenpusament de las mans. Lo .7. es ordenament de preyres e de diaques. fol. 88^b.

To sum up then, briefly; after the most important fact--the determination of the true date of the Nobla Leyçon-- the primary result gained from the recovery of these manuscripts, and a comparison of them with what we already know of others of the kind, is, that, besides the Dublin collection, all of which seem to have been written in the 16th century, we have two miscellaneous volumes at Geneva (MSS. 207 and 209) and four at Cambridge (ABCD), as well as more than one copy of the New Testament, all assignable to the 15th century; and in addition to these, at Cambridge and at Grenoble, one incomplete and one complete copy of the New Testament, which may be ascribed to the close of the 14th century. It is a small collection, doubtless; but it is a very precious one, even though not carrying us back to the 10th and 12th centuries, as we were led to expect; and it is much to be hoped that the authorities at our University Press will soon offer some encouragement towards bringing out a careful edition of at least the most important treatises in the collection. Whatever Cromwell and his friends were politically, it is at least certain that, as a literary body, we owe them a debt which it would take us a long time to repay, and which at present we refuse to acknowledge even in our annual commemoration of benefactors. We have for two hundred years ignored both the gift and the giver, and it is time that we should begin to make some reparation.

[NOTE. Sept. 1862. I have just received the welcome news from Dr. Todd, that he intends to republish, in a separate form, the Catalogue of the Ussher Collection of Waldensian MSS., which he furnished to the British Magazine in 1841. The new volume would contain some remarks on the various points connected with the subject, as well as a detailed description of all the Waldensian MSS. now known to exist in Dublin, Cambridge, Geneva, and elsewhere. H.B.]

Notes

1. It must be borne in mind that ever since the death of William Moore (in 1659), under whom every part of the library seems to have been thoroughly explored, all the librarians and their assistants have uniformly, though unaccountably, declined to make themselves in any way acquainted with the manuscripts under their charge. So, when fresh catalogues were required, both Mr. Nasmith and, more recently, the laborious compilers of the printed catalogue, were employed at a large cost to the University, as being supposed to know a good deal of the subjects of the works existing in MS., but a knowledge of the history of the individual volumes was not to be expected from them. These facts afford the only possible explanation of the reputed loss of the Waldensian MSS. as well as others from our library. Their history was lost sight of, and they had come to be regarded as miscellaneous pieces, apparently in Spanish, of no particular importance.

2. An examination of Dr. Gilly's facsimiles rather confirms than weakens the suggestion made in the text. To judge from these, the Grenoble MS. must bear a very strong resemblance to our F, and the Zurich MS. to our C, the former of which I should assign to the close of the 14th, and the latter to the early part of the 15th century. The truth is that so very few volumes bear an actual date, that persons who are familiar with MSS. may gain a fairly correct notion of the relative age of different volumes, and yet

differ from other critics as to the <u>actual</u> age. I have very little doubt that most <u>judges</u>, if the four copies were placed open before them, would range them (1) Cambridge, (2) Grenoble, (3) Zurich, (4) Dublin. Of the Lyons copy I can say nothing, as no facsimile is given.
3. The divisions mark the ends of the lines on the page in the MS.; the italics denote the abbreviations of the original.
4. A better acquaintance with the language would have enabled me to print this piece much more correctly. But the primary object of this paper has been to draw the attention of scholars to these genuine remains of the Waldenses of the 15th century, and while I only vouch for accuracy of reading where <u>names</u> and <u>numbers</u> are concerned (and this is <u>of</u> no small importance here), the reader, if at all gifted with an eye for conjectural criticism, will readily correct what, from ignorance of the language, I have mis-read.

2. LETTER ON THE CODEX SINAITICUS

The Guardian, 28 January, 1863. p. 85. (Supplement)

This letter is part of the correspondence on the subject of the Codex Sinaiticus in The Guardian in 1862-63. The long letter of Simonides to which H.B. replied is in the issue for 21 January 1863. Other correspondents, besides Simonides and H.B., were W. A. Wright; John Eliot Hodgkin; William Thomas Newenham; S. P. Tregelles.

Sir,

As Dr. Simonides has cited a letter which he wrote to me in uncial characters in October last, while he was at Cambridge, and as I have with my own eyes seen and examined the Codex Sinaiticus within the last few months, perhaps you will allow me to say a few words.

The note which Dr. Simonides wrote to me was to convince me and my friends that it was quite possible for him to have written the volume in question, and to confirm his assertion that the uncial character of the MS. was as familiar and easy to him to write as the common cursive hand of the present day.

He had invited some of us to Christ's College to examine his papyri and to discuss matters fairly. He could speak and understand English pretty well, but his friend was with him to interpret and explain. They first taxed us with believing in the antiquity of MSS. solely on the authority of one man like Tischendorf, and they really seemed to believe that all people in the West were as ignorant of Greek as the Greeks are of Latin. But the great question was, "How do you satisfy yourselves of the genuineness of any manuscript?" I first replied that it was really difficult to define, that it seemed more of a kind of instinct than anything else. Dr. Simonides and his friend readily caught at this as too much like vague assertion, and they naturally ridiculed any such idea. But I further said that I had lived for six years past in the constant, almost daily, habit of examining manuscripts,--not merely the text of the works contained in the volumes, but the volumes themselves as such; the writing, the paper or parchment, the arrangement and numbering of the sheets, the distinction between the original volume and any additional matter by later hands, etc.; and that, with experience of this kind, though it might be difficult to assign the special ground of my confidence, yet I hardly ever found myself deceived even by a very well-executed facsimile. All this Dr. Simonides allowed and confirmed. He gave the instance of the Jews in the East, who could in an instant tell the exact proportion of foreign matter in a bottle of otto of roses, where the most careful chemical analysis might fail to detect the same. Indeed, any tradesman acquires the same sort of experience with regard to the quality of the particular goods which are daily passing through his hands; and this is all that I claimed for myself. Dr. Simonides afterwards told me himself that this was the only safe method of judging, that there was no gainsaying such evidence, and that he only fought against persons who made strong and vague assertions without either proof or experience. Yet when I told him that I had seen the Codex Sinaiticus, he spoke as if bound in honour not to allow in this case the value of that very criterion which he had before confessed to be the surest; and he wrote me the letter to which he refers, in the hope of convincing me. I told him as politely as I could that I was not to be convinced against the evidence of my senses.

On the 18th of July last I was at Leipzig with a friend, and we called on Professor Tischendorf. Though I had no introduction but my occupation at Cambridge, nothing could exceed his kindness; we were with him for more than two hours, and I had the satisfaction of examining the MS. after my own fashion. I had been anxious to know whether it was written in even continuous quaternions throughout, like the Codex Bezae, or in a series of fasciculi each ending with a quire of varying size, as the Codex Alexandrinus, and I found the latter to be the case. This, bye-the-bye, is of itself sufficient to prove that it cannot be the volume which Dr. Simonides speaks of having written at Mount Athos.

Now, it must be remembered that Dr. Simonides always maintained two points--first, that the Mount Athos Bible written in 1840 for the Emperor of Russia was not meant to deceive any one, but was only a beautiful specimen of writing in the old style, in the character used by the writer in his letter to me; secondly, that it was Professor Tischendorf's ignorance and inexperience which rendered him so easily deceived where no deception was intended. For the second assertion, no words of mine are needed to accredit an editor of such long standing as Professor Tischendorf. For the first, though a carefully made facsimile of a few leaves inserted among several genuine ones might for a time deceive even a well-practiced eye, yet it is utterly impossible that a book merely written in the antique style, and without any attempt to deceive, should mislead a person of moderate experience. For myself, I have no hesitation in saying that I am as absolutely certain of the genuineness and antiquity of the Codex Sinaiticus as I am of my own existence. Indeed, I cannot hear of any one who has seen the book who thinks otherwise. Let any one go to St. Petersburg and satisfy himself. Let Dr. Simonides go there and examine it. He can never have seen it himself, or I am sure that, with his knowledge of MSS., he would be the first to agree with me. The Mount Athos Bible must be a totally different book; and I only regret, for the sake of himself and his many friends in England, that he has been led on, from knowing that his opponents here have seen no more of the original book than he has himself, to make such rash and contradictory assertions, that sober people are almost driven to think that the Greek is playing with our matter-of-fact habits of mind, and that, as soon as he has tired out his opponents, he will come forward and ask his admirers for a testimonial to his cleverness.

Cambridge, Jan. 24, 1863.   Henry Bradshaw.

3. LETTER ON THE ORIENTAL MANUSCRIPTS IN THE LIBRARY OF KING'S COLLEGE, CAMBRIDGE

Catalogue of the Oriental Manuscripts in the Library of King's College, Cambridge, by Edward Henry Palmer. Royal Asiatic Society's Publications, June 1867.

Prothero records (Memoir, p. 128) a letter of Bradshaw, dated June 18, 1865, which reads, in part,: "I have just set a Hungarian rabbi [Dr. Schiller-Szinessy] at work on our Hebrew manuscripts, ... what with this, and young Palmer [afterwards Professor Palmer] for the Arabic, and Miss Shields for the Vaudois manuscripts, all being paid out of my own pocket, it leaves me but little prospect of going abroad this summer."

Palmer, who was at this stage 25 years of age, was at the beginning of a remarkable and tragic life which led eventually to the burial of his remains in St. Paul's Cathedral. A short account of his career may be found in J. W. Clark's Old friends at Cambridge and elsewhere, 1900, pp. 201-281 (reprinted from Church Quarterly Review, October 1883) and a fuller one in Walter Besant's The Life and Achievements of Edward Henry Palmer..., 1883.

Bradshaw's whole career, with manuscripts and printed books, emphasized the importance of provenance of copies. Time and again he unraveled and explained the history of collections and of individual copies as an essential starting point to an investigation.

In this letter to Palmer, Bradshaw gave the

background history to the collection which Palmer was describing.

King's College, 12th November, 1866.

Dear Mr. Palmer,--The manuscripts, of which you have been good enough to draw up the list, which I trust the Asiatic Society will print, came to us at the end of last century. The donor, Edward Ephraim Pote, was a son of Mr. Pote, of Eton, and was elected a scholar of this College in 1768. He took his degree in 1773, and seems to have entered the Civil Service of the East India Company very soon after that.

In his letter to the College, dated "Patna, 6th February, 1788," he says: "... from the time of my arrival in the East I have exerted my utmost endeavours to obtain some Asiatic writings worthy the acceptance of our societies; and have the pleasure to inform you that at length I have acquired a collection of Persian Manuscripts amounting to more than 550 volumes. I propose doing myself the honor of presenting one-half of these books to our College and the other half of them to the College at Eton.... I have been disappointed in my hopes of sending you these manuscripts by the ships of this season, yet I cannot restrain my desire of communicating the acquisition I have made..."

The collection, contained in eight chests, arrived in England in 1790; and by an agreement made between the Provosts of the two colleges, the chests marked A, B, C, D, were allotted to King's College, and the remaining four were sent to Eton.

A glance at your list will show that the books were arranged roughly in alphabetical order according to their titles, and in that order packed in the chests; so that, with very few exceptions, we have at Cambridge the first half of the alphabet, while those which fall into the latter half may be looked for at Eton.

I only mention these details with a view of showing that the responsibility of this mode of division (which has been the cause of amusement to many persons) does not rest with the donor; and that, therefore, if an examination of the two collections, such as that to which you have subjected ours, should make it appear desirable that some of the volumes might with advantage change places, there could be no possible difficulty in adjusting the matter.

But the most interesting circumstance about the collection is one which is not generally known. The books bought by Mr. Pote evidently formed part of the Oriental library of Colonel Polier, who is known as the first person who brought to Europe a complete copy of the Vedas. His seal, "Major Polier, A.H. 1181," occurs, as you remember, in a large number of the volumes, and his autograph, "Ant. Polier," in several. A full account of Polier and of his family is given by M. M. Haag in La France Protestante, derived chiefly from information supplied by M. Dumont, the librarian at Lausanne.

Born at Lausanne, in 1741, Polier entered the service of the East India Company at an early age. He won the confidence and respect of Lord Clive and of Warren Hastings; but, through a great portion of his thirty years' stay in India, he was enabled to devote himself to Indian literature, solely by reason of that illiberal spirit of English jealousy which first resented and then cancelled the appointment of a foreigner to a post of military authority.

His biographers mention the fact of his return to Europe in 1789; and they further mention the choice collection of manuscripts which he brought home: the Vedas, which he presented to the British Museum, and (besides a few others) forty-two volumes of Arabic, Persian, and Sanscrit manuscripts which were obtained from his heirs, and are now in the Imperial Library at Paris. No mention, however, is made of the bulk of his library; but putting the facts side by side, there seems no doubt that the collection acquired by Mr. Pote in 1788 contains a large portion of Polier's library as he left it; and as such, as the collection of one of our earliest orientalists, it merits examination.

One advantage of the books having been thus early brought together is apparent; namely, that there are to be found here many small historical pieces which may serve to unravel the intricacies of Indian history during the sixty or seventy years before the rise of the English power, which it is almost hopeless to look for in any other collection. It is from this point of view especially that I hope to see good results arise from the publication of your catalogue. Yours very truly,

Henry Bradshaw.

E. H. Palmer, Esq.,
St. John's College.

4. LETTER ON THE LAMBETH LIBRARY

Times, 7 October, 1867.

> Bradshaw was not a writer for the popular press. There is nothing in his papers similar to Pollard's article on "The Salaries of Lady Teachers" (1888) or Greg's letter on "The Price of Sugar" (1915). This present letter is a rare occurrence, but it shows the eternal vigilance of the librarian in protecting the interests of his collection.

THE LAMBETH LIBRARY.

TO THE EDITOR OF THE TIMES.

Sir,--In the recent discussions about the Lambeth Library I find it suggested that the Archbishop might be relieved altogether from the responsibilities attaching to its custody, and it has been tacitly assumed in letters written on the subject that the books would, as a matter of course, be transferred to the British Museum. I beg, however, to suggest that, if for any reason the collection should be removed from Lambeth, the University of Cambridge is the body to whose care it should on all reasonable grounds be intrusted.

Any one who is acquainted with the history of the library knows that it was established by Archbishop Bancroft by his will in 1610, under the express stipulation that it should be reserved to his successors if they would enter into covenants to hand it over intact to their successors; or, failing this, that it should go to the King's College at Chelsea if such College were erected within six years, which did not come to pass; and again, failing this, he bequeathed it to the public library of the University of Cambridge.

On the execution of Archbishop Laud and the abolition of episcopacy, the University presented a petition to Parliament claiming the library on the ground that the first two conditions of Bancroft's will were no longer capable of fulfilment. The justice of the claim was readily allowed, and by order of the Lords and Commons the whole library, including the additions made by Bancroft's successors, was removed without delay to its new home. A large room was set apart for the collection; various catalogues (still preserved here) were made, so as to render it as useful as possible; and there is ample evidence that the new acquisition was well cared for and highly prized by the University. At the restoration the University at once yielded to the representations of the then Archbishop of Canterbury, and the library was restored to Lambeth.

The fact that the original library was contingently bequeathed to the University, and that, on the contingency arising, the whole collection was transferred to Cambridge by the authority of Parliament, affords a strong argument in favour of a like proceeding now if it should be found impracticable to fulfil the first condition of the founder's will. I may further mention that by the rules of our University the books would be accessible to all real students from whatever quarter they come, and capable of being borrowed under such regulations as form a perfect safeguard for their custody without being a bar to their free use, a boon fully appreciated by those who have enjoyed the privilege of access while the books have been in their present keeping.

Your obedient servant,

Henry Bradshaw.

University Library, Cambridge, Oct. 5.

5. THE PRINTER OF THE HISTORIA S. ALBANI

Published as Memorandum No. 1, February 1868. Reprinted in Collected Papers, 1889, pp. 149-163.

This paper is worthy of study not solely because of the subject matter but even more because of Bradshaw's treatment. The descriptions of the thirteen books mark important advances in this area of bibliographical work and their influence will be traced in later models.

Every one who has spent any time in the study of early printed books must have met with a number of small quarto volumes bearing a great resemblance to each other, and all attributed to various early presses at Cologne. In the Stadt-Bibliothek at Cologne, in the Royal Library at the Hague, in the Bodleian Library at Oxford, not to mention other places, there are large collections of these volumes, by means of which there are opportunities of comparison, without which it is impossible to arrive at any satisfactory results. The bibliographers have divided these books roughly into two sets, and have attributed the one set to Ulric Zel, and the other to Arnold ter Hoernen, or Veldener, or the Brussels press. A good deal more research is needed before the class of books formerly attributed to ter Hoernen, Veldener, and the Brussels press can be accurately assigned to their respective printers, though Mr. Holtrop has cleared away many of the difficulties; but almost all who have described the class of books commonly given to Ulric

Zel, have followed each other with very little hesitation. Hain sometimes adds, 'Typi Zellianis similes,' but this is the extent of the hesitation.

There are many variations in the mode of printing adopted in these books which may help to settle the dates with greater certainty; but I wish now to draw attention to thirteen volumes which have been almost uniformly attributed to Zel, which yet I cannot believe to be the productions of his press. They are palpably all from the same press; the type is almost identical with Zel's; but the typographical characteristics, the mode of working, &c., are so different from his, that they must for the future be kept separate. If they are examined with this view, I have no doubt that the number will be largely increased, and it is quite possible that some clue may be found to the name of the printer.

Until the eye becomes accustomed to the differences between Zel's type and that of the Printer of the Historia sancti Albani,[1] as I shall call him for the present, there are certain points which can be recognised with ease. One is the frequent use of the semicolon (;) at the end of a sentence, while it is never used at all by Zel. Another is the use of the small double hyphen, whereas Zel's hyphens are very peculiar. They are not found at all, I believe, except in what are supposed to be his earliest books; and then they are single strokes and always stand out beyond the end of the line. Again, of Zel's books there are very few in which the lines are not fully spaced out to the end; while the Printer of the Historia sancti Albani, in several of the books described below, exhibits many instances of the peculiarity of even spacing on the recto, and uneven on the verso, of a leaf. This is a matter which was first noticed, I think, by Mr. Blades in connexion with Caxton's early books, and he has shown most ably how much aid may be obtained in settling the dates of books by noticing the habits of the printers and their gradual improvements in working. Indeed, where we have no date on the face of the book, the unconscious evidence afforded by the methods of working is of course of the greatest value.

In the collations, as there are no printed signatures, I have examined the books by the quires of which they are composed, and have called the quires a,b,c, &c., as if they had been so marked by the printer.[2] Where, as sometimes happens, a single leaf is inserted in a quire owing to some miscalculation on the part of the printer, the leaf will be found described by the number of the preceding leaf, only with the addition of an asterisk (6* if inserted after 6, 5* if inserted after 5, &c.), and the first word of the inserted leaf is given, so as to enable the collator to identify it at once. Thus in the Seneca (No. II. below), the expression c(+6* 'zenocrates')[6] means that the quire c consists of six leaves, besides (+) a leaf inserted after the 6th leaf (hence called 6*), which inserted leaf commences with the word 'zenocrates.' The great advantage of this systematic method of collation over the plan of merely counting the leaves is that every leaf is accurately accounted for, deficiencies are noticed at once (even if only a blank leaf), and it is made clear what pieces are printed together, and what are only bound together. Hitherto every treatise which happens to begin on the recto of a leaf has been assumed to be the commencement of a volume, and scores of books have been ruthlessly cut up in consequence of this erroneous impression. In Zel's famous volume, for instance, containing St. Augustine's De vita christiana and De singularitate clericorum, printed in 1467, where the first treatise ends and the second begins in the middle of the third quire, all the bibliographers for the last seventy years have, I believe, without exception described them as two separate books; in some cases even different dates (three or more years apart) have been assigned to what must have been worked by one pull of the press. But this is beyond my present purpose. I shall be most thankful if any one who has access to collections of this kind, will examine and report upon any books that he finds printed by the Printer of the Historia sancti Albani. Hain's 12257 (Ovidii Liber trium puellarum) described by Dibdin (BS. No. 327) and there bound with No. XII below, I have not seen, but it is almost certainly one which may be added to the number; but there are most likely many more.

To explain the abbreviations used in the notes:

SBK means <u>Stadt-Bibliothek zu Köln</u>, the Town-Library at Cologne, the contents of which are described, so far as our purpose is concerned, in the <u>Katalog</u> printed by the learned Archivist and Librarian, Dr. Ennen, in 1865.

BRH means <u>Bibliotheca Regia Hagana</u>, the Royal Library at the Hague, the fifteenth century books in which have been described in the <u>Catalogus</u> published in 1856 by the Librarian, Mr. J. W. Holtrop, to whom all students in this branch of bibliography owe a debt which they can best repay by following in his steps. What was before the publication of his catalogue a shapeless unknown and unexplored mass, has become under his hands a system in which every book readily finds its place, and in which the very errors themselves afford the clue to their own rectification.

BS means the <u>Bibliotheca Spenceriana</u> described by Dr. Dibdin, 1814-23. It is not to be expected that we should find thoroughly accurate descriptions of these books in an English work published fifty years ago; but the great value of the book lies in the fact that it is the catalogue of an existing library, which the liberality of its owner will allow to be examined.

I may add that the descriptions here given, so far as they relate to books preserved at Oxford, are only portions of a similar catalogue, which I made in 1866, of about 100 quarto books, all printed (apparently) at Cologne, before the introduction of printed signatures, and all preserved in the Auctarium of the Bodleian Library. In the summer of that year I was able, through the kindness of Mr. Coxe the Librarian, to examine every early printed volume in the Auctarium with the view of finding books printed in England, Holland, or Belgium, or at the early Cologne presses. The result was highly satisfactory; and I do not suppose that many were overlooked. Where I found books described in the Hague catalogue, Mr. Holtrop was kind enough to compare notes and verify his descriptions. Where his catalogue is corrected in any point, the correction is due to his own later investigations, which he is ever ready both to make and to communicate.

The books here described are placed roughly according to their typographical characteristics. I have made no attempt to assign a date to any of them; but it may be fairly presumed that they were all printed before 1475.

With reference to the contractions used by the early printers, as there is so little demand in England for bibliography of this kind, our printers cannot be expected to indulge us with the luxury of special types cut to represent every contraction used, as may be seen in Hain's Repertorium printed at Tübingen. I have therefore adopted the common plan of printing in italics all letters which are represented by a contraction in the original. The double hyphen of the original is represented by the ordinary modern hyphen. Any attempt to give some of the contractions by clumsy expedients would only disfigure the page without effecting its purpose.

I.

L. Annaei Senecae Liber de remediis fortuitorum. No place, no printer's name, no year. 8 leaves in 4^0.

Collation. a^8; 8 leaves, 27 uneven lines (especially uneven on the versos), no printed signatures, no initial-directors, no hyphens, except on 1^a.
Leaf 1^a-8^b text.

Beginning (1^a li 1):
    (H) Vnc librum composuit Seneca nobilissimus

End (8^b li 15):
    autem quam rara domi sit ista felicitas;

(li 16 blank)
Annei lucij Senece de remedijs
fortuitorum liber explicit
(li 19-27 blank)

Copy examined. Oxford, Bodleian: Auct. N.5.5 (Nº 3); perfect.

Not in SBK.
BRH. Nº 79 part I (Zell c. 1470), but wrongly identified with Hain *14655.
BS. Nº 422 part I (Zell).
The Mainz public library contains a copy; see Fischer, Lief. iv, p. 103, Nº 72 (Zell), and a facsimile of the first three lines on Pl. 4.
Not in Hain (not *14655).

II.

L. Annaei Senecae Liber de quatuor virtutibus. Ejusdem Liber de moribus. Epitaphium ejusdem. Tres orationes (Aeschinis, Demadis, Demosthenis) in senatu Atheniensi de recipiendo Alexandro magno vel armis repellendo. Demosthenis Oratio ad Alexandrum. Bernardi Silvestris Epistola super gubernatione rei familiaris. Adagia. Architrenius in laudem civitatis Parisiensis. No place, no printer's name, no year. 21 leaves in 4⁰.

Collation. a⁸bc(+6* 'zenocrates')⁶; 21 leaves, 27 uneven lines (especially uneven on the versos), no printed signatures, no initial-directors, no hyphens.
Leaf 1ª-6ª De quatuor virtutibus; 6ᵇ-10ª De moribus; 10ª Epitaphium; 10ᵇ-11ᵇ Tres orationes: 11ᵇ-13ª Demosthenes ad Alexandrum; 13ᵇ-16ª Bernardus; 16ª-21ª Adagia; 21ᵇ Architrenius.

Beginning (1ª li 1):
Annei lucij Senece de quatuor
virtutibus liber Jncipit;
(li 3 blank)

(Q) Vatuor virtutum species multorum sapien

End (21ᵇ li 14):
Omne bonum si sola bonis fortuna faveret;
(li 15-27 blank)

Copy examined. Oxford, Bodleian: Auct. N. 5. 5 (Nº 4); perfect.

Possibly SBK. Nº 16. 67; but if so, not carefully described.
BRH. Nº 79 part 2 (Zell c. 1470).
BS. Nº 422 part 2 (Zell).
British Museum; see Grenville catalogue, p. 654 (Zell perhaps before 1466). From the Heber and Sykes collections.
The Mainz public library contains a copy; see Fischer, Lief. iv, p. 99. Nº 71 (Zell).
Not in Hain.

III.

Historia sancti Albani martyris metrice. Historia ejusdem prosaice. No place, no printer's name, no year. 8 leaves in 4⁰.

Collation. a⁸; 8 leaves, 27 mostly even lines (more uneven on the versos), no printed signatures, no initial-directors, no hyphens (except once).
Leaf 1ᵃ Hist. metr.; 1ᵃ-8ᵇ Hist. pros.

Beginning (1ᵃ li 1):
Martiris albani venerabilis ecce legenda.
Vtilis erranti. quia fertilis est relegenda.
Historia ejusdem metrice.
(Q) Vem mater genuit fuit hec sibi soror et vxor.

End (8ᵇ li 14):
et super niuem dealbari; Amen
(li 15 blank)

Et sic est finita historia sancti albani
martiris
(li 17-27 blank)

<u>Copies examined</u>. 1. Oxford, Bodleian: Auct.
N. 5. 5 (N⁰ 7); perfect. 2. In the possession of Mr.
Boone (1866); perfect, and forming N⁰ 5 in a volume
of tracts given to the library of the convent "Marie
laudis ordinis fratrum sancte crucis prope opidum los-
sense borchloen dyoces' leodiensis" in 1475. Of the
other pieces in the volume, N⁰ˢ 1, 2, 4, are by the
Printer of <u>Dictys Cretensis</u>; and N⁰ˢ 3, 6, 7, 8, by
Ulric Zel.

Not in SBK.
BRH. N⁰ 88 (Zell c. 1470).
Borluut (1857) 3014 (Zell). Bound alone.
British Museum; see Grenville Catalogue, p. 17
(Zell c. 1470).
Not in Hain.

IV.

Tractatus de successionibus ab intestato. Casus
breves trium partium tractatus successionum. No place,
no printer's name, no year. 16 leaves in 4⁰.

<u>Collation</u>. a b⁸; 16 leaves, 27 mostly even lines
(on the rectos, but sometimes very uneven on the versos), no printed signatures, no initial-directors, with
hyphens, with reference-letters in the outer margin.
Leaf 1ᵃ-15ᵇ Tractatus; 16ᵃ-16ᵇ Casus breves.

<u>Beginning</u> (1ᵃ li 1):
Jncipit tractatus de successionibus ab intestato;
(li 3 blank)
(E) xquo materia successionum
cuius noti

<u>End</u> (16ᵇ li 11):
non amplius in stirpes.

(li 12 blank)
Hic deseruiunt Autentice Jtaque Cessanti Post
fratres Jn hoc ordine aptissimo
(li 15 blank)
Nota littere .C L L A. significant.
vbi in textu
isti casus breves poni debent
(li 18-27 blank)

Copy examined. Cambridge, University Library: AB. 5. 107;* perfect. A facsimile of the first page, photographed by Mr. W. Nichols of Cambridge, accompanies this paper.**

Not in SBK.
Not in BRH (not 137).
Not in Hain (not *15110).

V.

Beati Hieronymi Ordo sive regula vivendi deo. No place, no printer's name, no year. 30 leaves in 4^0.

Collation. $abc^8 d^6$; 30 leaves, 27 mostly even lines, no printed signatures, no initial-directors, with hyphens.
Leaf 1^a-30^b text.

Beginning (1^a li 1):
Jncipit prologus in ordinem viuendi deo.
eximij
doctoris Jhieronimi ad Eustochium sacram
deo virginem quam Bethlee cum pluribus
deo
dicatis virginibus in monasterio sub istius
ordinis obseruationibus conclusit;
(li 6 blank)
(T) Epescens in membris. procliuum corpus

---

*[Now AB. 12. 59. J.]
**[See Prefatory Note. J.]

End (30ᵇ li 20):
vestris iuuare oracionibus;
(li 21 blank)
Explicit ordo siue regula viuendi deo.
docto
ris eximij Jheronimi. ad Eustohium
sacram
deo virginem. quam bethlehem. cum pluri
bus. deo dicatis virginibus. in monasterio
sub istius ordinis obseruacionibus conclusit
(li 27 blank)

Copies examined. 1. Oxford, Bodleian; Auct. N.
5. 5 (Nº 8); perfect. 2. Cambridge, Trinity College:
Grylls 6672;* perfect, but the quires b and c are trans-
posed, and a half-sheet of the Augustinus super orationem dominicam by the same printer is bound into the
middle of sig. b.

Not in SBK.
Not in BRH (not Nº 156).
BS. Nº 1138.
Not in Hain (not *8569).

VI.

Antonini archiepiscopi Florentini Tractatus de
instructione seu directione simplicium confessorum.
Sancti Johannis Chrysostomi Sermo de paenitentia. No
place, no printer's name, no year. 144 leaves in 4⁰.

Collation. abcdefghiklmnopqrs⁸; 144 leaves,
27 sometimes uneven lines, no printed signatures,
no initial-directors, with hyphens.
Leaf 1ª-139ª Antoninus; 139ᵇ-143ᵇ Chrysos-
tomus; 144 not known.

---

*[Now Grylls. 3. 371. J.]

Beginning (1ᵃ li 1):
 Ncipiunt Rubrice super Tractatum de
  instructione
 seu directione simplicium confessorum.
  Et primo
   De potestate confessoris in audiendo
 confessiones et absoluendo   .i.

End (143ᵇ li 10):
 domino nostro ihesu xpō in secula seculorum benedicto Amen;
    (li 12 blank)
  Explicit sermo de penitentia
  Johannis Crisostimi;
    (li 15-27 blank)

Copies examined. 1. Oxford, Bodleian: Auct. N. 5. 5 (N⁰ 6); wanting leaf 144. 2. In the possession of A. J. Horwood, Esq.;* wanting leaf 144.

Not in SBK (not 74 or 75).
BRH. N⁰ 98 (Zell c. 1470).
Possibly either Kloss 275 (Zell 1472-73), or 276 (Zell 1474-75), or 277 (Zell 1476 identified with Panzer i. 326. 376).
Not in Hain (not *1162).

VII.

Matthaei de Cracovia Liber de arte moriendi. No place, no printer's name, no year. 18 leaves in 4⁰

Collation. a⁸b¹⁰; 18 leaves, 27 almost wholly even lines, no printed signatures, no initial-directors, with hyphens.
Leaf 1ᵃ-17ᵇ text; 18 blank.

Beginning (1ᵃ li 1):
 Jncipit prologus in librum de arte morien

---

*[Now in the University Library, Cambridge. J.]

di magistri mathei de Cracouia sacre the
ologie professoris;
(li 4 blank)
(C) Vm de pre͟se͟n͟tis exilij miseria mor

End (17ᵇ li 6):
mors occupat terminos eius: mori discat;
(li 7 blank)
Explicit liber vtilis de arte mori
endi Ma͟g͟i͟s͟t͟r͟i Mathei de Cracouia;
(li 10-27 blank)

Copy examined. In my possession; perfect, bought in January 1868, from M. Tross, who obtained it at the Yemeniz sale (299) in 1867.

SBK. Nº 5. 19.
Not in BRH.
The Public Library at Mainz appears to contain a copy; see Fischer, Lief. iv, p. 80 (Zell).
Hain 5801 (Zell), not seen.

VIII.

Beati Augustini Sermo super orationem dominicam. Ejusdem Expositio super symbolum. Ejusdem Alia expositio super symbolum. Ejusdem Sermo de ebrietate cavenda. No place, no printer's name, no year. 8 leaves in 4⁰.

Collation. a⁸; 8 leaves, 27 even lines, no printed signatures, no initial directors, with hyphens.
Leaf 1ᵃ-3ᵃ Sermo; 3ᵃ-5ᵃ Expositio; 5ᵃ-6ᵃ Alia exp.: 6ᵇ-8ᵇ Sermo de ebr. cav.

Beginning (1ᵃ li 1):
Jncipit sermo beati Augustini episcopi.
super orationem dominicam;
(li 3 blank)
(Q) Voniam domino gubernante. iam
estis

End (8ᵇ li 27):
  per omnia secula seculorum Amen

Copies examined. I. Oxford, Bodleian: Auct. 7Q. 5. 9 (N⁰ 1); perfect. 2. Cambridge, Trinity College: C. 4. 80 (N⁰ 5); perfect. 3. Two leaves (2 and 7) are bound in the centre of quire b of a copy of the Hieronymi Ordo vivendi deo by the same printer, in Trinity College Library (Grylls 6672 described above, N⁰ V).

Not in SBK.
Not in BRH (not N⁰ 89).
Hain *1990 (typis ed praeced. sc. Zell).

IX.

Maphaei Vegii Dialogus inter Alithiam et Philaliten. No place, no printer's name, no year. 16 leaves in 4⁰.

Collation. ab⁸; 16 leaves, 27 even lines, no printed signatures, no initial-directors, with hyphens.
  Leaf 1 blank; 2ᵃ-3ᵃ Prologue; 3ᵃ-15ᵇ Dialogue; 16 blank.

Beginning (2ᵃ li 1):
  Maphei Vegij laudensis dialogus inter Alithiam et Philaliten Jncipit feliciter.
       Prologus
      (li 4 blank)
  (M) Apheus Vegius. Eustochio fratri.

End (15ᵇ li 7):
  sequor libens.
      (li 8 blank)
    Explicit feliciter Mafei vegei dilogus inter Alithiam et Philalitena
      (li 11-27 blank)

Copy examined. Cambridge, Trinity College: C. 4. 80 (N⁰ 3); perfect, but leaf 1 folded so as to follow leaf 16.*

    Not in SBK.
    BRH. N⁰ 77 (Zell c. 1470), but wrongly identified with Hain 15928.
    The Mainz public library appears to contain a copy; see Fischer, Lief. iv, p. 105 (N⁰ 73).
    Possibly BS. N⁰ 794 (Zell).
    Possibly Kloss 3654 (Zell 1471-72 identified with Panzer ix. 226. 274) or 3656 (Zell 1480).
    Not in Hain (not 15928).

X.

    Libellus de raptu animae Tundali et ejus visione. No place, no printer's name, no year. 20 leaves in 4^0.

    Collation. $a^8 bc^6$; 20 leaves, 27 even lines, no printed signatures, no initial-directors, with hyphens.
    Leaf 1ᵃ-18ᵇ text; 19-20 not known.

    Beginning (1ᵃ li 1):
        Jncipit libellus de Raptu anime Tundali
        et eius visione Tractans de penis inferni
        et gaudijs paradisi;
            (li 4 blank)
    (A) Nno domini Millesimo centesimo quadra-

    End (18ᵇ li 16):
        dam sermone de omnibus sanctis contrarium
        innuere videatur
            (li 17 blank)
        Explicit libellus de raptu anime
        Tundali et eius visione. Tractans de
        penis inferni et gaudijs paradisi;
            (li 21-27 blank)

---

*[This volume now stands VIᵉ. 5. 1. Of the other pieces contained in it Nos. 1 and 4 are by Ulric Zell, 2 by Arn. ter Hoernen, 6 by the Printer of Dictys. J.]

Copy examined. Oxford, Bodleian: Auct. N. 5.
5 (N⁰ 2); wanting leaves 19-20.

> Not in SBK.
> Not in BRH.
> The Mainz public library contains a copy; see
Fischer, Lief. iv, p. 96, N⁰ 69 (Zell).
> BS. N⁰ 790 (ter Hoernen!).
> M. Fr. Vergauwen of Ghent has a copy; see
Van der Meersch, Recherches, T. i, p. 264, N⁰ LXXVI
(attributed to ter Hoernen on Dibdin's authority).
> Hain *15542 (typi Zellianis similes).

XI.

Petri Blesensis Libellus de amicitia christiana.
No place, no printer's name, no year. 16 leaves in 4⁰.

Collation. ab⁸; 16 leaves, 26 even lines, no printed signatures, no initial-directors, with hyphens, the lines closer together than in the other books.
Leaf 1ᵃ-15ᵃ text; 15ᵇ, 16, blank.

Beginning (1ᵃ li 1):
> Jncipit libellus magistri Petri Blesensis
> de ami cicia cristiana.
> (li 3 blank)
> (S) Vbsannabit aliquis et arguet. quod

End (15ᵃ li 6):
> eam enormitas reatus eliminet.
> (li 7 blank)
> Explicit libellus magistri Petri
> blesensis de amicicia cristiana.
> (li 10-26 blank)

Copies examined. 1. Oxford, Bodleian: Auct. N. 5. 5 (N⁰ 5); wanting leaf 16. 2. In the possession of A. J. Horwood, Esq.; perfect.*

---

*[Now in the University Library, Cambridge. J.]

Not in SBK.
Not in BRH.
BS. N⁰ 1050 (Zell).
Possibly Kloss 2799 (Zell 1475).
Hain *3241 ('Dibdin Ulrico Zell dat').

XII.

P. Ovidii Nasonis Liber de nuncio sagaci. No place, no printer's name, no year. 8 leaves in 4⁰.

Collation. a⁸; 8 leaves, 24 lines, no printed signatures, no initial-directors, with hyphens, with the initials of the speakers on the left-hand margin.
Leaf 1 blank; 2ª-8ª text; 8ᵇ blank.

Beginning (2ª li 1):
 Ouidij Nasonis Sulmonensis poete
 de nuncio sagaci liber incipit;
   (li 3 blank)
 (S) Vmmi victoris fierem cum victor
 amoris

End (8ª li 8):
 Hijs verbis tuta. fuit illum virgo secuta;
   (li 9 blank)
 Ouidij nasonis Sulmonensis poete
 De nuncio sagaci liber Explicit
   (li 11-24 blank)

Copy examined. Oxford, Bodleian: Auct. N. 5. 4 (N⁰ 1); perfect.

Not in SBK.
Not in BRH.
BS. Supplement N⁰ 275 (Zell).
Hain 12258 (Zell), not seen.

XIII.

P. Ovidii Nasonis Libri tres de arte amandi.

Ejusdem Libri duo de remedio amoris. Dictamen ordinatum per fratrem Arnoldum de Buerik magistrum noviciorum in monasterio de rubea valle in Sonia ordinis sancti Augustini. No place, no printer's name, no year. 70 leaves in 4^0.

<u>Collation</u>. abcdefgh^{8}i^6; 70 leaves, 24 lines, no printed signatures, no initial-directors.

Leaf 1^a-49^b De arte amandi; 50^a-67^a De remedio amoris; 67^b blank; 68^a-70^a Buerik; 70^b blank.

<u>Beginning</u> (1^a li 1):
 Ouidij Nasonis Sulmonensis de
 arte amandi liber primus incipit;
    (li 3 blank)
(S) J qu̅is in hoc arte̅m populo no̅n nouit ama̅ndi

<u>End</u> (70^a li 10):
 Sint pre me̅nte tibi. dilige stare domi
    (li 11 blank)
 Explicit Dictamen Buerik
    (li 13-24 blank)

Copy examined. Oxford, Bodleian: Auct. N. 5. 4 (N° 2); perfect.

Not in SBK.
Not in BRH.
BS. N° 326 (Zell), but leaves 68-70 are not noticed. Arnold Buderik (according to Val. Andreas) was an Augustinian monk in the Rooden Kloster at Soignies near Brussels, and in the year 1417 became Prior of a newly founded house at Elzinghem near Audenarde.

Hain 12215 (Zell), not seen; and leaves 68-70 not noticed.

Brunet iv. 279 ('exécutée avec des caractères qui ont beaucoup de rapport avec ceux de Conrad Winters de Homburg, imprimeur à Cologne'); described carefully from the d'Ourches copy.

Notes

1. I have selected this book for the purpose partly because it is the commonest (copies being, 1. at the Hague, 2. in the British Museum, 3. in the Bodleian, 4. in a volume belonging to Mr. Boone, and 5. one formerly in the Borluut collection, bound separately), and partly because it is almost the only one which has no risk of being confused with other editions differing in type, but resembling each other page for page.
2. Signatures have existed as long as books have required binding; they are easily traceable for more than 1200 years back. The early Strasbourg (and some Italian) books afford examples of the clumsy devices resorted to for printing them before the simple method was devised of appropriating a line at the bottom of the page for their reception.

The photographed facsimile (opposite) taken from the first page of the Tractatus de successionibus ab intestato is, as nearly as possible, the exact size of the original. The large initial E is inserted by hand in red, and the same rubricator has touched all the capitals throughout with a dash of red. In this page both the semicolon and the double hyphen, which at once characterise these books, are easily to be noticed; and I am confident that any one who has before his eyes either this facsimile or any of the volumes described in the present paper, will readily be able to recognise any books that he may possess by the Printer of the Historia S. Albani, and to separate them from the Zels in his collection. It is possible that, as M. Brunet seems to suggest, they may be early specimens of the press of Conrad de Homborch; if so, those who have greater facilities than I have, of studying the early Cologne books, should be able to give us a solution.

⁊ Incipit tractatus de successio‑
nibus ab intestato ;

Ex quo materia successionū c9 noti‑
cia vtil' ē. a sepe i mltis casib9 ne‑
cessaria i corpe iuris ciuil' tā i textu
bz q̄ i glo. no sat mmū eē dispsa   A
Ita vt etiā eis q̄ libros legales ad manum hr̄e
put difficile sit valde i mltis casib successionū
se et alios expedie l' certificae. Ideo no parū ne
cessariū e marie p iapieaū directōne. vt de illa
materia heat aliq̄d opediose collcm et coportatū
no min9 tn solide positū et fūdatū. quo se miuae
possint ne forte ipi dictoʒ textuū a glo. plixita
te mltitudie a varietate detrim. ab h9 materie tā
vtilis a ncaarie se subtrahāt studio et iquisitōe
Quae ego ipos eosde iapietes mltis de laboibz
fū portae cupiens x/ hunc qui sequitur tractatū
magno cū laboē studui opilae i modū p vt hic
sub nectit (Vt autē i oib9 casib9 successionū ō‑
curtētib9 stati q̄s sciat i qua pte hui9 tractat9   B
cuiuslibet coʒ requirēda sit discussio. sūmopere
ncāa est. huius tractat9 bona. dara. et plana
distmctōz. ergo vt mōcōnfuse et distincte preses
materia ptractet x/ sit hec pūtis tractat9 ptiō pti
apalis trimembʒ. q̄ scz i eo p̄ mo dicet de suc‑
cessione descendencui. sedo de ascendecui. tao de

Specimen of types used by the Printer of the
Historia Sancti Albani at Cologne

INDEX

Adagia	II.
Aeschines, Oratio in senatu Atheniensi	II.
Albanus (S.), see Historia.	
Antoninus archiep. Florentinus, Tractatus de instructione seu directione simplicium confessorum	VI.
Architrenius, in laudem civitatis Parisiensis	II.
Arnoldus, see Buderik (A. de).	
Augustinus (S. Aurelius), Expositio super symbolum	VIII.
--Expositio alia super symbolum	VIII.
--Sermo de ebrietate cavenda	VIII.
--Sermo super orationem dominicam	VIII.
Bernardus Silvestris, Epistola super gubernatione rei familiaris	II.
Blesensis, see Petrus Bl.	
Buderik (Arnoldus de), Dictamen	XIII.
Buerik, see Buderik.	
Chrysostomus, see Johannes Chr.	
Cracovia (Matthaeus de), Liber de arte moriendi	VII.
Demades, Oratio in senatu Atheniensi	II.
Demosthenes, Oratio ad Alexandrum	II.
--Oratio in senatu Atheniensi	II.
Epitaphium Senecae	II.

Hieronymus (B.), Ordo sive regula vivendi deo, ad Eustochium	V.
Historia S. Albani martyris	III.
Johannes (S.) Chrysostomus, Sermo de paenitentia	VI.
Libellus de raptu animae Tundali et ejus visione	X.
Matthaeus, see Cracovia (Matth. de).	
Ovidius Naso (P.), De arte amandi libri tres	XIII.
--De remedio amoris libri duo	XIII.
--De nuncio sagaci	XII.
--Liber trium puellarum	[p. 108]
Petrus Blesensis, Libellus de amicitia christiana	XI.
Seneca (L. Annaeus), Liber de moribus	II.
--Liber de quatuor virtutibus	II.
--Liber de remediis fortuitorum	I.
--see Epitaphium.	
Successiones ab intestato, see Tractatus.	
Tractatus de successionibus ab intestato	IV.
Tundalus, see Libellus.	
Vegius (Maphaeus), Dialogus inter Alithiam et Philaliten	IX.

6. ANCIENT GREEK MANUSCRIPT OF THE GOSPELS

Notes and Queries, 4th. S. II, July 25 and August 15, 1868.

Notes and Queries is a journal, well represented by long runs in many libraries throughout the world, but seldom sufficiently well-known or well-used by students. It is one of the ideal journals for browsing by students of bibliography and it can teach them that serendipity is the most useful tool in their bibliographical armory.
  Note in particular that Bradshaw's clarification of the problem, as well as the understanding of the misdescriptions of the past, lay in being "in the least familiar with the services of the Eastern Church."

Ancient Greek Manuscript of the Gospels.

  In Bridges's History of Northamptonshire, under the parish of "Loddington," occurs the following curious notice, which, although possessing perhaps more of individual than of general interest, yet the Editor of "N. & Q.," with his accustomed and well-known courtesy, will, I feel sure, permit me to place before his readers, in the hope that some one or other of them may have seen the manuscript referred to, and be able to inform me where it may be found.

In the list of rectors is mentioned a Mr. George Tew, incumbent from 1693 to 1702, of whom Bridges says:--

> Mr. Tew, the late incumbent, found, walled up in the chancel, a Greek MS. of three of the Gospels, the Gospel of St. Mark being wanting, conjectured to be about 600 years old. It was communicated by him to Dr. Cumberland, then bishop of the diocese, of whom it was borrowed by Dr. Moore, Bishop of Ely, who, when pressed to return it, said he had mislaid or could not find it. From this circumstance it hath been suspected that the manuscript was much older than it was thought to be, and is perhaps preserved with the books he gave to the University of Cambridge.

Should the MS. have been lodged in the public library of that University, the curators can scarcely be unaware of its existence, and from them I would especially ask the favour of any information they may possess respecting it.

Edmund Tew, M.A.

Oxon.

P.S. The extraordinary conduct of Bishop Moore in this affair forms, I fear, but one out of many such instances. Some years ago an old friend of mine lent a MS., which he prized very highly, to a church dignitary in this very diocese--neither a bishop nor yet a dean; and upon requesting that it might be restored to him, received the very same reply as that given by this good bishop and honourable man to my ancient and worthy but too confiding relative. My old friend is no more, but the MS. has never yet found its way back to the true and lawful owner. E.T.

GREEK MS. OF THE GOSPELS.
(4th S. ii. 80.)

The following letter, which speaks for itself, will, I trust, be deemed worthy of insertion in an early number of "N. & Q." With a promptitude and courteousness demanding my best thanks, Mr. Bradshaw sent it to me direct; but, under his full permission, I am desirous that it should meet the public eye, containing, as it seems to me, information of very general interest, and at the same time affording proof of the usefulness and convenience of such a periodical as "N. & Q." as a medium of inter-communication between scholars and men of letters. Edmund Tew.

University Library, Cambridge,
27 July, 1868.

Dear Sir--With reference to your communication which appeared in Notes and Queries on Saturday last, I am very happy to give you all the information which it is, I believe, possible to give at the present time.

We have only two manuscript εὐαγγέλια in the Library. Both of these came to us with Bp. Moore's library in 1715. They are marked Dd. 8. 23 and Dd. 8. 49 respectively.

Mill, in his Greek Testament (Oxford, 1707, folio), gives a collation of one εὐαγγέλιον in Bp. Moore's possession which he calls M.2; this corresponds to our MS. Dd. 8. 49.

In the great Oxford Catalogue of 1697, the last of Bp. Moore's Manuscripts contains one εὐαγγέλιον, numbered 34. It is there described as follows: 34. Evangelistarium Gr. ante Annos 600 Conscriptum. Codex Membr. fol.

This copy has always been identified here with our MS. Dd. 8. 49.

The other εὐαγγέλιον mentioned above as coming

to us with Bp. Moore's books in 1715, bears the mark 20 on its first page, and is no doubt No. 20 in the Oxford Catalogue of 1697, where it is thus wrongly described as a copy of the Gospels:--

'20. <u>Evangelia Graece. Codex Membranaceus ante annos quingentos scriptus folio majore.</u>'

Neither of these two volumes contains any memorandum showing whence Moore obtained them; and neither of them contains any traces of English or other <u>Western</u> ownership before Bp. Moore's time. We can be certain that they were in his possession before 1697, when the list was printed.

Unfortunately both were rebound about a hundred years ago in the rough calf binding with which almost all our Greek MSS. were then honoured.

MS. Dd. 8. 23 (Moore 20) contains no trace of its former binding; but Dd. 8. 49 (Moore 34) has several waste leaves of paper, the condition of which strongly resembles that of the outer leaves of several books which I know to have been walled up in churches.

Moreover the ages of the two MSS. are accurately enough given in the Oxford Catalogue, where Moore 20 (our Dd. 8. 23) is described as 500 years old (xiith century), and Moore 34 (our Dd. 8. 49) as 600 years old (xith century). You will notice that the age and description here given correspond remarkably with what is said by Bridges of the book mislaid by Bp. Moore.

I have always felt satisfied in my own mind for years past that our Dd. 8. 49 was the mislaid manuscript, but of course there is no possibility of proving it.

Many persons have thought that it must be easy to identify, in some of our libraries, a copy which is described as containing only three of the four Gospels. But the truth is, that to any one in the least familiar with the services of the Eastern Church, the words 'a Greek Manuscript of three of the four Gospels, the Gospel of St. Mark being wanting,' are only an ignorant description of an εὐαγγέλιον, or Gospel book of the Greek Church, i.e. the book which contains the Gospels read in the service every day throughout the year, arranged in what we should call their Prayer-book order. In the Eastern Church St. John is read from Easter to Pentecost, St. Matthew from Pentecost to New Year (Holy Cross day in September), St. Luke from New Year to Lent; while St. Mark is only used in part of Lent, and to furnish supplementary week day Gospels at other times. Hence, as the MSS. commonly have greater ornaments at Easter, Pentecost, and New Year, and sometimes also portraits of St. John, St. Matthew, and St. Luke at these places, it is easy to see how an εὐαγγέλιον may come to be described as a copy of the Gospels wanting St. Mark.

Many persons use the term Evangelistarium for this Gospel-book or Εὐαγγέλιον, being misled by the fact that the Εὐαγγελιστάριον, or table of the Church lessons from the Gospels, is commonly found accompanying the Εὐαγγέλιον. It is just as if people were to call our Prayer-book a Kalendar.

If you ever come this way, I shall be most happy to show you the MS., and I think you will be inclined to allow that it is in good keeping.

Yours very truly,

Henry Bradshaw.

The Rev. Edmund Tew.

7. LIST OF THE FOUNTS OF TYPE AND WOODCUT DEVICES USED BY PRINTERS IN HOLLAND IN THE FIFTEENTH CENTURY

Published as Memorandum No. 3, June 1871. Reprinted in <u>Collected Papers</u>, 1889, pp. 258-280.

    Bradshaw had an especial affinity for the books of the Low Countries. In part this may have been due to the historical connections between the Netherlands and that bulge of Eastern England where he spent most of his life. It was certainly augmented by his friendship and close professional ties with J. W. Holtrop, librarian of the Royal Library at the Hague, and with Holtrop's successor, M. F. A. G. Campbell.

    In this paper Bradshaw's dictum of arranging the facts and allowing them to speak for themselves is clearly demonstrated. His proposed arrangement for early printed books as established here is that which was later used by Robert Proctor and has since always been known as Proctor order.

    The following pages contain a list of all the different founts of type and woodcut devices used during the fifteenth century by the Dutch printers, which are described and figured in Mr. Holtrop's <u>Monuments typographiques des Pays-Bas au</u> xve <u>siècle</u>, together with one or two which are either accidentally omitted there, or have come to light since the publication of that remarkable work. I used the term Dutch printers with reference to those who practised the art in the northern portion of the Low Countries which now forms the kingdom of the Netherlands. The printers of Belgium, in the modern acceptation of that term, will form the subject of a similar list.

The towns are placed in chronological order, the earliest book which has any date attached to it being taken as the guide. Under the towns the presses are arranged in the same way; and under each press the several founts of type find their place according to the date of their first use, so far as it has been ascertained. The same arrangement holds with the printers' devices. Sometimes two or more towns, as Deventer, Delft, and Gouda, come under the same year; and here precedence is given to Deventer, because only the year 1477 is known, while the other two are placed under 10 Jan. 1477 and 24 May 1477 respectively. When there is a distinct break in any printer's career, and it is clear that he starts afresh with a new fount or founts of type, and that the old types disappear, as in the case of Ger. Leeu at Gouda, and Peter van Os at Zwolle, I have used the terms First press and Second press to signify that the types of the one do not pass to the other. At Deventer, for instance, Paffroed starts in 1477 with one type, and adds a second in 1479. With these two he goes on till 1485. At this point Paffroed breaks off, and Jacobus de Breda starts in 1486 with the two founts of type which Paffroed had been using. With these Jac. de Breda goes on until 1487, when his press ceases, and these two founts of type disappear altogether. In August 1488 Paffroed begins again with an entirely fresh set of types; and in August 1489 Jac. de Breda begins again also with fresh types. Under these circumstances, to make the investigation of the books easier, and their sequence clearer, I have gone so far as to put the first press of Jac. de Breda immediately after the first press of Ric. Paffroed; because there is no trace until August 1489 of two presses being at work at Deventer simultaneously. The same terms (First, Second, &c.) are also used where a printer moves from one town to another, Veldener's first press being at Louvain (1474), his second at Utrecht (1478), his third at Kuilenburg (1483), and so on.

As the series of facsimiles in the <u>Monuments typographiques</u> is almost exhaustive, I have everywhere referred to a plate in that work, in order to shew clearly and at once what type is meant in each case by Type 1, Type 2, etc.

If this list be accepted as a fairly accurate one, my principal object in drawing it up will have been gained. In making a catalogue, for instance, of all the specimens of these presses which are to be found in the libraries at Cambridge, the additional words, 'Type 2,' or 'Types 2 (text) and 3 (commentary)' would convey at a glance the very information which is most needed, and would allow the description to be compressed into a smaller space than would otherwise be needed. It would in many cases also supersede the necessity of any reference to the facsimiles. Suppose we have any five books in a particular type, and there are five books at the Hague in the same type, the chances are great that one at least of the five will be common to the two collections, and we can at once identify all the nine as from the same press. The real books are then of more service than any facsimiles, and we become possessed of more data for studying the history of the type. Further, as the list furnishes as far as possible the date at which each type began to be used at each press, a large number of purely conjectural dates would disappear from our catalogues, and instead of speculating as to what the date of a book may possibly be, that date would be assigned which best serves to connect the book with some well-defined characteristics of other books which bear a positive date, and the reason for assigning a date to a book would be self-evident, instead of being (as now) left to the conjecture of the reader of the catalogue.

If this practice were to be adopted in the long wished-for <u>Typographical Antiquities</u> of Holland and Belgium, and two or three words were to be added to each description to say which founts of type were used in each book, naming them numerically as I have done here, or with the greater accuracy which Mr. Campbell, the present Librarian of the Royal Library at the Hague, alone can furnish, it is not too much to say that the value of such a work would be increased tenfold. In some cases of course it would be impossible to add these points of distinction, because the books have not been examined with that view, and are now perhaps not easily accessible. But if only such as were of easy access in the Royal Library were so noted, the great gain of having so much firm standing ground for future investigation would more than compensate for the labour which would have to be bestowed upon it.

It may be said that mere specimens of woodcut printing, as the Biblia pauperum, and other such books, having nothing typographical about them, should not have been included in a list of founts of type like the present. Where however they are actual books, I have admitted them into my list, while excluding all single woodcut sheets, pictures, &c. The latter belong rather to a history of engraving, or to a list of woodcuts, whether single or in series, such as I sometimes hope to publish; but when once the art of wood-engraving is applied to the illustration of books, the very mode of working the plates so as to form a book, even though no type be used, will sometimes aid materially in solving questions concerning printed books which would otherwise be quite hopeless.

It is perhaps necessary to add a few words in explanation of the course I have followed in placing the Biblia pauperum, the Speculum humanae salvationis, and the whole class of books which have been attributed to a press at Haarlem. The method I have adopted prevents me from accepting any testimony at all except such printed or written documentary evidence as is found in the volumes themselves, or failing this, such evidence as is afforded by an unmistakeable family likeness between two or more founts of type.

Having no documentary evidence as to where the Biblia pauperum was executed, I am bound to leave it standing where I first find trace of it, that is, at Zwolle, where the original blocks appear, cut into several pieces, in a book printed in 1488. The fact of the working of the book being by single sheets and not by quires of two or more sheets, at once serves to connect it with the original Canticum Canticorum and with the original Ars moriendi, which are worked in this way. The connexion of all three works with Zwolle is evident, as has been shewn by Mr. Holtrop, from the fact that the blocks of the Biblia pauperum appear there in 1488; that a block of the Canticum Canticorum appears in the Rosetum exercitiorum spiritualium printed there in 1494; and that the closest reproduction of the original Ars moriendi is to be found in the Sterfboeck also printed at Zwolle in 1488. I may here mention another point serving to connect the latter two books with one another. In Trinity College Library in Dublin I found in November 1869 an imperfect copy of the Ars moriendi, patched here and there with shreds of <u>another copy</u> of the same work and of a copy of the Canticum Canticorum, a fact which points to waste sheets of these two works having been in the same binder's office, and that probably not far from their original home. Surely in one copy or another of one of these works we may hope to find some manuscript note which will afford some clue to the real date of execution. Meantime however the books must remain where they are. If we keep hard facts before our eyes, and discourage frivolous speculation, we are all the better prepared to catch the true significance of any fresh fact, the moment it is presented to us.

The same method applies to the Speculum and its kindred books, only here we have been more fortunate. I am compelled to leave the Speculum at Utrecht until I know anything positive to the contrary, because it is at Utrecht that the cuts first appear, cut up into pieces, in a book printed by Veldener at that place in 1481. Without further information it would have been necessary to place the printer of the Speculum last among the Utrecht presses and to affix as his date (before 1481). But there is such an unmistakeably close resemblance between seven several founts of type of which Mr. Holtrop has given facsimiles in his Monuments, that it is impossible not to investigate a little further. The types of the Yliada and of the Ludovicus de Roma being found in the same volume, there can be no doubt that they belonged to the same press. In comparing the Donatuses in the Ludovicus type with those in the Yliada type, the working of the former (uneven edges, &c.) claims priority over the working of the latter, so far as we can judge by the ordinary laws of investigating such matters. Further, Mr. Holtrop notices that some capitals of the Ludovicus type are identical with some used in the Facetiae morales which serves to connect these two. Again, the type of the Facetiae morales bears such a close resemblance to that of the stray sheet in what is called the mixed Dutch edition of the Speculum, that these two again must be connected. Lastly, it is but natural to believe that the stray sheet in the Dutch Speculum should have been printed at the same press as the rest of the book, however difficult it may be to assign the true cause of the printer's using a different type for this sheet. Here then we have a distinct sequence of types from that of the Speculum to that of the Yliada, and I have numbered them accordingly. As the Speculum compels us to place them at Utrecht, and before 1481, so the Yliada enables us to throw back the date of execution at least to 1471-74. Mr. Holtrop mentions that the Hague copy of the Tractatus de salute corporis et animae and Yliada was bought by a certain Abbat Conrad for the library of his house; and as the Abbat in question was Abbat only from 1471 to 1474, the book cannot have been printed later than 1471-74; and this is at present the only date which we can use for our purposes. It is a singular circumstance that this one fact should compel us to place the printer of the Speculum at the head of the Dutch printers, though it only just allows him to take precedence of Ketelaer and Leempt. Can no evidence be produced from any of the copies of any of these books now remaining, which will throw additional light on this point? If the Dutch antiquaries interested in these matters would but bestow upon the investigation of downright facts a tithe of the energy which they have devoted to speculation upon possibilities for more than a century past, our knowledge would be in a very different state at present. It is to be hoped that Dr. Van der Linde's lucid statement of facts lately published may produce some fruit; though it is hardly reasonable to suppose that the accumulated cobwebs of three hundred years can be swept away in a day.

Many specimens of early printing have been recovered from the bindings of other books; and these sometimes afford a very valuable evidence as to their history. Such fragments in the binder's hands are either sheets of books which have been used up and thrown away, and may be called binder's waste; or else they are spoiled sheets or unused proofs from a printer's office, and may be called printer's waste. In early times the printers were frequently their own binders; many instances can be found to confirm Mr. Holtrop's interesting notice of Veldener being his own bookbinder. It becomes therefore a matter of considerable importance to use all endeavours to ascertain where the volume was bound which contains any such fragments. If a fragment is found printed only on one side it has hitherto been described as "a remarkably interesting specimen of anopisthographic typography, probably executed in the infancy of the art, &c., &c.," instead of which it is simply a proof-sheet of the most commonplace description; and in no case does it seem to have inspired the discoverer to follow up the scent, or to inform the world of the one single fact which might give his discovery any real value. Surely there must be some trace of the binders who used some of the many fragments now existing in Holland, such as the Enschedé Abecedarium and the Donatus fragment in the same type, or any of the innumerable fragments of Donatuses and Doctrinals which exist in various collections. If it is not thought unreasonable to spend large sums of money upon such specimens, it seems at least reasonable to devote a little trouble towards ascertaining what they really are. This portion of the enquiry, however, seems at present almost wholly unattempted even in Holland.

Henry Bradshaw.

Cambridge,
June, 1871.

LIST OF COUNTRIES
Showing the Place Occupied by
HOLLAND
As Regards the Introduction of Typography,
So Far as Has Yet Been Ascertained
From Dated Documents

1. Germany (15 Nov. 1454).
2. Italy (29 Oct. 1465).
3. France (1470).
4. Holland (1471-73).
5. Belgium (1473).
6. Spain (23 Febr. 1475).
7. England (18 Nov. 1477).
8. Denmark (1482).
9. Sweden (20 Dec. 1483).

LIST OF TOWNS

HOLLAND (1471-73)

1. Utrecht (1471-73).
2. Deventer (1477).
3. Delft (10 Jan. 1477).
4. Gouda (24 May 1477).
5. St. Maartensdijk in Zeeland (Nov. 1478).
6. Nijmegen (23 Aug. 1479).
7. Zwolle (22 Dec. 1479).
8. Hasselt in Overijssel (1480).
9. Leiden (1483).
10. Kuilenburg (6 March 1483).

11. Haarlem (10 Dec. 1483).
12. 's Hertogenbosch (1484).
13. Schoonhoven (28 Febr. 1495).
14. Schiedam (1498).
15. Unknown places.

LIST OF PRESSES

HOLLAND (1471-73)

1. Utrecht (1471-73).
    1. Printer of the Speculum (not later than 1471-74).
    2. Nic. Ketelaer and Gher. de Leempt (1473).
    3. Wilh. Hees (1475).
    4. Printer of the 32-line Gesta Romanorum (   ).
    5. Printer of the Cambridge Pamphilus (   ).
    6. Joh. Veldener, from Louvain, Second press (4 Nov. 1478).
    7. G. t. or G. l. (7 May 1479).

2. Deventer (1477).
    1. Ric. Paffroed de Colonia, First press (1477).
    2. Jac. de Breda, First press (1486).
    3. Ric. Paffroed, Second press (9 Aug. 1488).
    4. Jac. de Breda, Second press (31 Aug. 1489).

3. Delft (10 Jan. 1477).
    1. Jac. Jacobszoen van der Meer and Maur. Yemantszoen van Middelborch (10 Jan. 1477).
    2. Jac. Jacobszoen van der Meer (12 Febr. 1480).
    3. Chr. Snellaert (2 Nov. 1488).
    4. Hen. Eckert van Homberch (15 Apr. 1498).

4. Gouda (24 May 1477).
    1. Ger. Leeu, First press (24 May 1477).
    2. Ger. Leeu, Second press (13 Dec. 1483).
    3. Printer of the Teghen die strael der minnen (23 June 1484).
    4. Printer of the Indulgence of 1486 (1486).
    5. Gotfr. de Os (13 Nov. 1486).

6. G. D. ( ).
7. Govaert van Ghemen, First press (before 24 March 1490).
8. Printer of the Opus minus primae partis ( ).
9. Printer of the Blaffert (1489).
10. Collacie-Broeders (10 June 1496).

5. St. Maartensdijk in Zeeland (Nov. 1478).
   1. Pieter Werrecoren (Nov. 1478).

6. Nijmegen (23 Aug. 1479).
   1. Printer of the Epistola Engelberti (23 Aug. 1479).

7. Zwolle (22 Dec. 1479).
   1. Peter van Os, of Breda, First press (22 Dec. 1479).
   2. Peter van Os, of Breda, Second press (26 May 1484).
   3. Printer of the Biblia pauperum (before 1488).

8. Hasselt in Overijssel (1480).
   1. Peregrinus Bermentlo, First press (1480).
   2. Peregrinus Bermentlo, Second press (1488).

9. Leiden (1483).
   1. Heynricus Heynrici (1483).
   2. Govaert van Ghemen, from Gouda, Second press (before 24 March 1490).
   3. Cornelis Kers (12 Apr. 1494).
   4. Hugo Janszoen van Woerden, First press (10 Dec. 1494).
   5. Hugo Janszoen van Woerden, Second press (1498).

10. Kuilenburg (6 March 1483).
    1. Joh. Veldener, from Utrecht, Third press (6 March 1483).

11. Haarlem (10 Dec. 1483).
    1. Jac. Bellaert (10 Dec. 1483).
    2. Joh. Andreae (1 March 1486).

12. 's Hertogenbosch (1484).
    1. Ger Leempt de Novimagio (1484).

13. Schoonhoven (28 Febr. 1495).
    1. Canons of St. Michael's in den Hem (28 Febr. 1495).

14. Schiedam (1498).
    1. Printer of the Vita Lydwinae (1498).

15. Unknown Places.
    1. Printer of the BRH 651 (MMW) Mandaville.
    2. Printer of the Enschedé Abecedarium.
    3. Printer of the MMW Liber Alexandri.
    4. Printer of the Deventer Donatus (woodcut in printer's ink).
    5. Printer of the BRH 12 Donatus fragments.
    6. Printer of the Komst van Keyser Frederijck te Trier.
    7. Printer of the Freeska Landriucht.

    Qu. if in Holland?

    8. Printer of the Dialogi Orationes et Tractatus.
    9. Printer of the Ant. Haneron de Epistolis.
    10. Printer of the Folio Doctrinale.

LIST OF FOUNTS OF TYPE AND WOODCUT DEVICES

HOLLAND (1471-73)

Utrecht (1471-73).

1. <u>Printer of the Speculum</u> (not later than 1471-74):
   Type 1 (   ). Pl. 17, Speculum (unmixed Latin edition).
   Type 2 (   ). Pl. 19, Speculum (leaves 49 and 60 of mixed Dutch edition).
   Type 3 (   ). Pl. 25, Facetiae morales.
   Type 4 (   ). Pl. 23 a, Ludovicus de Roma.

Type 5 (not later than 1471-74). Pl. 23 b, Pii secundi Tractatus de mulieribus pravis.
Type 6 ( ). Pl. 31 a, Donatus fragment (BRH 556) in the Meerman-Westreenen Museum.
Type 7 ( ). Pl. 32 a, Donatus fragments at Uden.
Device. None known.

2. Nic. Ketelaer and Gher. de Leempt (1473):
Type 1 (1473). Pl. 37. 1, Historia Scholastica.
Device. None known.

3. Wilh. Hees (1475):
Type 1 (1475; Press 2, type 1 with additional ¶). Pl. 38. 1, Anth. Haneron de coloribus verborum.
Device. None known.

4. Printer of the 32-line Gesta Romanorum ( ):
Type 1 Press 2, type 1 with additional J). Pl. 126 b, Liber Alexandri magni; but no sample of the additional J is here given. See Pl. 50* b, Pamphilus, line 2.
Device. None known.

5. Printer of the Cambridge Pamphilus ( ):
Type 1 (Press 4, type 1 with additional N). Pl. 50* b, Pamphilus (Wolfenbüttel copy of the quarto edition).
Device. None known.

6. Joh. Veldener, from Louvain, Second press (4 Nov. 1478):
Type 4 (brought from Louvain). See Pl. 47. 3 a, Fasciculus temporum. This type occurs as a supplementary type in the Dutch Fasciculus temporum of 1480; but no specimen of it is given among the Utrecht facsimiles.
Type 5 (4 Nov. 1478). Pl. 39. 1, Epistelen en Ewangelien of 1478.
Device 1 b (30 July 1479). Pl. 39. 2, Epistelen en Ewangelien of 1479.
Device 2 a (14 Febr. 1480). Pl. 39. 3, Dutch Fasciculus temporum.

7. G.t. or G.l. (7 May 1479):
   Type 1 (7 May 1479). Pl. 41, Wech van Salicheit.
   Device 1 (7 May 1479). Pl. 44. 2, Sielentroest of 7 May 1479.
   Device 2 (10 Nov. 1479). Pl. 44. 3, Sielentroest of 10 Nov. 1479.
   Device 3 (30 March 1480). Pl. 44. 1 e, Otten van Passau.

Deventer (1477).

1. Ric. Paffroed de Colonia, First press (1477):
   Type 1 (1477). Pl. 64 a, Petri Bertorii Reductorium.
   Type 2 (31 March 1479). Pl. 64 b, Dom. Sabinensis.
   Device. None known at this period.

2. Jacobus de Breda, First press (1486):
   Type 1 (Press 1, type 1). Pl. 66 a, Modus confitendi.
   Type 2 (Press 1, type 2). Pl. 66 c, Boethius.
   Device. None known.

3. Ric. Paffroed, Second press (9 Aug. 1488):
   Type 3 (9 Aug. 1488). Pl. 64 d 1 (imprint), Jo. Synthen super prima parte Doctrinalis Alexandri.
   Type 4 (9 Aug. 1488). Pl. 64 e (text), Somnium Scipionis.
   Type 5 (9 Aug. 1488). Pl. 64 d 1 (commentary), Jo. Synthen super prima parte Doctrinalis Alexandri.
   Type 6 (24 Dec. 1490). Pl. 65 a (title), Stella clericorum.
   Type 7 (1491). Pl. 64 f 2 (text), Sermones Mich. de Hungaria.
   Type 8 (14 July 1495). Pl. 65 c (text), Farrago.
   Device 1 (24 Dec. 1490).* Pl. 65 a, Stella

*[Read Device 1 (4 May 1489), and Device 2 (4 May 1489). MS. correction by H.B.]

clericorum.
Device 2 (   ). Pl. 65 b, Cato moralissimus.

4. Jacobus de Breda, Second press (31 Aug. 1489):
   Type 3 (31 Aug. 1489). Pl. 66 d 1 (heading),
       Aeneae Silvii Epistola de fortuna.
   Type 4 (31 Aug. 1489). Pl. 66 d 1 (text, lines
       1-5), Aeneae Silvii Epistola de fortuna.
   Type 5 (31 Aug. 1489). Pl. 66 d 1 (text, lines
       6-10), Aeneae Silvii Epistola de fortuna.
   Type 6 (1492). Pl. 66 e 2 (imprint), Doctrinale
       altum Alani.
   Type 7 (1492). Pl. 66 e 2 (text). Doctrinale
       altum Alani.
   Type 8 (1 March 1493). Pl. 66 f 2, Epistelen
       en Ewangelien.
   Device. None known.

Delft (10 Jan. 1477).

1. Jac. Jacobszoen van der Meer and Maur. Yemantszoen van Middelborch (10 Jan. 1477):
   Type 1 (10 Jan. 1477). Pl. 81 a, Bible in
       duytsche.
   Device 1 (10 Jan. 1477). Pl. 81 a (above the
       imprint), Bible in duytsche.
   Device 2 (10 Jan. 1477). Pl. 81 a (below the
       imprint), Bible in duytsche.

2. Jac. Jacobszoen van der Meer (12 Febr. 1480):
   Type 1 a (Press 1, Type 1). Pl. 82 a, Die
       duytsche Souter.
   Type 1 b (1481; Type 1 a, only with different
       capitals). Pl. 82 b, Epistelen en Ewangelien of 1481.
   Type 2 (1482). Pl. 82 d 1, Somme ruyrael (imprint).
   Type 3 (4 Oct. 1486). Pl. 82 f 1, Epistelen en
       Ewangelien of 1486 (title).
   Type 4 (4 Oct. 1486). Pl. 82 g 2, De spiritu
       Gwidonis (imprint).
   Device 1 (12 Febr. 1480). Pl. 82 a 2, Die

duytsche Souter.
Device 2 (25 March 1486). Pl. 82 e, Die vier uterste (imprint).

3. Chr. Snellaert 2 (Nov. 1488):
   Type 1 (Press 2, Type 1 b). Pl. 83 a 3, Dyalogus der creaturen (imprint).
   Type 2 (Press 2, Type 2). Pl. 83 a 1, Physiologus (title).
   Type 3 (Press 2, Type 3). Pl. 83 a 1, Dyalogus der creaturen (title).
   Type 4 (Press 2, Type 4). Pl. 84 d 2, Dionysius de particulari judicio dei (text and imprint).
   Type 5 (10 Aug. 1491). Pl. 83 e 2, Jhesus minnenbrief (text and imprint).
   Type 6 (17 July 1494). Pl. 83 f, Van den seven droefheden onser liever vrouwen.
   Type 7 (14 Apr. 1495). Pl. 84 c 1, Antidotarius animae (title).
   Type 8 (14 Apr. 1495). Pl. 84 c 2, Antidotarius animae (imprint).
   Type 9 (6 June 1495). Pl. 84 b 2 (text), Alphabetum divini amoris (text).
   Type 10 (6 June 1495). Pl. 84 f, Missale Trajectense (imprint).
   Device 1 (2 Nov. 1488). Pl. 83 a 2 (centre cut), Dyalogus der creaturen.
   Device 2 (10 Aug. 1491). Pl. 83 e 3 (centre cut), Jhesus minnenbrief.

4. Hen. Eckert van Hombergh, First press (15 Apr. 1498):
   Type 1 (Press 3, Type 2). Pl. 85 a 2 (over Device), Leven ons liefs heren J.C.
   Type 2 (Press 3, Type 6). Pl. 85 a 1, Leven ons liefs heren J.C. (text).
   Device 1 a (Press 3, Device 1). Pl. 85 b 3 (centre cut), Passionael.
   Device 2 (Press 3, Device 2). Pl. 85 a 2, Leven ons liefs heren J.C.

Gouda (24 May 1477).

1. Ger. Leeu, First press (24 May 1477):
   Type 1 (24 May 1477). Pl. 67. 1, Liden en passie ons heren J.C.
   Type 2 (1477, after 10 Sept.). Pl. 67. 2, Ewangelien van den gheheelen jaer.
   Device 1 (10 May 1478). Pl. 68. 1, Passionael, somerstuc.
   Device 2 (3 June 1480). Pl. 68. 4, Dialogus creaturarum moralisatus of 1480.

2. Ger. Leeu, Second press (13 Dec. 1483).
   Type 3 (13 Dec. 1483). See Pl. 79 d 2, Breviarium regularium (imprint); but no specimen of this type is given among the Gouda facsimiles.
   Type 4 (11 June 1484). Pl. 71 4, Van den seven sacramenten.
   Type 5 (11 June 1484). See Pl. 102 a, lines 1-8, Cato cum commento (commentary), but no specimen of this type is given among the Gouda facsimiles.
   Device. None known at this period.

3. Printer of the Teghen die strael der minnen (23 June 1484):
   Type 1 (23 June 1484). Pl. 33 b, Teghen die strael der minnen.
   Device. None known.

4. Printer of the Indulgence of 1486 (1486):
   Type 1 (1486). Pl. 78 (headings), Raym. Peraudi Litterae indulgentiarum (headings).
   Type 2 (1486). Pl. 78 (text), Raym. Peraudi Litterae indulgentiarum (text).
   Device. None known.

5. Gotfridus de Os (13 Nov. 1486):
   Type 1 (13 Nov. 1486). Pl. 72 a 3, Opusculum quintupertitum grammaticale (imprint).
   Type 2 (13 Nov. 1486). Pl. 72 a 2, Opusculum quintupertitum grammaticale (Explicit).
   Device. None known.

148 / Henry Bradshaw

6. G.D. ( ):
    Type 1 ( ). Pl. 75 a 2, Le Chevalier délibéré.
    Type 2 ( ). Pl. 77 a 3, Historie Godevaerts van Boloen.
    Device 1 ( ). Pl. 75 a 2, Le Chevalier délibéré.
    Device 2 ( ). Pl. 77 a 3, Historie Godevaerts van Boloen.

7. Govaert van Ghemen, First press (before 24 March 1490):
    Type 1 ( ). Pl. 73, Lantsloet ende Sandrijn.
    Device. None known at this period.

8. Printer of the Opus minus primae partis ( ):
    Type 1 ( ). See facsimile (text) at the end of the present List, from the only known fragment, at the Hague.
    Type 2 ( ). See facsimile (commentary) at the end of the present List, from the only known fragment, at the Hague.
    Device. None known.

9. Printer of the Blaffert (1489):
    Type 1 (1489). Pl. 79 b 1, Blaffert (text).
    Type 2 (1489). Pl. 79 b 3, Blaffert (Van nobels Haerlem Delff).
    Device. None known.

10. Collacie-Broeders (10 June 1496):
    Type 1 (Press 9, Type 1). Pl. 80 a 3, Leven van Liedwy (text and imprint).
    Type 2 (Press 9, Type 2). Pl. 80 d, Breviarium Trajectense (imprint).
    Type 3 (10 June 1496). Pl. 80 a 1 (line 1), Leven van Liedwy (title, line 1, O liedwi).
    Type 4 (3 Oct. 1496). Pl. 80 b 2, Devote ghetiden van den leven ende der passien J.C.
    Device 1 (3 Oct. 1496). Pl. 83 b 2, Devote ghetiden van den leven ende der passien J.C.

St. Maartensdijk in Zeeland (Nov. 1478).

1. Pieter Werrecoren (Nov. 1478):
   Type 1 (Nov. 1478). Pl. 86, Der Zielen troest.
   Device. None known.

Nijmegen (23 Aug. 1479).

1. Printer of the Epistola Engelberti Cultificis (23 Aug. 1479):
   Type 1 (23 Aug. 1479). Pl. 87 a 4, Epistola de symonia vitanda.
   Device. None known.

Zwolle (22 Dec. 1479).

1. Pet. van Os of Breda, First press (22 Dec. 1479):
   Type 1 (22 Dec. 1479). Pl. 88 a, Modus confitendi.
   Type 2 (1479). Pl. 89 c, S. Bonaventurae Sermones.
   Type 3 (before 26 May 1484). Pl. 90 d, Caroli Viruli Epistolae.
   Type 4 (before 26 May 1484). Pl. 90 e (commentary), Joh. de Garlandia Cornutus cum commento (commentary).
   Device. None known at this period.

2. Pet. van Os of Breda, Second press (26 May 1484):
   Type 5 (26 May 1484). Pl. 90 a, Psalterium of 1486.
   Type 6 (19 Nov. 1490). Pl. 94 a 1 (line 1), Baptistae Mantuani Secundae Parthenices opus (title, line 1).
   Type 7 (30 Apr. 1491). Pl. 90 c (text, except line 1), Rosarium B.V. Mariae (text).
   Type 8 (27 March 1493). Pl. 90 b, Epistelen en Ewangelien.
   Type 9 (1494). Pl. 91 a 3 (text), Rosetum exercitiorum spiritualium (text).
   Type 10 (1494). Pl. 50* c (lines 2-4), Rosetum

exercitiorum spiritualium.

Type 11 (1499). See Pl. 94 e (imprint), Aristoteles de moribus ad Eudemium (imprint), for this type as used by Tyman van Os; but no specimen is given among the facsimiles of the types of Peter van Os.

Device 1 (26 May 1484). Pl. 90 a, Psalterium of 1486.

Device 2 a (26 May 1484). Pl. 92 a, Gesten van Romen.

Device 2 b (21 July 1485). Pl. 92 b, Der Sielen troest.

Device 3 (1500). See Pl. 94 e, Aristoteles de moribus ad Eudemium, for this device as used by Tyman van Os; but no specimen is given among the facsimiles of the devices used by P. van Os.

3. Printer of the Biblia Pauperum (before 1488):
No type. Woodcut printing. Pl. 3, Biblia pauperum.

Hasselt in Overijssel (1480).

1. Peregrinus Bermentlo, First press (1480):
Type 1 (1480). Pl. 96, Gesta Romanorum.
Device. None known at this period.

2. Peregrinus Bermentlo, Second press (1488):
Type 2 (   ). Pl. 97, Volmaecte clargie.
Type 3 (1488). Pl. 98 a, Die passie ende dat liden ons heeren J.C.
Type 4 (2 Jan. 1490). Pl. 99 (imprint), S. Jheronimus Boeck.
Device 1 (2 Jan. 1490). Pl. 99, S. Jheronimus Boeck.

Leiden (1483).

1. Heynricus Heynrici (1483):
Type 1 (1483). Pl. 112 a, Epistelen en Ewange-

lien.
Device 1 (4 June 1484). Pl. 112 b, Tho. de Aquino Tractatus de humanitate Christi.

2. Govaert van Ghemen, from Gouda, Second press (before 24 March 1490):
   Type 1 (brought from Gouda). See facsimile at the end of the present List, from the Cambridge copy.
   Device 1 (before 24 March 1490). See facsimile at the end of the present List, from the Cambridge copy.

3. Cornelis Kers (12 Apr. 1494):
   Type 1 (12 Apr. 1494). Pl. 112 c, Seer minnelycke woerden die O.L. Heere Jhesus hadde met sijne moeder Maria.
   Device. None known.

4. Hugo Janszoen van Woerden, First press (10 Dec. 1494):
   Type 1 (10 Dec. 1494). Pl. 112 d, Ghetiden van onser liever Vrouwen.
   Device. None known at this period.

5. Hugo Janszoen van Woerden, Second press (1498):
   Type 2 (1498). Pl. 112 e, Oefeninghe van den leven ons heren J.C.
   Device 1 (1500). Pl. 112 f 2, Dat leven O.L. Vrouwen.

Kuilenburg (6 March 1483).

1. Joh. Veldener, from Utrecht, Third press (6 March 1483):
   Type 5 (brought from Utrecht). Pl. 115. 2, Spieghel onser behoudenisse.
   Type 6 (1484). Pl. 116. 1 a, Kruidboeck in dietsche (large type).
   Device 1 b (brought from Utrecht). Pl. 115. 2, Spieghel onser behoudenisse.
   Device 2 b (1484). See Pl. 116. 2 b (border)

among the Kuilenburg facsimiles, though this particular book belongs to Veldener's fourth press, after his return to Louvain.

Haarlem (10 Dec. 1483).

1. Jac. Bellaert (10 Dec. 1483):
    Type 1 (10 Dec. 1483). Pl. 34 a, Dat lijden ende die passie ons heeren J.C.
    Device 1 (10 Dec. 1483). Pl. 34 c (centre cut), Jac. de Theramo der Sonderen troest.
    Device 2 (15 Febr. 1484). Pl. 35 b 2 (centre cut), Jac. de Theramo der Sonderen troest (the mark in the right-hand window).

2. Joh. Andrae (1 March 1486):
    Type 1 (1 March 1486). Pl. 36 a, Formula noviciorum.
    Device 1 (31 May 1486). Pl. 36 b 5, Hen. de Hassia Tractatus de consolatione theologiae.

's Hertogenbosch (1484)

1. Ger Leempt de Novimagio (1484):
    Type 1 (1484). Pl. 59 c, Dat boeck van Tondalus vysioen.
    Type 2 (1487). Pl. 117 a 2, Proverbia seriosa (text).
    Type 3 (   ). Pl. 117 b (heading), Liber de vita religiosorum (heading).
    Device. None known.

Schoonhoven (28 Febr. 1495).

1. Canons of St. Michael's in den Hem (28 Febr. 1495):
    Type 1 (28 Febr. 1495). Pl. 118 a, Breviarum Trajectense.
    Device. None known.

Schiedam (1498).

1. Printer of the Vita Lydwinae (1498):
    Type 1 (1498). Pl. 119 a, Vita Lydwinae.
    Device 1 (1498). Pl. 119 a 1 (lower cut), Vita
        Lydwinae.

Unknown Places.

1. Printer of the BRH 651 (MMW) Dutch Mandaville
    (Qu. Ger. Leeu, at Gouda before 1477?):
    Type 1. Pl. 121, Mandaville.
    Device. None known.

2. Printer of the Enschedé Abecedarium (   ):
    Type 1. Pl. 12, Abecedarium.
    Device. None known.

3. Printer of the MMW Liber Alexandri (Qu. Ger. Leempt before 1479?):
    Type 1. Pl. 126 a, Liber Alexandri Magni.
    Device. None known.

4. Printer of the Deventer woodcut Donatus (   ):
    No type. Woodcut printing in printer's ink. Pl.
        10 a, Donatus.
    Device. None known.

5. Printer of the BRH 12 Donatus fragments (Qu. G. de Os at Gouda before 1484?)
    Type 1 (   ). Pl. 33 a, Donatus fragments,
        BRH 12.
    Device. None known.

6. Printer of the Komst van Keyser Frederyck te Trier
    (not before 1486):
    Type 1 (not before 1486). Pl. 119 c, Komst
        van Keyser Frederyck te Trier.
    Type 2 (   ). Pl. 119 b, Die jeeste van Julius
        Caesar.
    Device. None known.

7. Printer of the BRH 555 Freeska Landriucht (   ):
   Type 1 (   ). Pl. 124, Freeska Landriucht.
   Device. None known.

8. Printer of the BRH 648 (MMW) Dialogi, Orationes et Tractatus (   ):
   Type 1. Pl. 127, Dialogi, Orationes et Tractatus.
   Device. None known.
   Qu. if printed in Holland at all?

9. Printer of the BRH 650 (MMW) Ant. Haneron de Epistolis (   ):
   Type 1. Pl. 128, Ant. Haneron de epistolis brevibus edendis.
   Device. None known.
   Qu. if printed in Holland at all?

10. Printer of the MMW Folio Doctrinale (   ):
    Type 1. Pl. 129, Doctrinale Alexandri Galli, fragments in the Meerman-Westreenen Museum.
    Qu. if printed in Holland at all?

NOTE RELATING TO THE FACSIMILES WHICH ACCOMPANY THIS LIST

1. Epistelen ende ewangelien. Printed at Gouda, by the Printer of the Teghen die strael der minnen, 23 June 1484. Quarto.
A facsimile is here given of the page which contains the imprint, in order that others may have the opportunity of identifying the type with that of the Teghen die strael der minnen, which Mr. Holtrop has figured in his Monuments typographiques, Pl. 33 b, as the production of an unknown press. The copy in the University Library at Cambridge, from which the facsimile is taken, formed part of the De Meyer collection, which was sold at Ghent in November 1869.

2. Alexandri Galli Opus minus primae partis, cum commento. Printed probably at Gouda, by Gotfridus de Os or Govaert van Ghemen, about 1486-1489. Quarto.
The facsimile here given is of the two outer pages

of the half-sheet which is the only remaining fragment of the volume now known to exist. The type of the text and the woodcut initial, are known from the other Gouda books of this date; but the type of the commentary is only found here. It closely resembles Gerard Leeu's Type 5, but it is nevertheless different. It is somewhat curious that no facsimile of it should appear in the <u>Monuments typographiques</u>, because it is mentioned by Mr. Holtrop in his text, and the fragment belongs to the Royal Library at the Hague. It is owing to the kindness of Mr. Campbell, the present Librarian, that I have been enabled to examine it at my leisure.

3. Den gheesteliken minnebrief die Jhesus cristus coninck der glorien seyndt tot synre bruyt der minnender zielen. Printed at Leyden, by Govaert van Ghemen, probably about 1488. Octavo.

The existence of this press was altogether unknown when Mr. Holtrop published his Monuments. A copy was discovered in the Meulman collection, and at that sale passed into the Royal Library at the Hague. A brief notice of the book was sent by Mr. Holtrop to M. Paul Deschamps, and will be found in the Supplement to his Dictionnaire de Géographie (Supplément au Manuel de Brunet), p. 1450. Another copy since discovered is now in the University Library at Cambridge. The device is interesting, because it appears that the device of the Collacie-Broeders used at Gouda in 1496 is precisely a reverse copy of this, only that the arms of Leyden have been exchanged for those of Gouda. The facsimile represents the unbound book, as it lies open, shewing the first and last pages, with the title and illustrative woodcut on one, and the imprint and device on the other.

na vā verre Doe riep hi dten mēlche tot hē eū
vraghede hē vā sinē leuen doe seide hi dz hi ee
sondaer gheweest hadde eū dat hi daer indū ker=
kē hoerde predikē vand ōcfermherticheit gods
Eū god had hē betrou ghegheuen also dat hy
gheweent hadde voer sijn sondē: Hier om laet
ons dicwile ter kerckē gaē eū bidde gode d̄ ver
ghifnisse op dat wi moghē comē na dit leuen
int ewighe leuen Dat moet ons gonnē die va
der die sone die heplighe gheest   AMEN

  Hier gaen vot die epistelen eū die euāgelien
mettē sonnendaerhsen sermoenē vanden ghe=
heelen iaer eū vanden hepligen Eū sijn ghe=
prēt ter goude in hollāt Jnt iaer ons heren M̄
cccc eū lxxxiiij: op sinte ians baptistē auont

  Hier beghint die tafel vā desen teghēwoer
dighē boecke
 Pten eersten sonnendach inden aduent
  epistel euangelium eū sermoen   i
Des woensdaghes epistel euangeliū iiij
Des vridaghes euangelium   v
Opten tweedē sonnedach indē aduent epistel
euangelium ende sermoen   v

Capl'm p'mus   de declinacōe noīm

Si pueri p'mo nequeāt attēdere plane
Iīc tamē attēdat qui doctrīale ācē lōgē ē
Atq3 legēs puēis laycā lingua releuabit
Et pueris etiā p'ao maxima plane patebit
Posset aliqs dicere D alexāder tuū doctrinale ē multū oifficile. Ideo pueri nō valebūt intelligere Ad hoc respōdet alexād
licet pueri pse nō poterūt intelligere istā doctrinā sī eoy lecto
res et pceptores debēt intelligere et explanare seu declarare eis
hāc doctrinā lingua layca.i.materna, et tūc nō erit difficultas
intelligēdi imo sic maxima ps libri patebit eis.

    Oces in p'mis quas per casus variabis
    Vt leuius poterate declinare docebo
In ista pte incipit anctor dare ordinē libro suo ipm p cap'lis
distinguēdo. Et dicit s: ego docebo declinare vt leuius p'seo
in p'mis.i.iu p'mo capitulo voces qs variabis .i.declinabis
casy q' diceret p'mū capitulū erit de declāciōib3 noīm

Istis cōfinē retinēt heteroclita sedem
Dicit heteroclita noīa retinēt sedē p'finē.i.locū p'mū istis de
nacionib3 supdictis.i. scōm capitulū erit de heteroclitis.i. noī
nib3 variomō declinabilib3 ibi hec tibi signabis

Atq3 gradus triplicis collacio subditur istis
Dicit collacio.i.cōpacio triplicis gd° subdit³.i. immediate s
iūgit² istis s.heteroclitis Hoc ē terciū cap'lm erit de sb° gd°
cōpaciōis ibi hūc gd°ib3 tnis

Cuiq3 sit articulo que vox sociāda notabo
Dicit ego notabo q̄ vox sit sociāda cuiq3 articulo.i.p quos
culos q'neq3 vox sit declināda hoc ē quartū cap'lm erit d
nerib° noīm .ibi Inq'ptū potero

Hinc de p'teritis petrū sequar atq3 supinis
                                a 2

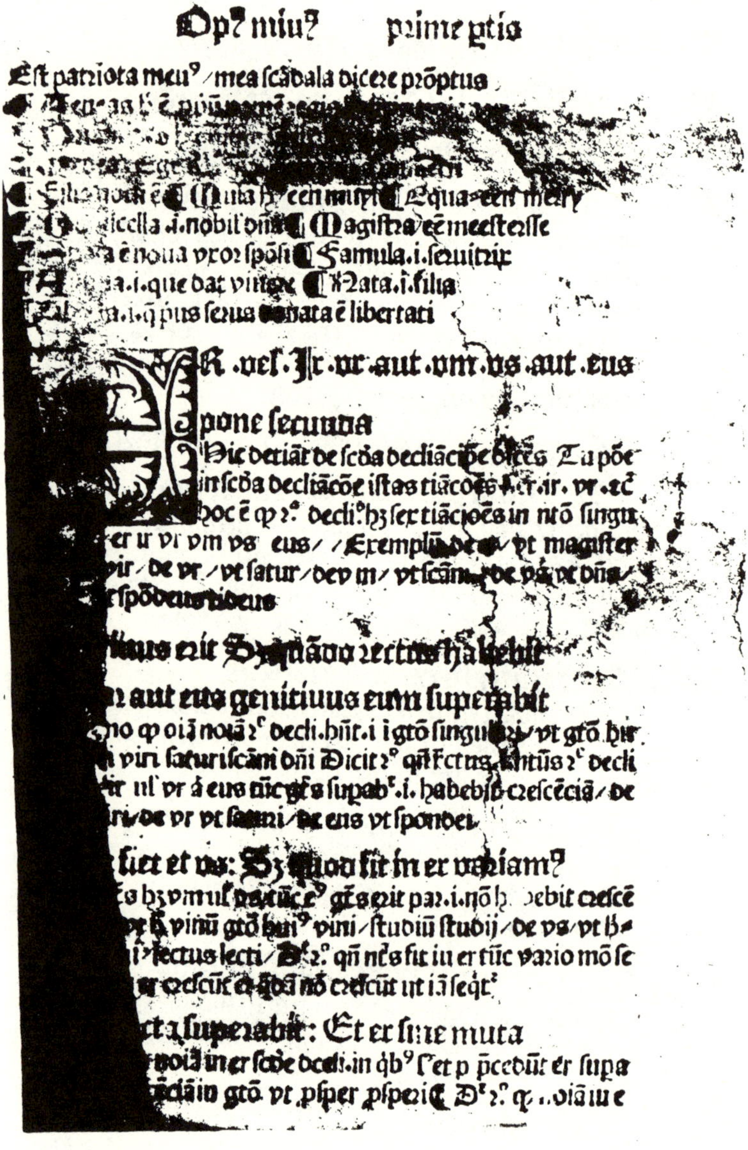
Op9 minu9 prime ptis

Est patriota meu9 / mea scādala dicere prōptus

Magistra ē meestresse

Famula .i. seruitrix

Nata .i. filia

R. vel. Ir. vr. aut. vm. vs. aut. eus

pone secunda

Hic deriuāt de scda decliācōe

lumus erit

aut eus genitiuus eum superabit

fiet et vs:

ta superabit: Et er sine muta

Excerpts from the Works / 159

⟨¶⟩ Den gheestelike minnebrief die Jhesus cristus coninck der glorien seynot tot sinen bruyt der minnender zielen.

Ghepeynt te leuen bi mi Gouaert van ghemen.

alle vpe ghene die mij mit gansser herten begherende syn.
Amen.

8. FRANCIS THYNNE'S <u>ANIMADVERSIONS ...</u>
Now newly edited by F. J. Furnivall. 1875.

Bradshaw's work on Chaucer's text, which occupied so many years, resulted in very little publication. The two communications which follow are among the contributions which he made to the Furnivall 1875 edition of Thynne. They typify the kind of general antiquarian research which gave Bradshaw great personal pleasure and which he embodied so successfully in his general bibliographical work.

In connection with this Preface comes one of those pretty discoveries which have made Mr. Bradshaw's name so famous among manuscript and black-letter men. He shall tell it in his own words, as he wrote it to me:--

"We know that Wm Thynne was 'Chief Clerk of the Kitchin,' that is, as we should now say, that he held an appointment in the Royal Household (the Board of Green Cloth) at Greenwich. Sir Brian Tuke was Postmaster, then an appointment in the same office. When Leland tells us that Sir Brian Tuke wrote a <u>limatissima praefatio</u> to the edition of Chaucer published by Berthelet, we are all puzzled; and when Leland tells us that Thynne edited the edition, we are still more puzzled, because no such edition is known. Now the woodcut frame round the title in Godfray's edition (Thynne, 1532) is that which, having belonged to Pynson, the King's Printer, was transferred to

Berthelet, his successor as King's Printer; and this is
enough to show that there were printing relations between Berthelet and Godfray, quite enough to allow
this to be the edition meant. Curiously enough, there
is a copy of Godfray's edition in one of the College Libraries here, in its original binding, in which, at the
top of Thynne's dedication, Sir Brian Tuke has written
with his own hand:

"'This preface I sir Bryan Tuke knight wrot at
the request of Mr Clarke of the Kechyn then being /
tarying for the tyde at Grenewich.'

"It would be difficult to find a prettier coincidence
in all points--the tarrying for the tide at Greenwich,
when we learn from quite other sources 1. that Thynne's
office was at Greenwich, and 2. that he lived down the
Thames at Erith. You will allow that it is not often one
has the pleasure of hitting things off so prettily. Observe the words then being. In 1532 Thynne describes
himself to the king as 'Wylliam Thynne, chefe clerke of
your kechyn.' In 1536 Tuke died. On the monument
to Wm Thynne in All-hallows Barking Church in London,
he is described as 'M. William Thinne esquire, one of
the masters of the honourable houshold to king Henry
the 8. our soveraigne Lord' (I quote from the Stemmata
Botevilliana, and M. Botfield probably quotes from
Stowe's London). The monument says he died August
10, 1546. It is possible that Thynne's position was
raised between 1532 and 1536 when Tuke died.--Ever
yours, Henry Bradshaw."

Mr Bradshaw's note on William Thynne's
cancelld one-column edition of Chaucer's Works

"I think the discovery of the long-missing Douce
fragment has settled, for good and all, the confusion
which Francis Thynne has fallen into about his father's
editions. The supposed cancelled edition by William
Thynne is a fiction. It is described as having one
column on a side, and containing the Pilgrim's Tale.
Tyrwhitt has shown conclusively that this Tale cannot

have been <u>written</u> before 1536; and it is clear that the
book, of which the Douce fragment is a part, must have
contained Chaucer's name on the title-page, and was
probably printed shortly before 1540 (when Bale was
exiled), or Bale would not have included among Chaucer's Works <u>De curia Veneris</u>, lib. 1, 'In Maio cum virescerent,' &c.; and <u>Narrationes diversorum</u>, tract. 1,
'In comitatu Lyncolninensi,' &c.

"Please remember that Bale went into exile in
1540, and that the first edition of his <u>Scriptores</u>, in
which these appear, was printed at Wesel in 1548, on
his return journey to England. This limits the date
pretty well to 1536-1540. In that edition the two items
occur in quite different parts of his list; but in the
later and fuller edition of 1557 the items come thus,
after enumerating the contents of Thynne's editions:--

De curia Veneris. Lib. 1. In Maio cum virescerent, &c.

Epigrammata quoque. Lib. 1. Fuge multitudinem,
veri. [Fle from the presse.--H.B.]

Narrationes diversorum. Lib. 1. In comitatu Lyncolniensi fuit.

"If Mr. Bright's fragment of the <u>beginning</u> of a
later edition of the 'Court of Venus' is forthcoming
(see Hazlitt's <u>Handbook</u>), you will probably find that
it begins 'In <u>Maio cum virescerent</u>' ... at least with
the English equivalent of those words.[1] Bale must
have seen the book, or he could not have given us
the <u>incipits</u>. It must (I think) have borne Chaucer's
name on the title-page, or Bale would not have put
it among Chaucer's works. It must have been printed
after 1536 (see Tyrwhitt) and before 1540 (when the
exile took place); and so it may be possible that
Thynne thought of including it in his 1542 edition,
but was prevented through Bonner's or Gardiner's
influence, not Wolsey's, which would put the matter
into a wholly different period.

"Remember that W. Thynne died (very soon after Francis Thynne was born) in 1546, and that, the report reaching Francis Thynne through the recollections of Sir John Thynne of many years previous, it is not wonderful that there should be some confusion. Francis Thynne, too, tells us that he had never seen the one-column edition himself. The result is, that I am convinced that the one-column edition of Chaucer with the Pilgrim's Tale can only mean the 4to Court of Venus, &c., printed between 1536 and 1540, which Bale saw. Whether the Douce and Bright fragments are parts of the original edition, or of the reprint licensed to Hen. Sutton in 1557, or to a later edition still, I cannot say,[2] and it does not very much matter for our purpose; as Bale's evidence, coupled with Tyrwhitt's statement, narrows the limit of printing to 4 or 5 years."

---

1. This Bright fragment is at Britwell, and Mr. W. Christie-Miller has been good enough to inform me that the first poem in it begins with
>In the moneth of May, when the new tender grene
>Hath smothly couered the ground that was bare

as Mr. Bradshaw expected. Mr. W. Christie-Miller adds: "Chaucer's name I do not see upon the sheet, nor any trace of the name of the author." But see Chaucer's name in the Douce fragment of the book, p. 98, I. 740, below.

2. The dropt lines and misprinted words show the Douce fragment to be part of some reprint.

9. NOTICE OF A FRAGMENT OF THE
FIFTEEN OES AND OTHER PRAYERS PRINTED
AT WESTMINSTER BY W. CAXTON ABOUT
1490-91, PRESERVED IN THE LIBRARY OF
THE BAPTIST COLLEGE, BRISTOL

Published as Memorandum No. 5, November 1877. Reprinted in Collected Papers, 1889, pp. 341-349.

    Many of Bradshaw's discussions relating to Caxton were conducted with William Blades, with whom he maintained a correspondence during several years.
    This paper is probably the most purely bibliographical, in a technical sense, of anything which Bradshaw published. It draws heavily on a knowledge of printing house practices and was related directly to the problems. It is particularly noteworthy in that it is an early attempt to gain insight into the activities of the compositor--later to be such a fruitful line of investigation.

    Among Dr. Gifford's Books in the Library of the Baptist College at Bristol is a copy of the second edition of Caxton's translation of the Mirror of the World, printed by him at Westminster probably in the year 1490. But that the book was re-backed while in Dr. Gifford's possession, the binding is very much in its original condition, wooden bevelled boards pierced by the ends of three stout bands fastened in by pegs of wood, and covered with dark brown leather, marked by double lines so as to form on each side a large panel, which again is crossed by diagonal double lines, each space thus left in the panel being ornamented with a lozenge-shaped device, being on the one side a sprig of flowers and on the other a fabulous animal. Whatever paper may have originally lined the board at the beginning of the volume, has long since disappeared; the only thing which now occupies the space is the College book-plate. At the end the board was lined with a sheet of printed matter, which after having suffered from various rough attempts to lift it from the cover, I have lately soaked off without any difficulty, by the desire of the Rev. Dr. Gotch, the present Principal of the College, to whose kindness I am indebted for the opportunity of examining the book at my leisure.

This fragment of printed matter consists of the chief part of a cancelled copy of the inner sheet (leaves 3, 4, 5, 6) of the first quire (sign. a) of the Fifteen Oes and other prayers, printed at Westminster by William Caxton about 1490-91. Each quire consists of two quarto sheets, one inside the other, so that the whole signature contains eight leaves or sixteen pages. The book when complete consists of 22 leaves, and evidently was printed as a supplement or appendix to a quarto edition of the Salisbury Primer or Horae now lost, and the two were incorporated into one volume in the reprint executed by W. de Worde within a very short time of Caxton's death. The only copy of the Fifteen Oes and other prayers, except the Bristol fragment, is one in the British Museum, which was purchased in 1851. It has been well described by Mr. Blades in his Life and Typography of William Caxton, and it has been completely reproduced in photo-lithography by Mr. Stephen Ayling. The Bristol fragment affords so much interesting evidence of the way in which the compositors of that day worked, and illustrates so many points in connexion with early printing in England, that I have thought it worth while to put down a few notes on the subject.

It has been assumed by many writers that the whole of one quire at least would always be in type at the same time; and they have calculated upon this basis the amount of type which a printer would possess at any one period. Now, so far from this holding true in Caxton's case, even at the end of his career, this book proves clearly that in a quarto book printed in 2-sheet quires (that is, with eight leaves to the signature) the outer and inner sheets of each quire were set up successively, the inner sheet after the outer sheet had been wholly worked off and the type distributed into its boxes. If any one will take Mr. Ayling's photolithographed reproduction of the British Museum copy of the <u>Fifteen Oes</u>, he will easily understand what I mean. Round each page are four border-pieces of different widths. Of each of these there are eight different kinds; four of which are used for the four pages which are imposed on the one side of the quarto sheet, and four others which are used on the four pages which occupy the other side of the quarto sheet. So that the eight pieces of each kind, which are found on the eight pages of the outer sheet of a 2-sheet quire, will all be found used again on the eight pages of the inner sheet of the same quire.

This book further shows us that, assuming that one compositor was employed on the outer four pages (1, 4, 5, 8) of a sheet, and another on the inner four pages (2, 3, 6, 7), the pressman would, when the compositor of the outer side was ready with his work, print off the required number of copies of these four pages, and then allow the type and border-pieces, used for these four pages, to be distributed, in order that the same compositor might proceed to use them for setting up his side of the next sheet, whatever it might be. Again, when the compositor of the inner side of the same sheet was ready with his work, the pressman would "perfect" the sheets, already printed on one side, by laying them on the form and so passing them through the press; after which the type and border-pieces of this form also would be distributed, and this compositor would proceed to use them for his side of the next sheet, that is to say, whichever side his fellow-compositor was not engaged upon. Now every one who has come into contact with the details of printing, must be aware that wrong "perfecting" is one of the most fruitful sources of printer's waste. If the pressman happened to lay the half-printed sheet the wrong way upon the form which contains the other side of the sheet, the necessary result would be that the pages of a quarto sheet would read 1, 6, 7, 4, 5, 2, 3, 8, instead of 1, 2, 3, 4, 5, 6, 7, 8, and the sheet so mis-printed would be for all practical purposes wasted. This is what has happened to the Bristol sheet of the Fifteen Oes, and it was consequently soon relegated to the bookbinder's department (for in Caxton's time printers were for the most part their own bookbinders), and it was there used for lining the boards of the first book which happened to want binding.

But the above facts are illustrated and confirmed in a remarkable manner by an examination of the Bristol fragment itself. The most cursory comparison with the British Museum copy, or with Mr. Ayling's photo-lithographed reproduction of it, shows that while the inner four pages of the Bristol sheet are precisely identical in composition with the British Museum copy, the composition of the outer four pages is entirely different. The following explanation of this peculiarity seems to me the only one possible. The mistake in "perfecting" must have been discovered after the type of the outer side (sign. a 3^a, 4^b, 5^a, 6^b) had been distributed and the compositor had gone on to the outer sheet of signature b, but while the inner side (sign. a 3^b, 4^a, 5^b, 6^a) was still standing in type, though after a number of copies had been printed off. The result is that the inner side was at once used again,[1] and the required number of copies worked on fresh sheets of paper; whereas the outer side had to be set up again completely by the compositor, and, when ready, was of course taken off on the blank side of the newly printed copies of the inner four pages.

This statement of details may perhaps be hardly intelligible to the ordinary reader, while it may be looked upon as a series of truisms by any one conversant with printing; but I have not scrupled to give them, because experience tells me that few even of those most conversant with modern printing can be trusted to form an accurate opinion of the very rudimentary methods which most of the early printers employed. It would hardly be believed that Caxton had been more than fifteen years at work before he arrived at the point of printing four pages at once; yet all experience shows that it was so.

A case of precisely the same mode of working attracted my attention some years ago in the Lambeth copy of the Primer or <u>Horae</u> printed in Caxton's house by Wynkyn de Worde, and probably the first edition which incorporated with the Salisbury Primer the English <u>Fifteen Oes and other prayers</u>, which form the volume of which the Bristol fragment is a sheet. The Primer I speak of must have been printed by W. de Worde, about 1494. Dr. Maitland in his <u>List of some of the early printed books ... at Lambeth</u> (London, 1843, 8vo.) has a note (p. 394) on this volume, in which he mentions incidentally that in one of the "two lytell prayers which kynge herry the syxte made," the words run "prout tibi placet" in the Lambeth copy. Now we have two copies of this Primer at Cambridge (G. 3. 61 and G. 4. 4 in the University Library, both from the Moore Collection of 1715), and though I had always thought, having only seen them apart, that they were identical with the one at Lambeth, yet an examination of our copies at once showed that the reading in the prayer was "prout tibi placeret." I borrowed the book from Lambeth by the kind offices of my friend Mr. S. W. Kershaw, and I was then still more puzzled, on going through the two books page by page, to find that they were absolutely identical in composition. When however I came to the outer side of the outer sheet of the quire signed f, I found the two were entirely different; but a little observation led me to the conclusion that, as the page was originally set up, the reading had been "prout tibi placeret," and that, after the type of the outer side of the sheet had been distributed, but while the inner side was still standing in type, the printer or editor had thought it better to correct the word "placeret" to "placet." Accordingly a fresh batch of copies was printed of the inner side (sign. f 1^b, 2^a, 7^b, 8^a), and this sheet was then "perfected" by a re-composition of the four outer pages (sign. f 1^a, 2^b, 7^a, 8^b); everything else in the book remaining the same. Having thus gone through this process in the case of the Lambeth volume seven years ago, it can easily be understood that, when the Bristol fragment came into my hands, I was prepared for the case at once, and saw in a very few minutes the real nature of the fragment, and how it came to be used as lining for the boards of a book printed in Caxton's office.

But this is not all that an examination of the Bristol fragment brings to light. Both sides are disfigured by a considerable amount of printer's ink, a "set-off" from wet pages which have themselves not been preserved to us. Those on the outer side, at least pages a 4^b and 5^a, contain a "set-off" from a form of four octavo pages in the type of the Book of good manners; and the length of the lines, the 17 lines to a page, and the traces of red printing, leave little doubt on my mind that they belong to a waste sheet of the octavo Primer or Horae with red printing, which is at present only known from the fragment (sign. d 1, 2, 3, 4) found by Mr. Maskell in the binding of a book, and given by him to the British Museum in 1858. From this we may infer that in all probability the octavo Primer and the Fifteen Oes were passing through the press about the same time. Mr. Blades and myself had come independently to the conclusion, that both books belong to the last year of Caxton's life (1490-91); so that this fragment affords an additional mite of evidence.

The inner side of the Bristol fragment is, however, still more interesting; as it gives us a "set-off" of two quarto 22-line pages in the type of the Book of good manners, and enclosed within woodcut borders. It is much blurred, and I have not yet been able to make out many words, even with the aid of a looking-glass and a strong magnifying glass. 22 lines of this type correspond very nearly to 21 lines of the type of the Fifteen Oes; and it is very natural that we should find traces of another book enclosed in the same woodcut borders. I can only say at present that no book in this type and with woodcut borders has come to light as yet; though so many specimens of Caxton's press have been discovered in the last few years, that I do not in the least despair of coming upon more satisfactory traces of this book than we can expect to obtain from the blurred "set-off" by means of which alone the fact of its existence has been revealed to us.

After all that has been said, it cannot be any matter of wonder that the fragments used for lining the boards of old books should have an interest for those who make a study of the methods and habits of our early printers with a view to the solution of some of many difficulties still remaining unsettled in the history of printing. I have for many years tried to draw the attention of librarians and others to the evidence which may be gleaned from a careful study of these fragments; and if done systematically and intelligently, it ceases to be mere antiquarian pottering or aimless waste of time. I have elsewhere drawn attention to the distinction to be observed between what may be called respectively binder's waste and printer's waste. When speaking of fragments of books as binder's waste, I mean books which have been in circulation and have been thrown away as useless. The value of such fragments is principally in themselves. They may or may not be of interest. But by printer's waste I mean such pieces as this Bristol fragment; waste, proof, or cancelled sheets in the printer's office, which, in the early days when printers were their own bookbinders, would be used by the bookbinder for lining the boards, or the centres of quires, of books bound in the same office where they were printed. In this way such fragments have a value beyond themselves; as they enable us to infer almost with certainty that such books are specimens of the binding executed in the office of the printer who printed them; and thus, once seeing the style adopted and the actual designs used, we are able to recognise the same binder's work, even when there are none of these waste sheets to lead us to the same conclusion. I will mention a few of the instances which have come under my notice; but it is a new field of enquiry altogether, and I am only now beginning to work at it systematically.

1. In the binding of the Bristol copy of the second edition of the Mirror of the world, printed by Caxton, probably in 1490, we find a cancelled sheet of the Fifteen Oes printed at the same press about 1490-91; the fragment which has led to the present remarks. I am led therefore to the conclusion that the binding itself was executed in Caxton's office. I have had the two sides of the book photographed, and I hope they may be the beginning of a collection which will some day see the light, and so increase our knowledge in that direction.

2. The Bedford copy of the Royal book has (or had, when I saw it first in 1863) the boards lined with unused (and therefore, after date, waste) copies of one of Caxton's two editions of the Indulgence of Johannes de Gigliis issued in 1480. The binding is therefore probably Caxton's own.

3. A fragment of a copy of another of Caxton's editions of the last named Indulgence, was discovered by Mr. Blades, with a mass of other specimens of printer's waste from Caxton's office, in the binding of a copy of Chaucer's Boethius in the Grammar School library at St. Alban's. There can be no doubt that this book was bound in Caxton's workshop.

4. In Jesus College library I lately found a copy of the Latin Bible, printed at Cologne by Nicolaus Gotz in 1480, in unmistakeable English binding, and with the centre of every quire lined with fragments of unused copies of two editions of an Indulgence issued by John Kendale in 1480 and printed in the type used in London by John Lettou in 1480 and 1481. On going over to Oxford soon after, I at once recognised in the Auctarium a book printed by Lettou, on the binding of which the very same tooling was used; and I have no doubt that both books were bound by him.

5. In a copy of the Dives and Pauper printed in London by Pynson in 1493, now in the Bodleian Library, I long ago noticed that the old boards were lined at one end with an unused fragment of a Grammar printed by Pynson himself about the same time; while the other board was lined with an unused fragment of a copy of the Servitium de Visitatione B.M.V., printed by W. de Machlinia in the type used by him in Holborn.

6. In the Minster library at Lincoln I found a copy of the Expositio Hymnorum and Expositio Sequentiarum, printed abroad, but containing at the end of each part a supplementary quire printed by Pynson. The book is in English binding, and the fly-leaves are portions of an octavo Primer or Horae printed in the type used by W. de Machlinia when living by Fletebridge. These last two books convey, to any one who works intelligently at these things, a fact which has hitherto not even been suspected, though nothing could be more natural. As Pynson is thus shown to have inherited W. de Machinia's waste, there can be little doubt that, on leaving his master Caxton, he took up W. de Machlinia's press and carried on the business himself. W. de Machlinia was our first law printer, and though, on his disappearance after 1486, Caxton and his successor W. de Worde were employed for a time to print the statutes, yet the law printing soon fell into Pynson's hands, where it remained as long as his press continued to work.

7. Some years ago I obtained from Mr. F. S. Ellis a pad of leaves which had served for the board of a small octavo volume, which had evidently been bound by John Byddell while living at the Sun in Fleet street, in which house he succeeded W. de Worde. The fragments were every one, where traceable, pieces of Sun-printed books, ranging from the Four Sons of Aymon, printed there by W. de Worde in 1504, and hitherto only known to exist from Copland's colophon in his reprint of 1554, down to an otherwise wholly unknown edition of Adam Bel and Clim of the Clough, printed there by John Byddell in 1536.

These are only a very few of the many instances I have come upon in my own work; and that, as I have said, is only in its first stage. When applied to foreign early printing, it is evident that if only Dutchmen or Germans could be persuaded to work patiently and methodically upon some such lines, the results would be infinitely more satisfactory and more fruitful than the baseless and frivolous speculations which disfigure even the best books at present written on the subject.

But I have said enough. I cannot regret the happy accident which led the Bristol book to find its way to Cambridge after the Caxton Celebration exhibition at South Kensington this summer. Neither can I sufficiently thank the Rev. Dr. Gotch, the Principal of the Baptist College at Bristol, for the ready kindness with which he has allowed me the free use of the volume for more than two months.

King's College, Cambridge,
November 13, 1877.

Note

1. I ought to mention that there is one variation noticeable between the Bristol and British Museum copies of the inner side of the sheet, though in other respects they are identical. The outer border-piece on sign. a 3^b is in the Bristol fragment upside down, while in the British Museum copy it is the right way up. This merely shows that just before printing off the new batch of the inner side of the sheet from the still standing type, it was noticed that this border-piece was upside down, and this having been rectified the copies were struck off.

10. THE IRISH MONASTIC MISSAL AT OXFORD

The Academy, 12 January, 1878.

Irish books in general and church service books were among the earliest and most enduring of Bradshaw's bibliographical enthusiasms. It was therefore only natural that he should be more than usually interested in an Irish Missal. At this time four only of this category were known: The Stowe Missal, in the collection of Lord Ashburnham; the Drummond Castle Missal, belonging to Lady Willoughby d'Eresby; the Rosslyn Missal in the Advocates' Library, Edinburgh; and the one about which Mr. Warren had written.

Bradshaw's hope that Warren would later "print the book" was fulfilled when <u>The Manuscript Irish Missal belonging to the President and Fellows of Corpus Christi College, Oxford</u>, edited, with an introduction and notes by F. E. Warren, was published by Pickering.

The Irish Monastic Missal at Oxford

King's College, Cambridge: January 5, 1878.

All who are interested in the study of the service-books of the middle period (by which I mean the five centuries preceding the Reformation and the Council of Trent) must be grateful to Mr. Warren for his notice of the Irish monastic missal in Corpus Christi

College library at Oxford, which appeared in a recent number of the <u>Academy</u> (Dec. 15, 1877). He tells us a good deal; and the care with which it is evident that he has gone through the book is, I hope, only an earnest of what he is going to do for us. Why should not Mr. Warren print the book in the same unpretending way in which Dr. Henderson has given us the Hereford Missal? It surely would not be a difficult thing to get either a subsidy from the Oxford Press, or a sufficient number of subscribers, or, indeed, both. So much valuable matter is to be found on this subject in the publications of the late Bishop of Brechin and his brother, the Rev. G. H. Forbes, of Burntisland, that it would be really a gain to dispense with much of the illustrative detail which too often delays for years the appearance of texts of this kind. We are not yet in a fit state to generalise upon these books. The very fact that we have such comparatively ample materials for studying the earlier and later periods, leads some liturgical writers to think that they know all about this middle period, which is nevertheless one of the darkest of all, because we have so few materials in print for forming an opinion based upon facts, while the tendency is rather to give us, in place of facts, opinions which are based only upon inference and speculation.

The Earl of Ashburnham's volume (formerly at Stowe) belongs to the earlier time; as do the smaller liturgical pieces in the Books of Dimma, Mulling, and Deer. The Drummond Castle Missal, which is in the Irish character, belongs also, I believe, to the later portion of this earlier period. On the other hand, a fair number of service-books exist, which may be taken to represent the Anglo-Irish community in various parts of the kingdom during the middle period; among them the extremely interesting Dublin <u>Troparium</u> of the thirteenth and fourteenth centuries, which Bishop Mant gave to Dr. Todd, and which afterwards, owing to the short-sighted apathy of the Trinity College authorities, found its way to the University Library at Cambridge, where its real nature and value were first brought to light. But for service-books of the "mere Irish" portion of the Church during the middle period, the Oxford missal stands, so far as I know, quite alone; and on this ground I would urge most earnestly that steps be taken to let us see the book in print.

It is only when in print that an ordinary person can study a book of this kind at leisure, that he can give the time which is necessary to let the characteristic features of such a book tell their own story to one who is content to keep them before him for this very purpose, instead of running hastily through it (in the reading-room of a library) to see how far it supports his own foregone conclusions on a subject of which after all he knows next to nothing. To take one point only: we know very little practically of the action of monastic and secular Uses upon each other, and of the influence exercised upon both by those rituals which they superseded. The wave of revived monasticism which spread over Western Europe in the early part of the twelfth century swept away the old Celtic communities, and replaced them by Benedictines, Augustinians, Cistercians, &c. These would be the means of introducing Roman and other foreign elements into the service of the Church. The English conquest would help to introduce various features of the Sarum Use. Synodical decisions on liturgical reform, and the service-books themselves, require a wholly separate, though parallel, course of investigation. It is never safe to argue from one to the other. Wherever we examine the manuscripts of this period, we find that the sweeping-away was far from complete. Survivals of the obsolete ritual are always liable to appear, sometimes where least expected. No mere description, therefore, of such a book as this is in any way enough to satisfy our wants; and one such book printed in an unostentatious form would be more precious than any number of dissertations without the text.

A happy accident brought me into contact with Mr. Laing, of Corpus Christi College, when I was at Oxford last July; and among the treasures of his

College library which he poured out before me he naturally showed me this Missal; and he very kindly allowed me to look through it at the Bodleian Library, where I was at work for a day or two. I had no leisure to go at all minutely through the book, or to compare it with other Missals; but, after looking right through the volume I took down some notes of two litanies which occur in it, one at Easter Eve, and one in the Baptismal Service (so my notes say, but I cannot now say whether it is the same which occurs, according to Mr. Warren, in the service for the Visitation of the Sick). These two litanies differ in a remarkable way, and seem clearly to belong to different periods; and as one of them contains a point which ought to bear upon the date of the book, but which has been passed over in silence by Mr. Warren, I may perhaps be allowed to give part of my extracts.

In the litany on Easter Eve the Saints run thus: --"S. Petre, S. Paule, S. Andrea, S. Zefane, S. Laurentii, S. Uincentii, S. Martine, S. Patricii, S. Benedicte, S. Maria Mag', S. Felicitas, S. Margareta, S. Petronilla, S. Brigida"; then, "Omnes sancti orate"; then, "Propitius esto, parce nobis domine"; and so on with this part of the litany, which then proceeds as follows:

> Peccatores te rogamus audi nos.
> Ut pacem nobis dones t.
> Ut domnum apostolicum nostrum in sancta relegione conseruare digneris t.
> Ut aeclesiam tuam immaculatam custodire digneris t. r.
> Ut regem hibernensium et exercitum eius conseruare digneris t. r.
> Ut eis uitam et sanitatem atque uictoriam dones t. r.
> Ut sanitatem nobis dones t.
> Ut pluuiam....

and so on. I see that in my notes I have called the handwriting twelfth-thirteenth century, and with this impression I am glad to find Mr. Warren sees reason to agree; but who can possibly be meant by "regem hibernensium et exercitum eius" at this period?

In the litany in the Baptismal Service the Saints are much more numerous. The confessors run thus:--"S. Martine, S. Siluester, S. Leo, S. Hilarii, S. Ambrosii, S. Augustine, S. Hironime, S. Grigorii, S. Benedicte, S. Patricii, S. Columbe, S. Brendine, S. Finniane, S. Ciarane, S. Fursee, S. Paule, S. Antoni, S. Nicolai." The Virgins close thus:--"S. Petronilla, S. Margareta, S. Brigida"; then, "Omnes sancti orate pro nobis"; then "Propitius esto...," and so on; then as follows:--

>Peccatores te rogamus audi nos.
>Ut pacem nobis dones t. r. a. n.
>Ut sanitatem nobis dones t. r. a. n.
>Ut aeris temperiem.
>Ut remissionem omnium peccatorum nobis dones.
>Ut domnum apostolicam in sancta relegione conseruare digneris.
>Ut ei uitam et sanitatem atque uictoriam concedere digneris.
>Ut dominum illum regem et exercitum christianorum in perpetua pace et prosperitate [conseruare?] digneris.
>Ut populo christiano pacem et unitatem concedere digneris.
>Ut aeclesiam tuam sublimare digneris.
>Ut istam congregationem in sancta relegione conseruare digneris.
>Filii dei... &c.

I see by my notes that this Baptismal service, with what follows, appears to be in the same handwriting as the preceding portion of the volume, but that it begins on a fresh quire, after the main part of the book, which ends with a blank page at the close of the preceding (seventeenth) quire. Particular care is, of course, needed to distinguish the original scribe's work from any later accretions, whether of parchment or writing; and my cursory examination enabled me to do but little towards this end; but now that the subject has come up, I sincerely hope that it may not be allowed to drop. With the richest liturgical collections in the whole kingdom, it is surely time that Oxford should contribute something towards making them of use to those who are not fortunate enough to have to spend their lives among them.

Henry Bradshaw

11. LETTER ON THE OVID MANUSCRIPT IN THE BODLEIAN

Ellis, R. "De Artis Amatoriae Ovidianae Codice Oxoniensi." Hermes, Vol. 15, 1880, pp. 425-432.

Bradshaw wrote a letter, which was quoted in this paper, regarding the Bodleian Manuscript, Auct. F. iv. 32.

The Ovid you mention in the Bodleian library is one of the standing authorities for what is called old Welsh. I am afraid to place it earlier than the latter half of the IXth century. The writing and ornamentation both resemble very strongly the Augustine de Trinitate written by Johannes son of Sulgen in the monastery of St. Paternus in Cardiganshire between 1080 and 1090, but the Ovid cannot possibly be so late as that. It seem[s] to have passed out of Welsh hands into Dunstan's possession at Glastonbury in the Xth century.

The volume as it now stands (Auct. F. IV 32) consists of* four wholly separate parts. No. 2 is an

---

*Nihil hic dicit Bradshaw de Excerptis Bibliae, quae foliis 24-36 continentur. Scripta sunt binis columnis, Latina exaduersum Graecis; haec interdum Graecis, plerumque uulgaribus litteris exarata. Nonnulla ex iis describenda curauit Westwoodius in Palaeographia sua.

Anglo-Saxon homily apparently put with the rest at Glastonbury--but everything in the volume which there is reason to place before Dunstan's time must, I think, have come out of Wales together in his time.

The* first piece "de coniugationibus verborum" is Breton and written in Brittany. There need be no hesitation in supposing it to have been brought from Brittany to Wales early in the Xth century, and the writing cannot be much older. This is now, I believe the generally received conclusion, though until Ebel gave it his imprimatur I had some difficulty in getting it accepted.

The middle piece (now no. 3) which I call the liber Commonei is undoubtedly the oldest in the volume. It is a quire of useful knowledge written for one Commoneus by his son, palpably a Welshman of Wales. It contains amongst other things the alphabet of Nemniu, and a lunar (19-year) cycle for common use, showing the cycle in which they were living, namely A.D. 817-835. This quire is the patriarch of all Welsh books known. The handwriting corresponds very much to that of the text of the Juvencus written by Nuadu in this library (the University library of Cambridge), and to that of the entry of gift in the Gospel now at Lichfield, in which it is recorded that one Gelhi son of Arihtiud gave the book to the church of Telian (now called Llandaff) in the presence of certain witnesses. All these may fairly be called early IXth century writing. But the Ovid in the Bodleian MS. is more like that of some of the later IXth century documents written on the margins of the Gospel of Telian, when a somewhat different and more set style of writing had come in; so perhaps the nearest phrase for the date of the Ovid would be late mid-IXth or late-IXth century.

---

*Fragmentum est Eutychis Artis de Verbo quam edidit Keilius Art. Script. Minor, pp. 442-459.

12. NOTE ON MEDIAEVAL SERVICE BOOKS

Cox, J. Charles and Hope, W. H. St. John. <u>The Chronicles of the Collegiate Church or Free Chapel of All Saints, Derby.</u> 1881.

In the first "Appendix" to this work Bradshaw published a "Note on Mediaeval Service Books."

<u>Note on Mediaeval Service-Books</u>

In the old Church of England, the services were either--

1. For the different hours (Mattins, Lauds, Prime, Terce, Sext, None, Vespers, and Compline), said in the choir,

2. For processions, in the church or churchyard,

3. For the Mass, said at the Altar, or

4. For occasions, such as Marriage, Visitation of the Sick, Burial, etc., said as occasion required.

Of these four all have their counterparts, more or less, in the English Service of modern times, as follows:--

1. The Hour-Services, of which the principal were Mattins and Vespers, correspond to our Morning and Evening Prayer.

2. The Procession Services correspond to our hymns or anthems sung before the Litany which precedes the Communion Service in the morning, and after the third Collect in the evening, only no longer sung in the course of procession to the churchyard cross or a subordinate Altar in the church; the only relic (in common use) of the actual procession being that used on such occasions as the consecration of a church, etc.

3. The Mass answers to our Communion Service.

4. The Occasional Services are either those used by a priest, such as Baptism, Marriage, Visitation and Communion of the Sick, Burial of the Dead, etc., or those reserved for a bishop, as Confirmation, Ordination, Consecration of Churches, etc.

All these services but the last mentioned are contained in our "Prayer-Book" with all their details, except the lessons at Mattins and Evensong, which are read from the Bible, and the hymns and anthems, which are, since the sixteenth century, at the discretion of the authorities. This concentration or compression of the services into one book is the natural result of time, and the further we go back the more numerous are the books which our old inventories show. To take the four classes of Services and Service-books mentioned above:

1. The Hour-Services were latterly contained, so far as the text was concerned, in the <u>Breviarium</u>, or <u>Portiforium</u>, as it was called by preference in England. The musical portions of this book were contained in the <u>Antiphonarium</u>. But the Breviary itself was the result of a gradual amalgamation of many different books:

(a) The <u>Antiphonarium</u>, properly so called, containing the Anthems (<u>Antiphonae</u>) to the Psalms, the Responds (<u>Responsoria</u>) to the Lessons (<u>Lectiones</u>), and the other odds and ends of Verses and Responds (<u>Versiculi et Responsoria</u>) throughout the service;

(b) The _Psalterium_, containing the Psalms arranged as used at the different Hours, together with the Litany as used on occasions;

(c) The _Hymnarium_, or collection of Hymns used in the different Hour-services;

(d) The _Legenda_, containing the long Lessons used at Mattins, as well from the Bible, from the _Sermologus_, and from the _Homiliarius_, used respectively at the first, second, and third Nocturns at Mattins on Sundays and some other days, as also from the _Passionale_, containing the acts of Saints read on their festivals; and

(e) The _Collectarium_, containing the _Capitula_, or short Lessons used at all the Hour-services except Mattins, and the _Collectae_ or _Orationes_ used at the same.

2. The Procession Services were contained in the _Processionale_ or _Processionarium_. It will be remembered that the rubric in our "Prayer-Book" concerning the Anthem ("In Quires and places where they sing, here followeth the Anthem") is _indicative_ rather than _imperative_, and that it was first added in 1662. It states a fact; and, no doubt, when processions were abolished, with the altars to which they were made, cathedral choirs would have found themselves in considerable danger of being swept away also, had they not made a stand, and been content to sing the Processional Anthem without moving from their position in the choir. This alone sufficed to carry on the tradition; and looked upon in this way the modern Anthem Book of our Cathedral and Collegiate Churches, and the Hymn-Book of our parish churches, are the only legitimate successors of the old _Processionale_. It must be borne in mind, also, that the Morning and Evening Anthems in our "Prayer-Book" do not correspond to one another so closely as might at first appear to be the case. The Morning Anthem comes immediately before the Litany which precedes the Communion Service, and corresponds to the Processional Anthem or

Respond sung at the churchyard procession before Mass. The Evening Anthem, on the other hand, follows the third Collect, and corresponds to the Processional Anthem or Respond sung "eundo et redeundo," in going to, and returning from, some subordinate altar in the church at the close of Vespers.

3. The Mass, which we call the Communion Service, was contained in the Missale, so far as the text was concerned. The Epistles and Gospels, being read at separate lecterns, would often be written in separate books, called Epistolaria and Evangeliaria. The musical portions of the Altar Service were latterly all contained in the Graduale or Grayle, so called from one of the principal elements being the Responsorium Graduale or Respond to the Lectio Epistolae. In earlier times these musical portions of the Missal Service were commonly contained in two separate books, the Graduale and the Troparium. The Graduale, being in fact the Antiphonarium of the Altar Service (as indeed it was called in the earliest times), contained all the passages of Scripture, varying according to the season and day, which served as Introits (Antiphonae et Psalmi ad Introitum) before the Collects, as Gradual Responds or Graduals to the Epistle, as Alleluia versicles before the Gospel, as Offertoria at the time of the first oblation, and as Communiones at the time of the reception of the consecrated elements. The Troparium contained the Tropi, or preliminary tags to the Introits; the Kyries; the Gloria in excelsis; the Sequences or Prosae ad Sequentiam before the Gospel; the Credo in unum; the Sanctus and Benedictus; and the Agnus Dei; all, in early times, liable to have insertions or farsurae of their own, according to the season or day, which, however, were almost wholly swept away (except those of the Kyrie) by the beginning of the thirteenth century. Even in Lyndewode's time (A.D. 1433), the Troparium was explained to be a book containing merely the Sequences before the Gospel at Mass, so completely had the other elements then disappeared or become incorporated in the Graduale. This definition of the Troparium is the more necessary, because so many old church inventories yet remain, which contain books, even at the time of

writing the inventory long since disused, so that the lists would be unintelligible without some such explanation.

4. The Occasional Services, so far as they concerned a priest, were of course more numerous in old days than now, and included the ceremonies for <u>Candlemas</u>, <u>Ash</u> Wednesday, <u>Palm</u> Sunday, etc., besides what were formerly known as the Sacramental Services. The book which contained these was in England called the <u>Manuale</u>, while on the Continent the name <u>Rituale</u> is more common. No church could well be without one of these. The purely episcopal offices were contained in the <u>Liber pontificalis</u> or Pontifical, for which an ordinary church would have no need.

5. Besides these books of actual Services there was another, absolutely necessary for the right understanding and definite use of those already mentioned. This was the <u>Ordinale</u>, or book containing the general rules relating to the <u>Ordo divini servitii</u>. It is the <u>Ordinarius</u> or <u>Breviarius</u> of many Continental churches. Its method was to go through the year and show what was to be done; what days were to take precedence of others; and how, under such circumstances, the details of the conflicting Services were to be dealt with. The basis of such a book would be either the well-known Sarum <u>Consuetudinarium</u>, called after St. Osmund, but really drawn up in the first quarter of the thirteenth century, the Lincoln <u>Consuetudinarium</u> belonging to the middle of the same century, or other such book. By the end of the fifteenth century Clement Maydeston's <u>Directorium Sacerdotum</u>, or Priests' Guide, had superseded all such books, and came itself to be called the Sarum <u>Ordinale</u>, until, about 1508, the shorter Ordinal, under the name of <u>Pica Sarum</u>, "the rules called the Pie," having been cut up and re-distributed according to the seasons, came to be incorporated in the text of all the editions of the Sarum Breviary.

From the Inventory of 1466, given above in

the text, we learn that the Church of All Saints, Derby, possessed at that time the following books:--

    1. For the Hour Services, eight <u>Antiphonaria</u> and one <u>Collectarium</u>. The absence of all trace of a <u>Legenda</u> might seem to imply that one or more of the <u>Antiphonaria</u> were really what are sometimes called noted Breviaries, containing the whole Breviary Service, only with musical notation to the choral parts.

    2. For the Procession Services, four Processionars.

    3. For the Altar Service, two Missals, a Gospelar, and three Grayles or <u>Gradualia</u>.

    4. For the Occasional Services, two Manuals.

    5. Two <u>Ordinalia</u>, one good and one not worth much.

    The Inventory of 1527 shows us, beyond these, one great Portos, among the chained books, possibly a copy of the "Great Breviary" printed in 1516; and three printed Missals, two of which were reserved for the Altar of Our Lady, and one for that of St. Nicholas.

                                                        H.B.

Cambridge,
March 17, 1881.

13. GODFRIED VAN DER HAGHEN (G.H.), THE PUBLISHER OF TINDALE'S OWN LAST EDITION OF THE NEW TESTAMENT IN 1534-35

Bibliographer, No. 1, December 1881. Reprinted in Collected Papers, 1889, pp. 354-370.

    This is an excellent example of Bradshaw's bibliographical method applied to a relatively limited topic. He set out to establish the identity of the printer who used the initials "G.H." Bradshaw wrote and spoke on several occasions of the necessity of setting out the basic facts of the problem and then allowing them to speak for themselves.

    In this present paper this dictum is emphasized by two statements, one at the beginning and the other at the end:

    "It seems to me that it only needs to be stated to be accepted; and I can but wonder that those who have given minute attention to the subject should have been driven to hazarding unsatisfactory conjectures, when the facts were patent before them."

    "I mention these things merely to show that what is wanted for the solution of a bibliographical problem is not ingenuity of speculation, but simply honest and patient observation of facts allowed to speak for themselves. When will our leading bibliographers adopt this method in practice, and cease merely praising it in others?"

[The following notes were made two years ago, but, for want of some congenial medium of publication such as that at last afforded by the <u>Bibliographer</u>, were never communicated to any one. I mentioned the bare facts to Mr. Fry and to Mr. Stevens at the time; but no notice of them has hitherto, so far as I know, appeared in print.--H.B.]

I hope that my indefatigable friends, Mr. Francis Fry and Mr. Henry Stevens, will not take it amiss if an outsider, who has made no study of Antwerp printing during the Tindale period, comes forward with a suggestion as to the G.H., whose mark appears on the text-title of the original edition of Tindale's final revision of his English version of the New Testament, printed in 1534-35. It seems to me that it only needs to be stated to be accepted; and I can but wonder that those who have given minute attention to the subject should have been driven to hazarding unsatisfactory conjectures, when the facts were patent before them.

Mr. Fry has recently published (4to. London, 1878), an invaluable work called <u>A Bibliographical Description of the Editions of the New Testament, Tyndale's Version in English, ... illustrated with seventy-three plates.</u> It is simply a storehouse of facts upon the subject; and it is here that we have for the first time a clear statement of Tindale's work upon the New Testament, unclouded by the confusion caused by the want of knowledge from which previous writers suffered. The sequence of the editions, certainly issued before Tindale's death in 1536, now stands out plainly for any one to see.

Let me here say one word as to the spelling of Tindale's name. It is not perhaps a matter of any grave importance; yet, if there be any approach to consistency observable in the man's own habit of spelling his own name, in a time when the greatest inconstancy prevailed, it is at least more respectful to him, to adopt his own fashion. In his miscellaneous works, the original editions (which alone have to be considered) display a slight fluctuation between "Tindale" and "Tyndale," though "Tindale" predominates. But in his editions of the New Testament, which more certainly passed through the press under his own eye, the name is uniformly "Tindale." In the uncompleted quarto edition (No. 1 of my list below, 1525) the name does not occur; and in the first complete edition (No. 2, 1525 or 1526), we know that his name did not appear. But in his own second complete edition (No. 4, Nov. 1534), we find "Willyam Tindale" on the general title, followed by "W. T. vnto the Reader," and "Willyam Tindale yet once more to the Christen Reader." Again, in his own third and last complete edition (No. 5, 1534-35) we find "Willyam Tindale" on the general title, followed by "Willyam Tindale vnto the Christen Reader." Further, in the only autograph letter of his as yet discovered, which has been given in facsimile by Mr. Fry, from the original in the Brussels archives, the signature is "W Tindal[9]," or as we should write it, without the mark of abbreviation, "W. Tindalus." It is a Latin letter written in the winter of 1535-36. With these facts before me, I am content to reject the casual spelling adopted by Mr. Fry and most writers on the subject, and to revert to what I feel justified in considering Tindale's own habitual mode of writing his own name; and I hope that others will follow my example.

I have said that, thanks to Mr. Fry's labours, the sequence of the early editions of Tindale's version of the New Testament, issued during his lifetime, stands out clearly. It may be put briefly thus:

1. 4to. Printed at Cologne, by Peter Quentell, in 1525. Only ten sheets had been printed, when the work was forcibly interrupted, and all further progress in the edition seems to have been stopped. One copy, wanting the first leaf (with the title) and the last two sheets, is preserved, in the Grenville collection in the British Museum. It has been reproduced in facsimile, with an introduction, by Mr. Edward Arber.

2. 8vo. Printed at Worms, by Peter Schoeffer,

in 1525 or 1526. This is Tindale's first complete edition. A copy, wanting only the first leaf (with the title), is preserved at the Baptist College, Bristol; and another, very imperfect, is in St. Paul's Cathedral library. The Bristol copy has been reproduced in facsimile, with an introduction, by Mr. Fry.

3. 16mo. Printed at Antwerp, by the widow of Chr. Endhoven, August, 1534. This is a freely altered reprint of Tindale's book (No. 2), by George Joye. One copy is preserved, in the Grenville collection in the British Museum.

4. 8vo. Printed at Antwerp, by Marten Emperowr [Martin de Keyser, Martinus Caesar], the text-title dated 1534, the general title November, 1534. Joye's edition (No. 3) was published before the printing of this commenced. Many copies of this (Tindale's own complete second edition) are preserved, at the British Museum, Oxford, Cambridge, and elsewhere.

5. 8vo. Printed at Antwerp, by an as yet unknown printer, for G.H. [Godfried van der Haghen, Godefridus Dumaeus], the text-title dated 1534, the general title 1535. Copies more or less imperfect are preserved in the British Museum, in the Bodleian Library, and in the Earl of Pembroke's collection at Wilton, all wanting the general title and preliminary matter. Mr. Fry is the happy possessor of a copy containing the general title and a good part of the preliminary matter belonging to it. His work has made it perfectly clear that in this book we have Tindale's own third complete edition of his English version of the New Testament.

6. 8vo. Place and printer as yet unknown, the text-title dated 1535, the general title not as yet discovered. This is a reprint of the preceding edition, and is chiefly noted for the very peculiar spelling found in it. An imperfect copy is in the British Museum; one more perfect is in the University Library, Cambridge; and a third is at Exeter College, Oxford. None of these, however, contain any of the proper preliminary matter, or the general title.

From this list it will be seen that our knowledge concerning the printing and publication of the first four books is fairly complete, but that the printer of No. 5 is unknown to us, and the publisher as yet only recognisable by his trade-mark; while of No. 6 printer and publisher are alike unknown to us. Of the printer of No. 5 I have nothing to say. My object at present is to offer a suggestion as to its publisher, whose trade-mark bears the initial G.H. In Mr. Fry's Bibliographical Description, page 13, he quotes Mr. Henry Stevens as writing thus: "Matthew's New Testament has recently been proved by Mr. Francis Fry, of Bristol, to be a reprint of Tyndale's last revision, the edition of 1534-5, with the combined initials of Tyndale and Van Meteren on the (2nd) title-page. Mr. Francis Fry, under his No. 4, calls this edition G.H., but has hitherto been unable to explain the monogram. Our suggestion is that the G.H. means the translator, Guillaume Hytchins, the assumed name of William Tyndale; the other letters being the initials of the printer and proprietor I.V.M., that is Jacob van Meteren." Mr. Fry adds: "I had made much search to discover the meaning of this monogram, but in vain. Mr. Stevens' suggestion probably is correct." But Mr. Stevens and Mr. Fry have both of them done far too much valuable work to allow their names to be connected with a suggestion which only shows a complete misconception of the essential nature of the old trade-marks. A merchant's device may bear his initial, or not; but the notion of combining the mark of one man with the initial of another wholly independent person is an absurdity. I believe, too, that I should not be far wrong in saying that the initial which a man uses in his trade-mark is the initial of his name or names in the vernacular, and not in Latin or any foreign language which he may be led to use in the imprint of a book, because the book is in that language. My own suggestions are offered here chiefly as a sample of the way in which bibliographical problems of this kind may be simply and satisfactorily worked out; so I will at once proceed to my story.

An accident led me, a short time ago (May 2nd,

1879), to refer to Dr. Boehmer's Bibliotheca Wiffeniana; and, on opening the book, my eye lighted upon an entry (page 88) of the title of the "Pro Carolo V. Imperatore Apologetici libri duo" of Alfonso de Valdés, published in 1527, at Antwerp, "apud Godfr. Dumaeum." After noting the Serrure and Le Tellier copies of this rare work, Dr. Boehmer suggests that an imperfect book in Mr. Wiffen's library may be a copy of the edition issued by Dumaeus. He describes it as defective at beginning and end, but as having at the beginning of Book ii. a merchant's mark with the initial G.H. Had Dr. Boehmer not been at the pains to reproduce this trade-mark and initial in his text, my attention would never have been arrested. As it was, I instantly recognised in it the very device which Mr. Fry's laborious investigations and numerous facsimiles had made familiar to us all as the trade-mark of Tindal's unknown publisher in 1534-35. I use the term publisher, rather than printer, because, assuming (as I did at that time on insufficient data) that the New Testament of 1534-35 was printed by the well-known Antwerp printer, Martin de Keyser, who had already printed Tindale's previous edition of November 1534, I had long ago concluded that the unknown G.H. was the publisher, or undertaker of the cost, of the edition of 1534-35, and not the actual printer of it. In Dr. Boehmer's words there is nothing to show whether the concurrence of the name and initial presented the same conclusion to his mind which they did to mine, or whether he made the remark at random, on the assumption that a book might easily bear the name "Godfridus Dumaeus" and the trade-mark of "G.H." without being in any way noticeable on that account. In any case he draws no attention to the point, and I may conclude, therefore, that it did not strike him as a fact of any particular interest.

For my own part, the moment I read his note, my instinct told me that I was on the track to discover the unknown G.H. The possible alternatives, if Dr. Boehmer's suggestion were true, were these: Either G.H. and Godfridus Dumaeus were the same person, or they were not; and the following results would become clear:

1. If they were not the same person, there were again two alternatives: either one would be the printer, and the other the publisher, of the book; or one would have succeeded to the business of the other, and so Dumaeus would have become the legitimate inheritor of the trade-mark of G.H., just as W. de Worde did of Caxton's at Westminster, and Redman of Pynson's in London.

2. If they were the same person, then G.H. would be the initial of the original Dutch name of a man who in Latin styled himself, after the fashion of the day, Godfridus Dumaeus. I believe this to be, as I have said before, the universal law of trade-mark initials; and an instance happened to be very familiar at the moment, in the case of Tindale's own printer of a few months before, all of whose devices bear the initial M.K., for his Dutch name, Martin de Keyser, which he uses in the imprints of his Dutch books, though he habitually calls himself Martinus Caesar, Martin Lempereur, and Marten Emperowr, in those of his Latin, French, and English books respectively.

But, as a matter of fact, long before all these alternatives and sub-alternatives had time to present themselves to my mind, I had arrived at the conclusion that Dumaeus, a name till then unknown to me, but evidently nothing more than a derivative of dumus, a thicket, could only represent the well-known Dutch name, Van der Haghen, and that Godfried van der Haghen was the single name which would at once afford G.H. as its trade-mark initial, and Godfridus Dumaeus as its Latin equivalent, to be used in the imprint of a Latin book. The first biographical dictionary that came to hand settled the point at once, by telling me of a Dutch Dominican friar of the sixteenth century, who called himself in literature Joannes Dumaeus, while his native name was Jan van der Haghen. I felt it desirable, however, to confirm the conjecture started by Dr. Boehmer's remark, and to see with my own eyes a book in which the name of Dumaeus or its equivalent stood on the same title-page with the G.H. device. This wish was very soon gratified.

Shortly afterwards, Dr. Westcott (to whom, from his interest in the history of Tindale's work upon the New Testament, I had at once mentioned my idea) sent me, from the Cathedral library at Peterborough, a small octavo volume containing Lily and Erasmus' <u>Libellus de octo Orationis Partium Constructione</u>, printed at Antwerp in May, 1529. It has at the end the early separate device of Martin de Keyser, with the initial "M.K.," the motto "Sola fides sufficit," and the date "1525," all in the cut, but without any imprint. At the beginning is the title, with the imprint, "Godfridus Dumaeus excudebat," all within a border of four pieces, of which the lower one, forming the sill, contains the trade-mark and initial G.H., and is identical with that used on the text-title of Tindale's New Testament of 1534-5, as reproduced by Mr. Fry. Here, then, was a further step reached in the investigation. The device, at the end, of the well-known Antwerp <u>printer</u>, Martin de Keyser, showed that the book was <u>printed</u> by him. The imprint and border of the title-page therefore showed conclusively that G.H., or Godfridus Dumaeus, was the <u>publisher</u> of the book.

The next point was to ascertain whether an examination of the received history of the Antwerp press would bring to light any connexion or association in work between Godfried van der Haghen or Godfridus Dumaeus and Martin de Keyser, or any one else engaged in the book trade at Antwerp. It is very necessary to trace out these business connexions, because it is only thus that we can get a true view of the nature of each man's proper line of business. If we find, where two names are associated in the production of one book, the one man's name connected with such phrases as <u>sumptibus</u>, <u>impensis</u>, etc., while the other uses of himself the word <u>imprimebat</u>, etc., we get a clue, which, taken as a guide in further investigation, frequently proves conclusively that the one man was a printer by trade, and perhaps occasionally a bookseller; while the other was a bookseller by trade, and never appears as a printer. Now the second portion of Panzer's <u>Annales Typographici</u> contains the best account of Antwerp printing from 1501 to 1536, which is at my disposal.

Panzer gives seven books as bearing the name of Godefridus Dumaeus. But of these seven, five bear also the imprint of Martinus Caesar, whose name is connected with twenty-six books in the same list. Now a bare reading of the titles of these is enough to show, not merely that the two men worked in concert, but that the one was the printer, and the other the publisher, or undertaker of the cost, of those books, to which their names are both attached. Indeed, it is worth notice that of all the books given by Panzer as printed by Martinus Caesar, in which he is associated with any one else as publisher or undertaker of the cost, that publisher is Godefridus Dumaeus; and of all the books given by Panzer as issued by Godefridus Dumaeus, in which he is associated with any one else as printer, that printer is Martinus Caesar.

In trying to show what I believe to be the simplest mode of solving a bibliographical problem, I can but point out the method which I adopted in this particular case. For this purpose I must give here the wording of the imprints of these books, as they stand in Panzer's list of books printed at Antwerp (Ann. Typ., vol. vi., p. 12 and onwards). I will then add a few notes upon these entries, derived from such books as we happen to have in our University Library. The brief title of each work will further enable any one to look for copies in any library which may be within his reach. The references are to Panzer's numbers.

    94. Apud Godofr. Dumaeum. 1527. 8vo. (Latin.)
    105. Apud Martinum Caesarem. Nov. 1528. 12mo. (Latin.)
    106. Per Martinum Caesarem. 1528. 8vo. (Latin.)
    107. Typis et impensis Martini Lempereur. 1528. 4 vols. 8vo. (French.)
    122. Apud Martinum Caesarem. Jan. 1529. 8vo. (Latin.)
    123. Godfridus Dumaeus excudebat. Mai. 1529. 8vo. (Latin.)

138. Martinus Caesar excudebat impensis honesti viri Godefridi Dumaei. Nov. 12, 1530. 8vo. (Latin.)
139. Par Martin Lempereur. 1530. Folio. (French.)
146. Apud Martinum Caesarem impensis Godefridi Dumaei. 1531. 8vo. (Latin.)
147. Impress. per Martinum Caesaris impensis honesti viri Godefridi Dumaei. April 24, 1531. 8vo. (Latin.)
148. Martinus Caesar excudebat. Jun. 6. 1531. 8vo. (Latin.)
149. Apud Martinum Caesarem. 1531. 8vo. (Latin.)
151. By Martin de Keyser. 1531. 8vo. (Dutch.)
152. Typis Martini Lempereur. 1531. 8vo. (French.)
164. Apud Martinum Caesarem. Apr. 1532. 8vo. (Latin.)
165. Apud Martinum Caesarem. 1532. 12mo. (Latin.)
166. Typis Martini Lempereur. 1532. 12mo. (French.)
178. Apud Martinum Caesarem. 1533. 8vo. (Latin.)
179. Apud Martinum Caesarem. 1533. 8vo. (Latin.)
191. Excudebat Martinus Caesar sumptu et opera Godefridi Dumaei. Febr. 1534. Folio. (Latin.)
192. Par Martin Lempereur. 1534. Folio. (French.)
193. By Marten Emperowr. 1534. 8vo. (English.)
212. Apud Martinum Caesarem. Aug. 1535. 8vo. (Latin.)
213. 1535. Impensis Godofr. Dumaei Martinus Caesar imprimebat. 8vo. (Latin.)
214. Martinus Caesar excudebat. 1535. 8vo. (Latin.)
215. Apud Martinum Caesarem. 1535. 12mo. (Latin.)
216. By Martin de Keyser. 1535. 8vo. (Dutch.)
226. Excudebat Martinus Caesar. 1536. 8vo. (Latin.)

I have given these imprints simply thus, in order that they may strike the eye more readily. I must now make a few remarks on them in order.

No. 94 is the book by Alfonso de Valdés, which is noticed by Dr. Boehmer. In the description of the copies with the above imprint there is no mention of any border or device. In Mr. Wiffen's copy the subordinate title is described as having the border and device of G.H., while the general title, which would contain the imprint, is wanting. They must therefore be incompletely described copies either of the same edition of the book, or of different editions of it issued by the same publisher.

No. 105 is a Greek version of the Roman <u>Horae</u> with a Latin title-page. It is really in 16mo., not 12mo., so that the title-page is too small to allow of any known border device. The Cambridge copy, moreover, wants the last two leaves, on one of which would probably be found the separate 1525 device mentioned above.

No. 106 is <u>Flores Senecae</u>. No. 107 is a French Bible. No. 122 is <u>Petrus Mosellanus, Tabula de schematibus</u>.

No. 123 is the <u>Lily and Erasmus</u>, the Peterborough copy of which I have noticed above as containing the separate 1525 device of Martin de Keyser at the end, and the imprint with the border-device of G.H. at the beginning.

No. 127, to which Panzer assigns no printer's name, is an edition of Horace, of which we have a copy in our University library. It is printed in two parts; 1. Odes and Epodes; 2. Satires and Epistles. Part 1 has on the title "<u>Apud Martinum Caesarem</u>," and at the end his separate device containing "M K," "1525," and the motto "<u>Sola fides sufficit</u>." The motto has been carefully inked out. Part 2 has on the title "<u>Apud Martinum Caesarem</u>," and at the end the imprint, "Antuerpiae: <u>Martinus Caesar imprimebat,</u>

sumptu et opera honesti viri Godefredi Dumaei. An. M.D.XXIX. Mense Maio." On the next leaf is the separate 1525 device, with the motto carefully inked out as in Part 1. There are no woodcut borders in either part.

Bound with this Horace is a copy of Juvenal and Persius, also printed in two parts, in small octavo. On the title of the Juvenal is "Apud Martinum Caesarem. An. M.D.XXIX. Mense Maio"; and at the end the separate 1525 device, as in the Horace, with the objectionable motto inked out. The Persius bears on the title "Apud Godefredum Dumaeum. An. M.D.XXIX. Mense Iunio." At the end there is no imprint, and no room for any device. These two also are without any woodcut borders. In matters of type and arrangement the Horace and the Juvenal and Persius are identical.

No. 138 is Theodorici Corthoevii Bellum discors Sophiae et Philautiae. I have not seen it.

No. 139 is a French Bible in folio. The title is within a border of four pieces, of which the outer one contains the device of M.K. The imprint is followed by the printer's new and less dangerous motto, "Spes mea Jesus." A copy is in our University Library.

No. 146 is Erasmus's Enchiridion militis Christiani. No. 147 is Herm. Bodii Unio dissidentium. No. 148 is an Oratio of Hen. Cornelius Agrippa. No. 149 is described as Paup. subvent. forma apud Hyperas Flandrorum. No. 151 is a Dutch New Testament. No. 152 is a French New Testament. No. 164 is Erasmi Declarationes. No. 165 is Psalmorum Interpretatio Jo. Campensis. No. 166 is a French New Testament. No. 178 is Gulielmi Gnaphei Acolastus. No. 179 is Galeacii Capellae de rebus nuper in Italia gestis libri octo. I have not seen any of these.

No. 191 bears the title Biblia. Breves in

eadem Annotationes. Panzer gives the date February 1534, but our Cambridge copy has Jan. 1534, both on the title and at the end, where the imprint runs Excudebat Martinus Caesar pro honesto viro Godefrido Dumaeo. Jan. 1534. The book is a Latin Bible with notes, in folio; and the title is within the same border of four pieces (with the M.K. device in the outer piece), as the French Bible mentioned above, No. 139. The title to the index is within the same border, and bears the imprint, Per Martinum Caesarem. 1534.

No. 192 is a French Bible in folio, which I have not seen.

No. 193 is Tindale's own second complete edition of the New Testament in English, No. 4 in my list given above. The title which commences the text has the imprint as above, with the date "Anno M.D.xxxiiij.," all within a border of four pieces, of which the lower one, forming the sill, contains the trade-mark and initial (M.K.) of Martin de Keyser, the printer of the book. The general title contains the date "...fynesshed in the yere of oure Lorde God. A. M.D. & xxxiiij. in the moneth of Nouember," and is within a border of four pieces, very similar to that round the text-title, but different, and having a blank shield in the sill.

Next to this comes Tindale's own third complete edition of the English New Testament, No. 5 in my list given above. It is in small octavo, like the rest. The text-title bears the imprint "Anno M.D.xxxiiii.," and is within a border of four pieces, with the G.H. device in the sill, as in the Lily and Erasmus (No. 123 above), described from the Peterborough copy. The general title, prefixed to the preliminary matter, bears the imprint, "Prynted in the yere of oure Lorde God M.D. & xxxv.," and is within a border of four pieces, with a blank shield in the sill. The borderpieces are, I believe, identical with those surrounding the general title of the edition of November 1534 (No. 193 above), in spite of certain apparent and perplexing points of difference.

No. 212 is <u>Joannis Coleti aeditio</u>. No. 213 is a reprint of the <u>Lily and Erasmus</u> (No. 123 above), only that here the full imprint is to be seen, showing precisely the relations of the printer and the publisher to each other. No. 214 is <u>Jo. Lud. Vivis De communione rerum</u>. No. 215 is <u>Precationes Biblicae</u>. No. 216 is a Dutch New Testament. No. 226 is an edition of <u>Prudentius</u>. I have not seen any of these books.

Panzer's <u>Annales typographici</u> only come down to the year 1536. On turning, for information concerning the next few years, to his predecessor Maittaire, I found that both names, Martinus Caesar and Godefridus Dumaeus, had disappeared at once. In 1537 I find no trace of either; but as the succeeding years show evidence that both of them had successors in business, I must continue my list. My references are to the pages of the volume of Maittaire's <u>Annales typographici</u>, which deals with this period.

278. <u>Apud viduam Martini Lempereur</u>, 1538. 12mo. A French New Testament.

309. <u>Excudebat vidua Martini Caesaris impensis Joannis Coccii</u>. Ult. Feb. 1539. 8vo. G. Lilii De generibus nominum, etc.

310. <u>Apud Antonium Goinum</u>. 1540. Folio. This is described by Maittaire as <u>Biblia Latina</u>. We have at Cambridge an edition of the <u>Biblia. Breves in eadem Annotationes</u> (a reprint of the one noticed above, under Panzer's No. 191), which bears on the title, and at the end <u>Excudendum curabat Antonius Goinus</u> Anno MDXL. There are no borders or device, but the types and initials seem to be those of Martin de Keyser; and, if my suggestion below should be verified, no doubt Antonius Goinus succeeded the widow of Martin de Keyser. This may be the book intended by Maittaire.

312. <u>Impensis Antonii Dumaei</u>. 1540. 4to. The book is <u>De Melancholia ex Galeni, Rufi ... voluminibus collectanea ... Matthia Theodoro Melanelio interprete</u>.

202 / Henry Bradshaw

We have at Cambridge another book by the same translator, a version of Galen's <u>Utrum conceptus in utero sit animal</u>. At the end is the imprint, "Antverpiae <u>Impendio Antonii Dumaei excusum</u>, Anno Christiano MDXL. Mens. Sept." There is no border or device; but the book is in quarto, and I have not seen as yet any separate or border-device suitable for books of this size.

319. <u>Imprim. Antonio Dumaeo AEgidius Copenius</u>. 1540. 8vo. This is the incomplete way in which Maittaire notices the imprint of the <u>Didascalus autore Jacobo Zovitio apud Braedanos ludimagistro</u>.

322. <u>Per Antonium de la Haye</u>. 1541. Folio. This is no doubt Maittaire's inaccurate Latin rendering of one of the imprints to be found in the French Bible of Jan. 12, 1541, of which we fortunately have a copy at Cambridge. At the end, after giving the exact date, we read, "En Anuers <u>par Antoine</u> <u>des Gois</u>. Spes mea Jesus." At the beginning, on the title, is "En Anuers, <u>pour Antoine de la Haye</u>, demourant au Pan de nostre Dame. An. M.D. xli." The types, cuts, borders, and border-device, are all those of Martin de Keyser, as used in 1534, in the Latin Bible noticed above under Panzer's No. 191; and the two years privilege granted to him Nov. 21, 1533, is here reprinted. It seems therefore fair to infer, from this book:

(1) That in "par Antoine des Gois," a phrase strictly used of a <u>printer</u>, we may trace the "Antonius Goinus" of 1540; and that he was the successor of the "Vidua Martini Caesaris" of 1538 and 1539, and thus the legitimate inheritor of the trade-mark of Martin de Keyser, as a <u>printer</u>; and,

(2) That in "pour Antoine de la Haye," a phrase strictly used of a <u>publisher</u> or undertaker of the cost of a book, we may see the French name of the "Antonius Dumaeus," at whose <u>impendio</u> or <u>impensis</u>, as a <u>publisher</u>, certain books were printed at Antwerp in 1540; and that he was the successor in this business of Godefridus Dumaeus or Godfried van

der Haghen, who published so many of the books printed by Martin de Keyser.

But, whether all these inferences be accepted or not, two facts result, I think, clearly from Maittaire's and Panzer's lists, as verified where possible by actual copies:

First, we have three several devices, with the initial M.K., belonging to an Antwerp printer, whose name appears as Martin de Keyser when the book is in his native language, as Martinus Caesar or Caesaris when the book is in Latin, as Martin Lempereur when in French, and lastly as Marten Emperowr when in English.

Secondly, we have a border device, with the initial G.H., belonging to an Antwerp bookseller, who appears as Godefridus Dumaeus when the book is in Latin (as all his books mentioned by Panzer are); while one who is to all appearance his successor is called Antonius Dumaeus in Latin, and Antoine de la Haye in French books.

Judging from the fashion which we know to have been adopted by Martin de Keyser, and many other printers and literati of that day, I cannot but believe that both the Dumaei, Godefridus and Antonius, would appear with the name Van der Haghen, if we could but trace any Dutch books produced by or for either of them. Of my authorities, Panzer is eighty and Maittaire a hundred and fifty years old; so that a very moderate search in the present day would assuredly be rewarded by our finding more than one Dutch book of the kind.

After all that has been said, it will perhaps be assumed that I am prepared to maintain that Tindale's New Testament of 1534-35 was printed for Godfried van der Haghen (G.H., Godefridus Dumaeus) by Martin de Keyser. But although I have brought forward a considerable amount of evidence to show the business connexion existing between the two men, yet Mr. Fry's facsimiles, so far from leading me to assert that the

book was actually printed by Keyser, rather tend to make
me doubt the fact altogether. I have made no comparison of the originals, and Mr. Fry's copies, being litho-
graphed hand-tracings, are no doubt more or less un-
serviceable for purposes of minute comparison. But if
they are even moderately faithful copies, it is impossible to accept the results, which he offers, of his comparison of certain cuts in the editions of M.K., November 1534, and G.H., 1534-35. Mr. Fry says (page 59),
speaking of the edition of G.H., 1534-35: "It corresponds with the edition by Emperowr in the following
particulars. The border of the first title of this edition is identical with both the titles in 1534. The woodcuts of the four Evangelists, the seven-line capitals
A B F P T S ... are also identical." He proceeds to
say that nothing can be inferred as to the printer of
a book from the identity of materials used. Now, in
the first place, the borders of the two titles of the
edition of M.K., 1534, so far from being themselves
identical, as Mr. Fry states, are wholly different,
though showing a general resemblance in design. It
is only necessary to look at Mr. Fry's plate 3, to see
differences in all the four pieces of the border, apart
from the fact that the sill of the text-title contains
the device of Martin de Keyser, while the sill of the
general title contains a blank shield. In the edition
of G.H., 1534-35, the border of the text-title consists of four pieces, of which the sill contains the
device of G.H.; while the border of the general title
appears to be identical with that of the general title
of the preceding edition (Nov. 1534), and only differing in the presence or absence of certain perplexing breaks in the outer margin. Judging from this
title-page alone, there would be no inconsistency, so
far, in looking upon Martin de Keyser as the <u>printer</u>,
and Godfried van der Haghen as the <u>publisher</u>, of
the volume. Mr. Fry proceeds, however, to say that
the woodcuts of the four Evangelists (he might have
added, of the Pentecost at the beginning of the Acts),
and the seven-line initials A B F P S T, are identical. But on comparing his plate 4 (M.K. 1534) with
his plates 6, 7, 8 (G.H. 1534-35), it is true that
the identity of design is evident; but (if his tracings

are at all to be trusted) the total difference of execution in minute details is equally patent. It is difficult to believe that the same printer would have duplicate letters and cuts so closely resembling one another, unless they were such as to be wanted for use more than once on the same side of a sheet, which of course cannot be said of these. That at least is my experience of the cases where such duplicates are found. A careful comparison of the numberless Dutch, French, and English New Testaments and other small octavos which issued from the various Antwerp presses about this period, made by one who has an eye trained to observe these minute details of printing, would, I feel certain, reveal this unknown printer.

It must be borne in mind too that it was a dangerous thing at this time to avow sympathy with a man like Tindale. Martin de Keyser may have lost courage after printing the edition of November 1534. His bold motto "Sola fides sufficit," which he used (so far as I know) only from 1525 to 1529, evidently gave offence to some, as we may infer from the careful way in which it has been inked out in the Cambridge copy of the Horace and Juvenal of 1529. In 1530 he adopted the less compromising motto of "Spes mea Jesus," which was continued by his successor. Little is known of Tindale's own history during the two years which preceded his martyrdom in April, 1536; and as Martin de Keyser and Godfried van der Haghen both disappear in this very year, we can well believe that they must both have become aware of the perilous nature of their undertakings; and we cannot be surprised at the suppression of the name of the actual printer of such a book as the New Testament of 1534-35.

But, whoever may turn out to have printed the book, I cannot think that we need any longer hesitate to look upon Godfried van der Haghen as its publisher; and, this point being settled, the way stands open for a fresh investigation of the productions of the several Antwerp presses at which it may possibly have been printed.

If Panzer, the one true naturalist among general bibliographers, had more followers in the present day, our knowledge of these matters would advance very much more rapidly than it does. Put a book, about which you are anxious to learn something, among its fellows, that is, among the productions of the same and neighbouring presses, look at its surroundings for a few minutes, and your questions will solve themselves. You will be saved from all inducement to rash speculation. The facts will speak for themselves before you even have time to hazard a foolish conjecture. An examination of the actual books in Panzer's list alone would be sure to bring out many interesting points; and if my friend M. Ferdinand vander Haeghen will examine, with this view, some of the precious stores under his charge in the University Library at Ghent, I feel sure that his bibliographical instinct and well-trained eye could not fail to solve all these difficulties in a very short space of time. I have myself made no investigations worth mentioning, and at this moment I have neither leisure nor materials for pursuing the subject. I was struck by an entry of Dr. Boehmer's in his catalogue. I took down Panzer and Maittaire, wrote out the several entries of the kindred books, and looked at the half-dozen volumes on the list which our University Library affords. Certain conclusions were at once forced upon me. The book from Peterborough put the matter in a still clearer light, by just giving me that evidence at first hand, without which it is so difficult to feel anything like conviction. I mention these things merely to show that what is wanted for the solution of a bibliographical problem is not ingenuity of speculation, but simply honest and patient observation of <u>facts allowed to speak for themselves</u>. When will our leading bibliographers adopt this method in practice, and cease merely praising it in others?

[Note. Page 201. I may add two books which give earlier dates for Martin Keyser's widow and Antoine des Gois than those quoted from Maittaire.

Catalogi duo operum Erasmi ... Antwerpiae apud viduam Martini Caesaris, expensis Ioannis Coccij circiter Calen. Augu. anno MDXXXVII. 8°.

Commentaria Viti Amerbachii in Ciceronis tres libros de Officiis. Antwerpiae excudendum curabat Antonius Goinus, Anno M.D.XXXIX. 8°.

Page 202. In 1884 the Vergauwen Catalogue (Part 2) enabled him to verify his conjecture. No. 27 is a Eusebius in Dutch "Gheprent in ... 1534 Tantwerpen by my Govaert van der haghen." F°.

Mr. E. Gordon Duff informs me that in the Registers of St Luke's Gild at Antwerp, edited by Messrs. Rombauts and Van Lerius, "Govaert (van der Haghen), in de Pant, prynttere," occurs under the year 1533. He also gives me the description of a book (which may possibly be the same as that in the Vergauwen catalogue): Die Historie die men heet Ecclesiastica, gheprent md ende XXXIIII Tantwerpen in onser Liever Vrouwen Pant by my Govaert Van der Haghen. 4°. J.]

14. A WORD ON SIZE-NOTATION AS DISTINGUISHED FROM FORM-NOTATION

An appendix which was attached to the publication of the President's Address which Bradshaw delivered to the Library Association of the United Kingdom at Cambridge, September 5, 1882.

Published as Memorandum No. 7, October 1882. Reprinted in Collected Papers, 1889, pp. 406-409.

> The problem which Bradshaw discussed here, and which had been presented to the Conference by a Committee, remains a difficulty for many students to the present day. There is widespread confusion regarding the correct meaning of format and its relationship to size. Bradshaw's viewpoint was a highly individual one, shaped above all by the practices of the Cambridge University Library. It also draws attention in some degree to the different outlooks of the librarian and the bibliographer, with Bradshaw seeing the issue equally clearly from both sides.

The careful Report presented by the Size-notation Committee to the Cambridge meeting of the Library Association was discussed to some extent, but it was unreasonable to expect any immediate agreement upon such a question, and the matter was reserved for future consideration.

The truth is, that the case has evidently not been fully stated. One thing is patent and acknowledged: that all are anxious to represent a fact, whatever be the notation they propose; while opinions are divided as to the best mode of representing this fact. Two other points, however, appear to me not to be so clearly or universally apprehended:

(1) That the terms Folio, Quarto, Octavo, &c., represent strictly not size-notation but form-notation; and

(2) That the modern methods of making paper and of printing books combine to render any accurate application of form-notation to such books not so much difficult as impossible.

The logical conclusion from these two facts is, of course, that the form-notation expressed by the terms Folio, Quarto, Octavo, &c., should be given up in the case of modern books to which it is wholly inapplicable; and that a size-notation, which does represent an undoubted fact, should be adopted in its place. This logical conclusion was seen, accepted, and acted upon, at Cambridge in the year 1854; and I confess that it is difficult to resist the conviction that this principle must sooner or later be accepted by others, though there will no doubt be differences of opinion as to the most advisable form of notation to adopt. A librarian cannot afford to be eccentric in this matter; whatever method is adopted, it must be adopted by all the great libraries, and it must commend itself to the general reader. Now I feel sure that I shall not be taxed with dogmatism or with any predilection for some crotchet of my own devising, if I say that the complicated and artificial systems, recommended by the Committee and others, are such as cannot possibly become familiar, even if they become intelligible, to the general run of readers.

In the old Cambridge size-notation of "London, 1856, 8 x 5," meaning 8 inches high by 5 inches across, the second number, denoting the breadth, very soon fell out of use, except in writing; and for years we always spoke of books as eights, sevens, sixes, &c., meaning that they were eight, seven, or six, inches high.[1] This does but point to the undoubted fact that, unless the book is actually oblong (that is, broader than it is high), its breadth is a matter of only secondary importance. We want, above all things, a notation which shall bring the book to our mind's eye, and, by showing us its height, at once place it, to our imagination, side by side with books which we already see upon our shelves.

No vote of the Library Association, indeed no amount of external authority, will compel, or even enable, an ordinary person to keep in his head the number of inches, or fractions of an inch, which distinguish (for instance) the term "sm. 8vo." and "la. 8vo." If these expressions, couched some of them in unfamiliar phraseology, are proposed, as they are avowedly proposed, with the sole object of their serving as equivalents for certain definite measurements by inches or millimètres, let us rather, in the name of common sense, resort to the inches or millimètres themselves, which are facts of everyday life, such as can be understood by the most ordinary reader. If we wish to distinguish between an Englishman's inches and a Frenchman's millimètres, let each use simple letters or an index-letter to notify the fact. Take the Englishman's "London, 1882, 8in.," or the Frenchman's "Paris, 1882, 215^m." These could not fail to be intelligible, and would very soon become familiar enough. Each nation would use its own size-notation for books, precisely as it does for every other commodity; and our neighbours would find no greater difficulty in converting our inches into millimètres, than we experience every day in reversing the process, when we examine any ordinary catalogue of engravings.

Further, if ever, as in a detailed description, more minute accuracy of size-notation were desired, it would be equally easy and intelligible to add the fraction ("London, 1882, 8-3/4in."); and, if the breadth were considered of importance, we could in each case express the fact in the usual way ("London, 1882, 8 x 5 in." or 8½ x 5¼in.), and thus the utmost demands of bibliographical accuracy could be met without the slightest departure from the simple principle of making the size-notation represent a fact, with more or less minute exactness according to the taste of the owner of the books. For an ordinary alphabetical catalogue, however, which is always rather a finding index than a minutely descriptive catalogue, it would probably be found sufficient to denote only the height of the volume.

If then we could arrive at an agreement upon the question of size-notation by the adoption of a plan which secures, what is of all things most wanted under the circumstances, <u>easy accuracy</u>, we could proceed without difficulty to fix upon some form-notation, which would satisfy the conscience, while gratifying the conservatism, of all real lovers of old books.

To denote books in quarto (for instance), a term which means that a page or leaf of the book is, in size, one-fourth part of the whole sheet of hand-made paper on which the book is printed, the French use the formula "in-4.," the Germans use "4.," while the English use indifferently "4to." or "4°." The single index-letter °, representing the termination of the word, whatever it may be, seems to my mind the simplest formula to employ, as it is also the least likely one to mislead the reader. Every possible form of folded sheet (the French <u>format</u>), F°, 4°, 8°, 12°, 18°, 16°, 24°, 32°, &c., could thus be represented by a perfectly uniform expression, which we never, even at present, find any difficulty in interpreting.

Only let this form-notation immediately precede the real size-notation in the case of all old books to which it is applicable ("London, 1662, F°.12in." or "Cantabrigiae, 1638, 4°.7in."), and we have all the elements of certainty which can well be desired. It appears indeed to me that it would be difficult to combine the two necessary elements of simplicity and accuracy under any more easily intelligible or more thoroughly commonplace formula.

It may perhaps have been thought superfluous for me to define the meaning of the term "quarto," a definition which *mutatis* *mutandis* applies to all such terms. But the truth is that, although Frenchmen seem to be generally taught these things as elementary facts, I am bound to say that I have not found, during the last twenty years, five Englishmen, either librarians or booksellers, who knew how to distinguish a folio from a quarto, or an octavo from a 12° or a 16°. It is surely high time then, that we should make a serious effort to arrive at some common understanding as to a matter of such purely practical concern; seeing that we are all agreed that it is desirable to convey some idea of the size of a book by the notation we use to describe it.

Note

1. The practice in use with us has been to measure the height of the book from the top to the bottom of the page, disregarding the covers. We compute inches as we compute a man's age; a book is 8 in. until it is 9 in.; only, seeing that bound books are so often cut not quite square, anything short of the number used in the size-notation, by an eighth of an inch or less, we call by that number for ordinary purposes. I have said, ... that in our General Library Catalogue, we have reverted to the common form-notation, 8vo., 12mo. &c.; but pure size-notation is still retained in other departments, while in Trinity College library it has never been given up since it was first adopted in 1856 or thereabouts.

15. QUERY CONCERNING "THE TOYES OF AN IDLE HEAD"

<u>Notes and Queries</u>, 6th. S. x, 6 September 1884, p. 187.

So far as I have been able to trace, no answer was ever forthcoming to this query from Bradshaw.

"The Toyes of an Idle Head."--What is the book of which the above is the running title? Two leaves are used as fly-leaves in the contemporary English binding of a book printed in 1600. The "Toyes" are printed in quarto, the text of the poems in Elizabethan black-letter, the headings or rubrics in Roman letter. The running title, in Roman capitals, has on the left-hand page, "The Toyes of," and on the right "an Idle Head." The leaves cannot be consecutive. One contains, on both sides, part of a poem in which the author recounts a dream, in long rhyming couplets, each verse having seven accents. The following is a specimen:--

> Who knocketh at the doore, quoth one? A
>   silly wight, quoth I,
> cast vp of late, on sorrowes shore, by
>   tempests sodainly:
> Brought in the Barke of weary bale, cast
>   vp by waues of woe,
> since when to seeke some place of rest, I
>   wandred too and froe.

The other leaf contains, on the first side, the end of

another poem about a dream, also in long rhyming couplets; but here the first verse of each has six accents, the second seven; and the lines are printed so as all to range together, while in the preceding poem the second line of each couplet is indented. Here is one couplet, reminding one faintly of Chaucer's account of his dream of the Parlement of Foulis:--

> Some thinke in sleepe they are, in field
>   with foe at fight,
> And with their fists they buffet them, that
>   lye with them by night.

Over leaf is a "Toy" in four six-line stanzas, of which I give the heading and the first stanza:--

> ¶ Another Toy written in the praise of a Gilliflower, at the request of a Gentlewoman, and one aboue the rest, who loued that flower:--

> If I should choose a prety Flower,
> For séemely show, and swéetest sente:
> In my minde sure, the Gillyflower,
> I should commend, where so I went.
>   And if néede bée, good reason too,
>   I can alledge why so I doe.

Below this is the first line of the heading of the poem which should follow, only all below this line is wanting:--

> ¶ A pretty toye written in the praise of a straunge Spring.

Is this some well-known book, which I cannot find for want of knowing the author's name? Or is it, by chance, a fragment of the lost "newe booke in English verse intituled <u>Tarlton's Toyes</u>," licensed to Richard Jones, Dec. 10, 1576? I see nothing like it in the excellent index of English books of poetry in the new <u>British Museum Catalogue</u>, and I see no "Toyes" except Tarlton's in Mr. Arber's <u>Transcript of the Stationers' Registers</u>. I have no familiarity with Elizabethan literature; but perhaps some one of the many who have this knowledge will kindly name my fragments for me. Attention was duly called to them in the catalogue in which I found them, issued by Mr. Cornish, of Manchester. Such fragments are always worth preserving; for, however well known their contents may be, the particular volume of which they form part is never likely to be common.

Henry Bradshaw.

16. DISCOVERY OF A ST. ALBANS BOOK

<u>The Academy</u>, 17 January 1885.

    A number of very happy associations surround this letter of Bradshaw's. Only two provincial towns possessed a printing press in England in the fifteenth century: Oxford and St. Albans. In St. Albans an unnamed printer worked from 1479 onwards and the most that we know of him is the description in a colophon of "one somtyme scole master of saynt Albons." The case is one of the many historical riddles of bibliography which have always intrigued research workers. It is a curious little problem which has still not yielded all its answers. It is also a pleasant circumstance which links Bradshaw with two of the younger generation of bibliographers. Edward Gordon Duff (1863-1924) is remembered, although not well as he deserves to be, for his work on early English printed books. He carried on a spirited correspondence with many of the leading bibliographers and bookmen of his day. Falconer Madan (1851-1935) is associated primarily with his researches into Oxford books and his work is often cited as an admirable model for the investigation of the books of a specific locality. He also provided an admirable guide for students with his <u>Books in Manuscript</u>, which has been an influential introduction for hundreds of beginners since it first appeared in 1893.

Discovery of a St. Albans Book

Wadham College, Oxon.

The history of the first English presses, and of their early typographical productions, has always been a subject of great interest both to the antiquary and the bibliographer; but to no press is more mystery attached than to that situated at St. Albans, and worked by the unknown schoolmaster, at the time when Caxton was spreading the productions of the first English press over the country.

To the extreme rarity of the volumes from the St. Albans press we must ascribe the poverty of bibliographical detail concerning them. Herbert's edition of Ames' Typographical Antiquities, to which we first look for information, gives but the scantiest details, although it contains the only facsimile of the type used throughout this volume, namely, the smallest of the three types used at St. Albans. Dibdin, in his enlarged but unfinished edition of Ames, does not treat of the provincial presses. From this press there issued in the fifteenth century eight works, of which two are in English and the rest in Latin. Of the former, doubtless the best known is the Book of Hunting and Hawking, ascribed to Dame Juliana Berners, and brought recently into notice by the facsimile edited by W. Blades, Esq.; and the rarity of the original may be gathered from the fact that the sum of £630 was, within the last few years, paid for a copy by Mr. Quaritch.

It will no doubt interest many of your readers to hear that a copy of the Antonii Andreae Questiones super Logica (which is almost the rarest of the St. Albans books, and of which up to now only one copy has been known, discovered by Mr. Bradshaw at Cambridge) has recently been discovered at Oxford.

During my work at the fifteenth century books in the library of Wadham College, I found a fine and perfect copy of this book in a seventeenth century binding, and considering how little is known about it, a full and careful collation cannot fail to be of use.

Collation.--328 leaves.

a-z (omitting j, v, w), 2. 9. ., est, am̄,
A-O (omitting J, L) all in eights.
a1 is the only blank leaf.

Typographical Particulars.

There is no title-page. The lines, which are not always spaced out, form a page measuring about 3-3/4 x 5-3/4in., and there are thirty-two in a page. Signatures are used in the first half of each section, but there are no catchwords, nor are the leaves numbered.

The text ends on the recto of the 328th leaf with the following words:--

Explicit scriptū Antonii in sua logica
venetiis correctum.

The volume contains the following five treatises:--

Super librum Porphyrii, super librum
praedicamentorum Aristotelis, super 6 principia,
super primum librum periermenias, super
librum divisionum boecii.

The signatures of the first two gatherings are very incorrectly printed, and it is to be noticed that no capital L was used in the signatures (being, in fact, entirely absent from the book), whence probably arose the mistake in Mr. Blades's introduction to the book of St. Albans, where--in the tabular collation of this book--he gives the number of leaves at 335 printed, counting a gathering too much.

The water-mark throughout is a variety of the bull's head.   Ed. Gordon Duff.

Cambridge: Jan. 8, 1885.

Mr. Duff has kindly allowed me to read his note about the Antonius Andreae at Wadham College before sending it on to the Academy.

The existence of the book remained unnoticed, so far as I know, until September, 1861, when I lighted upon a copy in exploring the library of Jesus College in this University. It is in its original English binding; but it unfortunately wants the outer half-sheet of the first quire, the blank leaf 1 and the printed leaf 8.

An excellent photolithograph of leaf 275a (sig. G 3) appeared in the Annales du Bibliophile Belge et Hollandais (no. 8, p. 149, Bruxelles, Juin, 1865), at the end of an article headed "Un Incunable anglais inconnu," by M. Ch. Ruelens, of the Bibliothèque Royale. M. Alph. Willems had recently presented to the Brussels library a fragment of thirteen leaves, rescued from a book-cover, and M. Campbell, of the Hague, had recognised it as St. Albans type; but the book was, naturally enough, not identified. On reading the article I wrote at once to M. Ruelens, who published a translation of my letter to him in the August number of the Annales; and I was able to tell him that the thirteen leaves of his fragment were D 1, D 3, D 6, E 4, E 5, F 2, F 5, F 7, G 1, G 3, G 6, H 2, and H 7, of the Antonius Andreae.

Some years afterwards Mr. R. L. Bensly discovered another copy in the old library at Norwich; and, happening to spend a few hours there in 1880, I went to the museum to examine the book with my own eyes. I found that it was in the original binding, closely resembling that of the Jesus College copy, and also that it was happily quite perfect. A few months ago Dr. T. W. Bensly kindly brought the Norwich copy with him to Cambridge, and I was able to examine and collate it at leisure.

I am sorry to find that the Wadham College copy wants the whole quire signed L (leaves 305-312). It is certainly to be found in both the copies I have seen. The book actually consists of 336 leaves in forty-two quires. The apparently incorrect printing of the signatures at the beginning, noticed by Mr. Duff, is really a matter of particular interest. This is not the place to enter into technical details of typography; but it is lawful to mention that this book displays the first attempt, on the part of the St. Alban's schoolmaster, to print a quarto book by whole sheets, instead of by half-sheets, as he had done in his previous books. It may safely be assigned to the date 1481-82, by which I mean that it is later than the books bearing the printed date 1481. When these things come to be studied methodically, all such phenomena will have a plain meaning for the trained student, where the ordinary bibliographer would pass them over in silence, or treat them as perhaps careless mistakes. It is not too much to say that every one of the early St. Alban's books shows clear characteristics, by which its sequence in connection with its fellows may be traced and laid down with accuracy and with confidence. It is very encouraging to see the work that is at last being done in this field at Oxford by Mr. Madan, and others following (<u>longo intervallo</u>) in his footsteps. It may be looked upon as certain that, as soon as the College libraries there come to be explored with any intelligence, the search will be rewarded, as in the cases of Mr. Madan and Mr. Duff, by the discovery of volume after volume which will throw light upon the history of printing, and so, indirectly, upon the history of literature, in England.

HENRY BRADSHAW.

17. THE EARLY COLLECTION OF CANONS COMMONLY KNOWN AS THE HIBERNENSIS: A LETTER ADDRESSED TO DR. F. W. H. WASSERSCHLEBEN, PRIVY COUNCILLOR, PROFESSOR OF LAW IN THE UNIVERSITY OF GIESSEN

Published as Memorandum No. 8, June 1885. Reprinted in Collected Papers, 1889, pp. 410-420.

This paper demonstrates two things very clearly. The first is the close association which Bradshaw felt to exist between philology and bibliographical studies. In Bradshaw's case it is particularly apparent in connection with work which he did in the area of Celtic studies. It is important to remember that the three traditional areas of research in all textual studies have been literary, historical and linguistic. For the past hundred years or so bibliographical evidence has provided a fourth prop and its relationship with the other three must always be apparent.

The second point to be noticed is the clarity with which Bradshaw sets down his twelve propositions. The text under discussion is a complicated one, but the nature of Bradshaw's approach to the problem is to enumerate a number of individual points which need solution before the whole structure is clear.

King's College, Cambridge.
May 28, 1885.

My dear Sir,

As I find it is impracticable for me at present to put before you, as fully as I could wish, the results of several years' work upon the origin and earliest history of the collection of canons known commonly as the Hibernensis, I feel bound, after the communications which have recently passed between us, to send you a series of twelve propositions into which I have compressed some of the principal conclusions which I have been led to adopt chiefly from a study of the manuscripts in which the work has been preserved. You on your part cannot keep the press waiting, and I am absolutely without leisure during this portion of the year, so I must ask you to take what I am able to put together in the course of a few hours. In the propositions which I now submit to you, your own researches are only so far touched upon as they appear in your edition of 1874 and in your previous work on the Bussordnungen der abendländischen Kirche (Halle, 1851, 8vo.). If I have leisure during the next few months to present my work to you more in detail, I shall have had the further advantage of studying the results of your fresh researches in the new edition of the Hibernensis, which I hope to see before many weeks are over.

You must always bear in mind that my investigations started from a wholly different point from your own. The Hibernensis, which first came to my notice when Haddan and Stubbs were preparing their edition of the Councils, came afterwards to be a subject of more special study when I was engaged in searching for any volumes which might with certainty be looked upon as written (that is, transcribed) within the limits of Wales, Cornwall, and Brittany before the close of the eleventh century (A.D. 1100). Whatever I then found in the nature of contributions to the vernacular dialects, either new glosses or corrections of old ones, or scraps of verse, &c. I sent to Mr. Whitley Stokes, who printed them from time to time with a commentary of his own; and they have since been published in a more accessible and convenient form by M. J. Loth, being included in his <u>Vocabulaire Vieux-Breton avec commentaire</u> (Paris, 1884, 8vo.). My own primary object was to see and to learn what books these early people read and used and transcribed for their own use, and to observe what peculiarities they displayed in handwriting and other details connected with the production of books. In this way I hoped incidentally to provide a safer foundation, than then existed, on which the philologist might carry on his speculations, by seeing that the glosses to be expounded were more accurately read and that they were at any rate assigned to their right Latin words, thus saving much fruitless speculation. I soon found that the Latin books themselves, which contained the glosses, were of no interest to the Celtic philologist; whereas, for my purpose, even where the books contained specimens of classical literature, they never failed to present features of interest peculiar to themselves, while in cases where they had the appearance of being native productions, their interest in my eyes was naturally increased a hundred-fold.

I feel that a few words are necessary, on my part, to explain the persistence with which I have been led to bring the claims of Brittany into notice. My conclusions in this direction were wholly unforeseen by myself, and were only forced upon me from my constant work among the manuscripts. It was about 1871 that I first drew attention to the continental character of the handwriting of the Oxford manuscript of <u>Eutyches</u> formerly at Glastonbury, and of the Luxemburg fragments of the <u>Hisperica Famina</u> formerly at St. Wilbrord's monastery of Epternach. It seemed to me clearly impossible that they could have been written in Wales, though treated by Zeuss as Welsh. Further, in spite of a rooted determination to avoid all semblance of trespassing on the domain of philology, I could not help noticing that some of the grammatical forms appearing in these two manuscripts were, wherever distinguishable, rather

Breton than Welsh. The Celtic philologists, however, were unwilling, or did not care, to accept the suggestion. In point of fact, as no Breton literature was traceable back beyond the fifteenth century, and no scraps of the Breton dialect earlier than the twelfth century were known to exist, except those which occurred in stray names or phrases in the two eleventh-century cartularies of Redon and Landevennech, the suggestion was treated as almost too good to be true, and was certainly not to be accepted without caution. When, however, in 1876, book after book came to light, as I went from place to place in search of them, the philologists began gradually to waver. In the course of three or four weeks I came upon a Hibernensis at Oxford, an Amalarius at Cambridge, and two more copies of the Hibernensis in Paris; then, after training my eyes in undoubted Breton writing by a study of the cartulary of Landevennech at Quimper and of that of Redon at Rennes, I returned to England and found a fourth Hibernensis in the British Museum, all then first examined from this point of view and all containing in their vernacular glosses abundant evidence of Breton origin. And when, a year later, in 1877, I went to Orleans and found a fifth copy of the Hibernensis, with some 320 of these glosses, almost every page being sprinkled with them, all doubt was finally removed even from the minds of the philologists. This however did not concern my own particular studies. By the light of such overwhelming evidence it became clear that Brittany had been overlooked; that its long-forgotten history must be re-examined with care; and that a continuation of the search for scattered manuscripts bearing evidence of their having been written in the country, could not fail to be productive of fruitful results. By the accession of these new materials the study of the Breton dialect had been placed on an entirely new footing; and from the same cause it seemed to me as if the whole question of the origin of the Hibernensis and its associated literature would have to be reconsidered. At this point, as might be expected, your edition of the Hibernensis and your Bussordnungen der abendländischen Kirche, as well as Prof. Maassen's History,[1] came in for their share of criticism. The absolutely perfect methods adopted by yourself in editing these two books and by Prof. Maassen in his History, had naturally made me all the more eager to pursue my investigations into the subject when provided with such aids, the very using of which gave a double pleasure to the work. These three books had literally become my daily companions for several years. Now the more I worked at the contents of the manuscripts and the more I analysed their component parts and, above all, the evidence of origin afforded by the apparently miscellaneous entries in them (really the most instructive of all for this purpose), the more it became clear to me that the very perplexities exhibited in your books respecting the origin and earliest history and spread of the Hibernensis, and indeed of the whole group of these primitive British-Irish documents, would in great measure have been removed, if the true place of Brittany in the development of this literature had ever been recognised by you. And so my investigation went on, until, in 1880, circumstances occurred which compelled me to devote all my scanty leisure to a wholly different subject, though I fondly hoped that the discussion of the Hibernensis was laid aside only for a time.

In spite of the extremely egotistical nature of these remarks, I do not scruple to send them to you, as they will enable you to see at once that, since we start from such completely different points of view, our conclusions, however much they differ, can hardly be said to clash. My conclusions are, I believe, in no case directed against any arguments which have been brought forward by you, but serve rather to fill up the gaps which are left in your account of the development of the work.

I will only now interpose a very brief list of the manuscripts referred to in the ensuing propositions as either containing the Hibernensis or bearing most closely on its origin and early history. The

---
[1] (see page 233).

numbers follow those given in the Introduction to your edition of 1874, where they exist; and I have added numbers to those which are not so marked by you or are from other causes added by me to the list. The supposed Lyons manuscript does not, and never did, exist. The idea of its existence originated in a slip of the pen in Klee's notice in the Serapeum, from which all subsequent writers have gained their information instead of going back to Libri's original note in the Journal des Savants, which Klee was translating for the benefit of his German readers. I have marked with an asterisk those which I have examined myself.

No. 1. St. Gallen, Stiftsbibl. MS. 243. (I have photographic copies of two pages.)
No. 2. *Cambrai, Bibl. Comm. MS. 619 (formerly in the Cathedral library).
No. 3. *Paris, Bibl. Nat. MS. Lat. 12021 (formerly at St. Germain's, previously at Corbie, originally in Brittany).
No. 4. *Paris, Bibl. Nat. MS. Lat. 3182 (formerly in the Bigot collection, previously at Fécamp, originally in Brittany).
No. 5. Cologne, Dombibl. MS. 2178.
No. 6. Rome, Vallicelliana, MS. A. 18.
No. 7. *British Museum, MS. Cotton Otho E. XIII (formerly at St. Augustine's, Canterbury, originally in Brittany).
No. 8. *Chartres, Bibl. Comm. MS. 127 (formerly in the Cathedral library).
[No. 9. Strassburg, now lost.]
No. 10. *Orleans, Bibl. Comm. MS. 193 (formerly at Fleury on the Loire, originally in Brittany).
No. 11. *Oxford, Bodl. Libr. MS. Hatton 42 (formerly at Glastonbury, originally in Brittany).
No. 12. *Tours, Bibl. Comm. MS. 556 (formerly at Marmoutier).
No. 13. *Cambrai, Bibl. Comm. MS. 576 (formerly in the Cathedral library).
No. 14. *Cambridge, Corpus Christi College, MS. 279 (formerly at Worcester, originally in what is now Belgium or France).

The following are some of the propositions,

which I hope to be able to substantiate, or to see substantiated by others, when the materials at our disposal have been more fully and methodically studied.

I.

That the thirteen existing manuscripts (nos. 1, 2, 3, 4, 5, 6, 7, 8, 10, 11, 12, 13, 14), which either contain the Hibernensis or bear most closely on its origin and early history, were all written on the continent, and none of them in England or Ireland.

II.

That five of these manuscripts (nos. 1, 5, 6, 8, 12) afford no independent evidence concerning the origin and earliest history of the Hibernensis.

III.

That five others of these manuscripts (nos. 3, 4, 7, 10, 11) contain [not Irish, as has been stated, but] Breton interlinear or marginal glosses, and must have been written in Brittany, one by a Breton scribe Arbedoc for a Breton abbat Hael-Hucar (no. 3), another by a Breton scribe Maeloc (no. 4), and a third by a Breton scribe Junobrus (no. 10).

IV.

That the remaining three of these manuscripts (nos. 2, 13, 14), though not themselves written in Brittany, show marks of very close relationship with one or more of the above five Brittany manuscripts.

V.

That two clearly marked recensions of the Hibernensis are traceable:
    (1) the A-text, arranged under 65 tituli, where the latest author cited is Theodore, who died in 690, and he only from that form of his Penitential which has been preserved exclusively in our Brittany manuscripts; and

(2) the B-text, arranged under 68 tituli, where the latest author cited is Adamnan, who died in 704, and he only from that form of the Canons attributed to him which has been preserved exclusively in our five Brittany manuscripts; and that both of these texts are found in an unsophisticated state in these Brittany manuscripts (no. 3, A-text; no. 4, A-text; no. 7, A-text, with supplement of B-text; no. 10, A-text; no. 11, B-text).

VI.

That these five Brittany manuscripts (nos. 3, 4, 7, 10, 11) are distinguished by the peculiarity that they all, and they alone, contain annexed to the Hibernensis the two pieces known as the Excerpta ex libris Romanorum et Francorum and the Canones Adamnani; and that the titles thus given to these two pieces may without difficulty be shown to point to Ireland as the quarter in which these titles would most naturally be assigned to them.

VII.

That three of the manuscripts more or less closely connected with Brittany (no. 3 written there, and nos. 2 and 14 not written there) bear undeniable marks of being derived from manuscripts which had been in Irish hands, though evidently themselves written by scribes unacquainted with the Irish language.

VIII.

That the Hibernensis was compiled at the opening of the eighth century by an Irish monk or abbat of Dairinis in the south-east of Ireland, and that the name and home of the compiler may yet be recognised, although buried in the Breton scribe's corruptly written rubric, which stands thus

Hucvsq; nubeN & cv. cuiminiae. & du rinis

in what is certainly the most primitive, although not

perhaps the oldest, of all the existing copies of the Hibernensis (no. 3).

IX.

That this hitherto unrecognised compiler of the Hibernensis may, without any strain either of language or of evidence, be looked upon as possibly identical with the Cummeanus abbas in Scotia ortus to whom the penitential literature of the eighth century is so much indebted; who, it is allowed, must of necessity have been an Irishman settled on the continent at the opening of the eighth century, thus being precisely contemporary with the compiler of the Hibernensis; while his materials stand in the closest possible connexion with the materials used in the Hibernensis, exhibiting, as they do, a combination of Frankish documents with others of British and Irish origin which are only known to us at present as preserved in and through Brittany by means of one or other of the manuscripts included in our list.

X.

That we shall not render ourselves liable to the charge of rashness or hasty speculation if we regard as one and the same person,
(1) the Gildas cited in the Hibernensis and in the kindred compilation which is included in one of the manuscripts (no. 14) which shows an intimate connexion with our Brittany series;
(2) the Gildas to whom we owe the formation of the only remaining collection of British Synods (the Synodus Luci Victoriae, the Synodus Aquilonalis Brittaniae, the Excerpta ex libro Davidis, with a Praefatio by Gildas himself prefixed to the collection), which has been transcribed, with additions from Theodore and Adamnan, into one of our Brittany manuscripts (no. 4) and thence into another (no. 13);
(3) the British Gildas, to whom (with Cadoc and David) the "second order" of Irish saints, the Catholic presbyters, owed their form of service; and

(4) the Gildas who, after working in Britain and Ireland, passed over into Brittany, where he spent the remainder of his life and died in the monastery founded by himself at Ruys in the south of Brittany.

XI.

That Brittany is the district,--long overlooked, so that even Wasserschleben and Maassen failed to recognise it,--the one district on the continent, where British and Irish documents existed side by side with those of Frankish origin, and where alone (so far as our present knowledge extends) such compilations as those cited in the <u>Hibernensis</u> and occurring in our Brittany and closely allied manuscripts (nos. 2, 3, 4, 7, 10, 11, 13, 14) were to be found in the eighth and early ninth centuries.

XII.

That the decay of the Celtic institutions in Brittany (as in Scotland and elsewhere) was completed under the influence of the new and revived religious life which permeated western Europe in the twelfth century; and that the most precious and useful books were then transferred from Brittany to the great monasteries of the new life, precisely as, owing to the religious and political movements of the sixteenth, the eighteenth, and the nineteenth centuries in England, in France and Germany, and in Italy respectively, the treasures of the dissolved religious houses were dispersed, and have now to be looked for in the national and municipal or university and collegiate libraries in their respective countries; while the old and faultily written copies, the <u>libri vetusti et inutiles</u>, which would now be priceless in our eyes for historical purposes, were left naturally to perish, so that the marvel is that any such remnants should have been allowed to survive to the present day.

Until you have fuller materials before you, these propositions may at least serve the purpose of suggestions. They may perhaps lead some student to take pleasure in pursuing the investigation further; and if they are but honestly pursued, light will assuredly come to clear up what is a deeply interesting, even though a most obscure, question in literary history.

Yours most sincerely,

HENRY BRADSHAW.

To Dr. F. W. H. Wasserschleben.

NOTE

It may be as well to print here certain extracts from the introduction to the Bussordnungen der abendländischen Kirche (Halle, 1851, 8vo.) and from Maassen's Geschichte (Gratz, 1871, 8vo.), to which allusion has been made in the preceding pages. They are passages which concern the problem of the coexistence of British-Irish and Frankish documents in the same volume, especially in the Paris manuscript (Lat. 3182) which is marked no. 4 in our list. Mr. Haddan, in the first volume of the Councils (Oxford, 1869, 8vo. p. 116), speaks of the canons of the British synods as "documents, preserved in the north of France, obviously through Brittany"; but unfortunately there is no trace of any independent research in that part of his book, and this suggestion, or rather assumption, on his part never led him on to any further investigations or conclusions. When treating afterwards of Brittany he makes no allusion to the subject. Had any of these writers realised that the great Paris manuscript and others containing similar literature were written in Brittany, had they made any anatomical study of the manuscripts themselves, I feel sure that almost all that I have said in the preceding pages would have long since been anticipated.

Zu den bestrittensten und dunkelsten Fragen in der Geschichte der Bussordnungen gehört die über Alter und Ursprung des Pönitentials, welches dem Kommean oder Kummean oder Kumian, (Kumin, Komin) zugeschrieben wird... Wasserschleben, Bussordnungen, p. 61.

In Betreff des Vaterlandes waren bis jetzt Alle einig, Kummean und sein Werk galt als irischen oder schottischen Ursprungs, und die Bezeichnung des Verfassers in der St Gallener Handschrift als abbas in Scotia ortus schien diese Annahme ausser Zweifel zu stellen. Gleichwohl ist diese eine irrige, und selbst jene Bezeichnung deutet entschieden darauf hin, dass Kummean seine Bussordnung nicht in seinem Vaterlande verfasste, sondern sich in einem andern Lande befand. Betrachten wir die Quellen, aus welchen Kummean schöpfte, so finden wir zunächst hibernische Kanonen und eine reiche Benutzung namentlich Theodor's... Id. ib., pp. 63-64.

Ausser Theodor ist von Kummean, wie ich schon oben erwähnte, eine andere Sammlung vielfach benutzt, welche auch ausserdem besonders durch ihr irisches Material interessant ist, und welch ich Poenitentiale Bigotianum genannt habe, nach der einzigen Handschrift, welche von ihr erhalten ist. Dieselbe befindet sich im Cod. Paris. reg. 3182, früher Bigot. 89, pp. 286-299, demselben, aus welchem ich die meisten irischen und altbritischen Bussordnungen mitgetheilt habe,... Ausser zahlreichen hibernischen Kanonen unter der Inscription: canones sapientium et Gregorii, canones patrum, u. A. auch aus dem Werke des Vinniaus, und ausser dem Theodor'schen Pönitential, sind fränkische Beichtbücher, Cassianus und die Vitae Sanctorum vielfach benutzt, so dass die Vermuthung, der Verfasser sei ein Irländer gewesen und habe diess Werk im fränkischen Reiche zusammengestellt, sehr nahe liegt. Id. ib., pp. 67-68.

Der Stamm dieser Zusammenstellung [Cod. Paris. Lat. 3182], wohin ich die irische Sammlung, die irischen, altbritischen, und angelsächsischen Busscanonen, die Excerpte aus der h. Schrift und aus den Kirchenvätern rechne, ist ohne Zweifel irischen Ursprungs. Ihrem Urheber stand im wesentlichen derselbe Quellenkreis zu Gebote wie dem Autor der irischen Sammlung. Wahrscheinlich ist, dass die übrigen Stücke erst auf fränkischem Boden an diesen Stamm gesetzt sind, dass also die Verbindung, wie sie in der Handschrift von Fécamp vorliegt, nicht irischen, sondern fränkischen Ursprungs ist. Maassen, Geschichte, p. 786.

[Note. This letter is printed at length by Dr. Wasserschleben in the introduction to his second edition (Leipzig, 1885, 8°), with criticisms which, as Mr. Bradshaw felt, shew little appreciation of the line of enquiry upon which these conclusions are founded.

As for the rubric quoted on p. 228, Mr. Whitley Stokes suggested "Ruben" for "nuben," and I remember Mr. Bradshaw regarded the second & as an error for "ex," the two being much alike. J.]

Note

1. Geschichte der Quellen und der Literatur des canonischen Rechts im Abendlande bis zum Ausgange des Mittelalters. Bd. I. Gratz, 1870-71, 8vo.

18. A HALF-CENTURY OF NOTES ON THE DAY-BOOK OF JOHN DORNE, BOOKSELLER IN OXFORD, A.D. 1520, AS EDITED BY F. MADAN FOR THE OXFORD HISTORICAL SOCIETY

Contributed by Henry Bradshaw. 1886.

    This little work holds a rather special place in the corpus of Bradshaw's work, because it is the last piece of bibliographical writing which he completed before his death. His letter to Madan is dated January 30, 1886 and he died on February 10, 1886.

    Falconer Madan had edited the <u>Day-Book of John Dorne</u> for the Oxford Historical Society and sent a copy to Bradshaw, whose reaction to this is made very clear by his letter of thanks to Madan. As was his wont, he noted and annotated the work out of the richness of his learning and experience, and returned the fruits of his endeavors to Madan.

    After his death Bradshaw's friends edited his "notes" for publication. The "J" of the footnotes is Francis Jenkinson.

'Whatsoever thy hand findeth to do, do it with thy might; for there is no work, nor device, nor knowledge, nor wisdom, in the grave, whither thou goest.' Ecclesiastes, 9, 10.

A
Half-Century of Notes

on the

Day-Book of John Dorne

Bookseller in Oxford, A.D. 1520,

as edited by

F. Madan

for the

Oxford Historical Society.

Contributed
by
Henry Bradshaw.

Cambridge:
1886.

+ 'Quasi morientes et ecce vivimus'.

[The Day-book, to which these notes refer, is preserved in the library of Corpus Christi College, Oxford. It consists of 16 leaves, upon which John Dorne has entered, in double column and on both sides of the paper, the books he sold and their prices. The mention of various saints' days, together with Dorne's habit of drawing a line at the end of a day's transactions, has made it possible for Mr. Madan to indicate throughout the list the exact day to which each entry belongs. He has also numbered the entries consecutively (1-1851); and the numbers placed by Mr. Bradshaw before the titles quoted in his notes refer to this numeration. The higher numbers (1852-1952) do not belong to Dorne's list at all, but to an older document (written on the fly-leaf of a volume in the Bodleian), which Mr. Madan has printed at the end of the Day-book of John Dorne. It is an inventory (with prices) of books received in 1483 for sale by John Hunt, stationer of the university of Oxford, from Magister Peter Actor and Johannes de Aquisgrano; to whom he promises to restore the books or pay the price affixed in the list. Of Mr. Bradshaw's notes nos. 9, 17, 22, 24, 25, 38, 40, 42, 43, 48 relate to this earlier collection. J.]

King's College, Cambridge.
January 30, 1886.

My dear Madan,

  The care and patience with which you have edited the Day-Book of John Dorne ought to have secured you an earlier acknowledgement on my part. The separate-copy reached me at the beginning of this week; and, as it happens that I have been unequal to much serious work during the interval, the interest and amusement which such a book naturally provides for me has come at a most welcome time.

  I have been through it over and over again, every time finding some new light which it throws upon the subject in which we both feel a strong interest. To show you the sincerity of my thanks, I have put down a few notes in which I have brought some of the entries to bear upon one another with very satisfactory results. You will be glad to have them, though I dare say many of them express rash views which may have been entertained by yourself for a moment, but have been rejected on the second thoughts which come before final publication. The notes are arranged in the order of your first Index, and I have added a small supplementary Index, in which I have endeavoured to follow your admirable method.

  It is not until such a book is actually in print, with the contractions and abbreviations all honestly marked, just as you have done here, that it becomes possible to investigate the further problems which such a document presents. It augurs well for your Historical Society, if the publications continue to show the same amount of intelligent care which you have brought to bear upon this.

       Yours very sincerely,

        HENRY BRADSHAW.

LIST OF ENTRIES ILLUSTRATED IN THE FOLLOWING NOTES

1. Esopus grecus 1 quaternus.
2. Miraculum sancti augustini.
3. Quaterni of barkely.
4. Modus viuendi omnium fo (qu. fidelium?).
5. Breuiarium romanum pro fratribus augustinianis.
6. Carmen juuenile (Stans puer ad mensam in latino).
" Stans puer ad mensam in englis.
7. The lyf of san kerasinus.
8. Cronica anglie van 2 quaterni.
9. Complot...(?)
10. Cokeri.
11. Ciclus vel almanack.
12. Diurnale sarum.
13. Colloquia erasmi alst.
" Colloquia erasmi lo(uanii).
14. Colloquia erasmi de 9^{es}(?).
15. ff vetus textus paruum.
16. Frans end englis.
17. Preceptorium godscalcj.
18. Hackū end hōtigle.
19. Husbandry.
20. Hymni cum nottis.
21. Festum de nomine Jhesu paruum.
" Primarium premonstra[ten]sium in 2^{bus} ant[iquum].
22. Glosa super apocalipsim.
23. Saint jon euuangeliste en trelute (?).
24. Johannes de vassolis in 4to sententiarum.
25. Postille de sancto laurentio.
26. Opusculum insolubilium (oxonie).
27. Lynwodde.
" Constitutiones prouinciales.
28. Epistole karoli.
29. Sant margerit lyf.
30. Lamentation of our lady.
31. The myracke of our lady ypsuwise (?).
32. Rosarium beate marie virginis.
33. The complant of sant magda(lene).
34. Medulla grammatice.
35. Mundus a play.
36. Opusculum de vera nobi(litate).
37. Pamphulus de amore.
38. Epistole petri blesensis.
39. Pronosticon in en bigls (?).
40. De Restitutionibus.
41. The lyf of sant rocke.
42. Sermones XIII.
43. Quinque specula.
44. Spera heginy.
45. Summa angelica.
46. Theologia naturalis.
47. Theorica planetarum.
48. Walensis super psalterium.
49. Virgilius in englis van 4 quaterni.
50. Tractatus sacer de^{ls} (?).

[XXIV.] A HALF-CENTURY OF NOTES ON
F. MADAN'S EDITION OF THE "DAY-BOOK OF
JOHN DORNE, BOOKSELLER IN OXFORD,
A.D. 1520"

Notes on Index I (Authors and Books)

1 Aesopus.

 1245 1 esopus grecus 1 quaternus (with 2 others). 4^d.
  This can hardly be an Esop in Greek. 'Esopus Grecus' is the usual title of the "Facecie morales Laur. Vallensis alias Esopus grecus," of which there were seven editions printed in the Netherlands alone in the fifteenth century, each consisting of one quire (6 leaves in 4°, '1 quaternus'); see CA. 31-37. [Throughout these notes CA stands for Campbell's Annales de la Typographie Néerlandaise au xve siècle, La Haye, 1874, 8°.]

2 Augustinus (S. Aurelius).

 127 1 miraculum sancti augustini. 1^d.
  This seems less likely to refer to St. Augustine of Hippo than to St. Augustine of Canterbury, one of whose miracles in raising a dead body at Long Compton forms the subject of a poem which was very popular in the xvth century. An edition of it printed at Canterbury stands first in the list of books printed there, as given by Herbert.

3 Barclay (Alexander).

 1254 7 quaterni of barkely. 3^d.

Surely the 7 here, as elsewhere in this Daybook, means seven copies of what was sold. The price shows that it must have been something very small, ½d each and one thrown in when half a dozen were taken.

4 Bernardus (S.) Clarae-vallensis.

133   1 modus viuendi ounn (= one?) fo[lio]. 3½d.
I think ounn must be written not oūn but oīm=omnium, and if fo can be read fi, the book is probably Gerson's De modo vivendi omnium fidelium, of which you will find a separate edition in CA. 815 (Louvain, Jo. de Westfalia, about 1484), and a combined but separable edition in CA. 821+818+818 note (Antwerp, Math. Goes, ab. 1487). See also Hain *7671 (with two other treatises by Gerson), 30 leaves 4°.

5 Breviarium.

764   1 breuiarium romanum pro fratribus augustinianis li'. 3s 4d.
This pro fratribus can hardly mean that this book was sold to them, but that it was printed for them. The Augustinian Friars or Hermits adopted the Roman use, so they naturally used the Roman Breviary. But further than this, we have an edition of the Roman Breviary (1508, 8°), with the Kalendar modified and an Appendix added to the book (printed with it) containing special offices for the use of the Austin Friars. A purchaser is mentioned differently; 730 to gybs; see also 174, 1790, and 830, 1179.

6 Carmen juvenile.

166a   1 stans puer ad mensam. 1d.
166c   1 Stans puer ad mensam. 1d.
377   1 stans puer ad mensam. 1d.
536   1 stans puer ad mensam in quarternis (with another). 11d.

565	2 stans puer ad mensam.	2ᵈ.
575	2 carmen juuenile (with 5 others of Stanbridge).	9ᵈ.
671	2 stans puer ad mensam.	2ᵈ.
684	5 stans puer ad mensam in quaternis (with 7 others).	4ᵈ.
929	1 Stans puer ad mensam 1 quaternus.	1ᵈ.
1069	1 Stans puer ad mensam (with two others).	5ᵈ.
1084	1 stans puer ad mensam 9 [1?] quater' (with two others).	4ᵈ.
1088	1 Stans puer ad mensam.	1ᵈ.
1221	6 stans puer ad mensam in 1a° [latino?].	6ᵈ.
1484	2 stans puer ad mensam in en[glis] (with two others).	6ᵈ.
1679	1 stans puer ad mensam (with another).	8ᵈ.

The original Latin is by Joh. Sulpitius Verulanus, and in W. de Worde's edition of 1518 is entitled 'Stans puer ad mensam. Iuuenile carmen de moribus puerorum in mensa seruandis.' In CA. 1623-1625 are three Deventer editions printed between 1490 and 1500. In these the title is 'Ioannis Sulpicii Verulani de moribus puerorum Carmen Iuuenile'; and here as in the London editions the work consists of a single quire, whether of 4 or 6 leaves. No. 575 may be a foreign edition, and the rest printed in London. From No. 929 we see that it consisted of a single quire. No. 1484 is Lidgate's version of the poem in 7-line stanzas, which was printed by Caxton (1477-78, 4 leaves, 4°) and again by W. de Worde, with the Book of Courtesy or Little John subjoined to it. We have copies of both editions here.

7 Cerasinus (St.).

1110	1 the lyf of sant erasmus.	1ᵈ.
1625	1 the lyf of san kerasinus.	1ᵈ.

I think these two entries must refer to the same book. Dorne is frequently at fault

when he has to deal with English books. The
addition of this life is what distinguishes the
second from the first issue of Caxton's large
folio edition of the Golden Legend (1st issue
about 1484, 2nd issue about 1490). This fact,
which was unknown to Mr. Blades when he wrote
his book, may serve to date the rise of the cultus of St. Erasmus, which had certainly become
widely spread by 1520. His name is written in
an extraordinary variety of ways, as may be
seen from the extracts from the parish accounts
of Trinity Church, Cambridge, which I printed
a short time ago in the Communications of the
Cambridge Antiquarian Society. The actual
book sold by Dorne is not unlikely to have
been a copy of the separate Life of St. Erasmus
printed by Julian Notary (London, 1520, 4
leaves, 4°) noticed by Herbert. It is in the
British Museum (296. h. 7).

8   <u>Chronica Angliae.</u>

993   1 cronica anglie 2 qua[<u>ternis</u>]. 1^d.
1027 1 cronica anglie van 2 qua[<u>terni</u>] (with
     2 others). 4^d.

The two quires are two single quarto sheets
(each of four leaves and printed separately),
the first containing the Kings' names in order
from the fabulous Kings of Britain downwards,
and the second starting from William the Conqueror and bringing the list down to Henry
VIII. whose accession it mentions (1509), but
adds no details of his reign, having all the appearance of having been compiled shortly after
the accession of Henry VIII. We have copies of
both, printed by W. de Worde, the second part
bearing the date 1530. (This copy is mentioned
by Herbert, p. 181.) It is natural to assume
that earlier editions were printed between 1509
and 1520, which may have been for sale in Dorne's
shop.

Excerpts from the Works / 243

9 Complot...

    1932   Complot...
    1933   Complot...p

    You must have overlooked the fact that these books were not sold by Dorne in 1520, but were offered for sale by Hunt in 1483, and therefore cannot "conceivably" have reference to the Complutensian Polyglot Bible.

10 Cookery.

    219   1 cokery (with another). 4^d.
    905   1 the bocke of kockery. 4^d.
    1442   1 the bocke of cokeri (with another). 4^d.
    1815   1 the bocke of kokery. 4^d.

    The edition printed by Pynson in 1500 consists of 62 leaves in 4°, so that the price is not unsuitable. It may interest some of your readers to learn that this "noble book of feasts" shown to Herbert by the Duchess of Portland (who, it may be remembered, was the only child and heir of Edward Harley, 2nd Earl of Oxford, the collector of the "Harleian Library") passed to her _eldest_ daughter, who was the wife of the 1st Marquis of Bath; and the book is consequently, by natural descent, now to be found in the library of her great-grandson, the present and 4th Marquis of Bath, at Longleat.

11 Cyclus.

    235   1 ciclus. 1^d.
    290   1 ciclus vel almanack. 1^d.

    All the 27 entries, which are not worth writing out, are with one exception (359 1 Ciclus pronosticon 1^d), either _Ciclus vel almanack_ or simply _Ciclus_, and always cost $\overline{1d}$ when sold separately. I cannot think that the word Ciclus has any reference to the circular form in which the months and festivals were disposed on the sheet, but rather that it was a sheet containing the current 19-year or 28-year cycle, or some other definite number of years, with the days of Easter and other moveable feasts added in successive columns. Such a cycle, sometimes called a Tabula, sometimes an Almanack, for so many years, is frequently found in Breviaries, occupying a page immediately following the Kalendar.

12 Diurnale.

298   1 diurnale sarum. 1s 4d.

The price is that of a single volume of the small Rouen edition of the Portos (Portiforium), as may be seen in nos 1131 and 1620; and the Diurnale, as containing all the day-hours, that is all the Hours with the omission of Mattins, would naturally run to about that size. A copy of the edition printed in Paris for sale in London (1512, 16°) is in the Lambeth Library, and mention is made, in the preface to this edition, of two earlier and less correctly printed editions. It is described in Dr. Maitland's List, and it is also in Mr. F. H. Dickinson's List of service-books.

13 Erasmus (Desiderius).

688   1 colloquia erasmi alst. 4d.
1141   1 erasmus de constructione louani. 3d. [You have printed this louani; are the italic and roman letters here accidentally changed about, or what does it mean?]
1195   1 colloquia erasmi alst. 4d.
1234   1 enchiridion paruum alst ligatum in pergameno. 10d.
1261   1 colloquia erasmi alst. 4d.
1272   1 formule colloquiorum erasmi alst. 4d.
1367   1 enchiridion erasmi paruum lo[uanii] ligatum in pergameno recepi. 2s. (With another book) 2s.
1377   1 Enchiridion erasmi lo[uanii?] (with another book). 1s 2d.
1389   1 enchiridion erasni lova[nii]. 6d.
1537   1 erasmus de constructione lo[uanii] liga-

tus in pergameno recepi 1^S. (With another book) 1^S.
1599   1 colloquia erasmi lo[uanii]. 4^d.
1739   1 colloquia erasmi lo[uanii]. 4^d.

  Aalst or Aelst is the vernacular name of the town which we know as Alost. Thierry Martens, the friend of Erasmus and printer of many of his books, having started as a printer in his native town of Alost, removed to Antwerp in 1493 and afterwards to Louvain; and he is called by himself and his friends indiscriminately either Theodoricus Martini or Theodoricus Alostensis. The above list of entries tend to shew that Dorne distinguished Thierry Martens' editions from others at first by the printer's name (Alst) and afterwards by the place of their publication (lo- or loua-nii).

14 Erasmus (Desiderius).

1387   1 colloquia erasmi de q^{es} [?] ⎫
1388   1 erasmus de constructione   ⎬ . 8^d.
                                          ⎭

  Is it possible that "de q^{es}" may have been Dorne's first entry of the De constructione, which, seeing that it was actually a separate book from the colloquia, he at once re-wrote on the next line, without erasing the first incorrect entry? Is the final letter of "q^{es}" quite clear, and is it the letter q or ꝯ =con?

15 Ff.

1359   1 ff vetus textus paruum ligatum. 2^S.

  You have placed the similar entry (629 1 codex paruum ligatum 6^S) under Justinianus in your index; so this ought to have been placed there also, being a copy of the Digestum Vetus (commonly written Ff vetus), the text only, without gloss, in small size.

16 French and English.

117   1 frans and englis (with 3 others).

1^s 2^d.
942   1 frans end english (with another). 2^d.
          Besides Caxton's edition, which you mention, there is one printed at Westminster by W. de Worde (ab. 1498), 4°, in the Grenville collection. In the Douce volume containing "Early Typographical Fragments" n° 6 is a fragment of Caxton's edition (ab. 1480), F°. and n° 18/ is a fragment of W. de Worde's 4°. There is also a third, printed by Pynson, in the British Museum, and Dorne's books may belong to any of these editions.

17 Godeschalcus (Johannes).

1905   Preceptorium godscalcj 1 7^s 4^d.
          Surely this is the <u>Praeceptorium divinae legis</u> of Gottschalcus Hollen, the Augustinian Hermit, of which Hain gives several editions (8765-8770), one of them at least early enough to find a place in Hunt's list.

18 Hackum and Hontigle.

1018   1 Hackum end hontigle. 4^d.
          You will think me very bold (or rather presumptuous), but Dorne shows himself so hopeless where he has to deal with English books, that I am quite prepared to see, through the mist of this entry, the little quarto pamphlet issues of "Hawking" and "Hunting" issued by W. de Worde about this time. We have the "Hunting" in our library, and the "Fishing" is well known. The price would suit perfectly for such a book.

19 Husbandry.

1323   1 husbandry. 1^d.
          Our copy of the edition you mention, which is certainly from W. de Worde's press, cannot be later than 1510 (12 leaves, 4°). It is attributed to Bp Grosseteste (Groshead) as translator.

20 Hymni.

   1346^b (not 1345)   1 hymni cum nottis lig' (with two
      others).   3^s 8^d.
   1802   1 liber hymnorum cum nottis li'.   1^s 4^d.
       The Hymni cum notis seem to have been
   first published in 1518, after which date several
   editions are found. The book thus exactly takes
   the place of the school-book Expositio hymnorum,
   which was published almost every year (sometimes twice in one year) from 1496 to 1518, when
   the latest known edition appeared.

21 Jesus Christ.

   968   1 primarium premonstra[ten]sium in 2^bus
            ant[iquum] [no price]
   969   1 festum de nomine Jhesu paruum   4^s 6^d.
   979   1 festum de nomine Jhesu par[is]   4^d.
   1013   2 festum de nomine Jhesu li[gatum] per-
            gameno   2^s 7^d.
       This seems to be a separate copy of the
   office for the Name of Jesus, which is kept on
   the 7th of August. Being quite a recent festival, it is not to be found in any of the old editions of the Breviary or Missal. It is worth notice that these copies are all entered by Dorne
   under August 5. [When I wrote this, I did not
   understand Dorne's mode of entry. I now see
   that two copies (969, 979) were sold on the actual festival of the Name of Jesus (August 7),
   and the third (1013) two days later, while the
   services of the octave were still going on.] The
   British Museum has a copy printed by Pynson
   about 1493, in 4°., and Mr. Horner, of Mells,
   has one printed by Pynson about 1497, also in 4°.
   In your first entry I cannot help thinking that
   the two books (968, 969) should have been
   bracketed together, with 4^s 6^d as the price
   for the two. I should then prefer to read
   breuiarium rather primarium, and it might then
   (being antiquum) refer to the Praemonstraten-
   sian Breviary printed by Thierry Martens at

Alost in 1488. It is difficult also to see how a Primer could either form two volumes or reach such a price. Besides all which it must be remembered that <u>Primarium</u> was a peculiarly Anglican name, and of the only other two similar entries you give (183 Cisterciense and 293 Car[thusianum?]), the second is at least very doubtful. In 979 I should prefer, if possible, that <u>par</u> should stand for par[<u>uum</u>] (see 969) rather than for par[<u>is</u>], as I believe you do sometimes expand it. All the recently Paris-printed breviaries contained the office in its place under August 7, and the only separate editions traceable are those printed in the interval between the introductions of the new festival and the incorporation of the office into the books, that is, between 1420 and 1500. I have never seen or heard of any foreign-printed edition of any of the English <u>Nova Festa</u>. We know, besides the two by Pynson of the Name of Jesus, one by Caxton, and one by W. de Machlinia of the Visitation of the BVM, and one by Caxton and one by W. de Machlinia of the Transfiguration, and one by Caxton of the Compassion of the BVM.

22   <u>Johannes (S.) Evangelista</u>.

1917   Glosa super apocalipsim 4 quilibet.   8^d.

This must be the work of Joannes Viterbiensis entitled "Glosa super Apocalipsim de statu ecclesie ab anno salutis presenti sc. M.cccc.lxxxj. vsque ad finem mundi et de preclaro et gloriosissimo triumpho Christianorum in Turcos & Maumetos quorum secta et imperium breuiter incipiet deficere ex fundamentis Joannis in Apocalipsi et ex sensu litterali eiusdem apertissimo cum consonantia et iudiciis astrorum." Editions printed at Louvain by Jo. de Westfalia and at Gouda by Ger. Leeu are given in CA. 1276 and 1277; and either would answer to the entry in Hunt's list of 1483. The Gouda edition is in your Auctarium, Q. inf. 1. 8.

23 Johannes (S.) Evangelista.

1553   1 saint jon euuangeliste en trelute [?]. 1ᵈ.
You will say I am too severe upon Dorne's English, but it seems quite within the range of possibility that this may be a short interlude, of which St. John formed the subject, resembling the similar productions which Bale mentions among his own writings as 'in idiomate materno comoedias sub diuerso metrorum genere.' Compare the price of 'Mundas a play' under N° 1530.

24 Johannes de Vassolis.

1895   Johanes de vassolis in 4ᵗᵒ sententiarum 1. 4ˢ 8ᵈ.
The letters v and b are often confounded in writing, reading, and speaking. Johannes de Bassoliis (or Bassolis) was a favourite disciple of Scotus himself, and Wadding, in his Scriptores Ord. Min., mentions a revised edition of this author's work on the four books of the sentences as having been printed at Paris (apud Nic. de Pratis) in 1517. It is not improbable that an earlier edition, now lost, may have found a place in Hunt's list of 1483. The school-name for this author as quoted by Wadding is Doctor ornatissimus, while in Mansi's Fabricius it is given as Doctor ordinatissimus. While speaking of Hunt's list may I ask whether it consists of two separate leaves, or of two leaves still forming a sheet? Unless they are necessarily joined together, would it not be more natural to look upon Hunt's heading as standing at the beginning of the whole list, so that what you have printed as Nᵒˢ 1889 to 1917 should take precedence of Nᵒˢ 1852-1888?

25 Laurentius (S.).

1911   Postille de scō laurentio 1. 3ˢ 4ᵈ.
The book here mentioned in Hunt's list must be the "Postille euangeliorum dominicalium

totius anni et aliquorum festorum" of Johannes de sancto Laurentio printed at Brussels in 1480, a small folio of 198 leaves (CA. 1041). You have a copy in your Auctarium, marked 6Q. 2. 7.

26 Logica.

482	1 Jnsolubilium oxonie.	1^d.
505	1 Jnsolubilium oxonie.	1^d.
1024	2 Jnsolubilium.	2^d.
1051	1 Jnsolubilum.	1^d.
1518	2 Jnsolubilium.	2^d.
1720	1 Jnsolubilium.	1^d.
1730	1 Jnsolubilium erasmi [sic].	1^d.
1800	1 opusculum J[n]solubilium.	1^d.
1806	2 J[n]solubilium.	2^d.
1813	1 jnsolubilium (with 2 others).	2^d.

As the price never exceeds a penny, it is inconceivable that these entries can refer to Swyneshed's Insolubilia, which is a fairly thick quarto volume, as printed at Oxford about 1483-85. It seems rather to be a single sheet of the same kind as the "Bene fundatum oxonie" which was sold with n° 1813.

27 Lyndewode (Gulielmus).

872	1 lynwodde ligatus.	6^s 8^d.
1356	1 lynwodde ligatus.	6^s 8^d.
577	1 constitutiones prouinciales ligate in corio (with another).	2^s 1^d.
1600	1 constitutiones prouinciales ligate in corio.	6^d.

The first two entries may well refer to the Provinciale with Lyndewode's large commentary, as it exists in the great folio edition printed at Oxford about 1483-85, though the price would seem rather to point to one of the less bulky Paris reprints of 1505. The last two entries are probably the bare text of the Constitutions as printed by W. de Worde in 1496 and 1499 in small 8°. You have copies of both among Mr. Douce's xvth cent. books, 12 (1496) and 2 (1499).

28 Maneken (Carolus).

    381   1 epistole karoli. 5^d.

Campbell mentions eleven editions of this book printed in the Low Countries alone in the fifteenth century (CA. 1201-1211), but in that printed at Deventer by Jac. de Breda June 16, 1496 (74 leaves, 4°), the title consists of the very words entered by Dorne, corresponding letter for letter.

29 Margaret (St.).

    387   1 sant Margerit lyf. 3½^d.
    675   1 sant margerit lyff (with another similar). 4^d.

Besides the edition by Mychell and an earlier one by Redman (12 leaves in 4°) Hazlitt mentions a fragment of 2 leaves as existing among the Douce fragments, which H. says was attributed by Mr. Douce to Pynson. I saw a volume in your library in 1866, lettered "Early Printed Fragments," which I was told had belonged apparently to Hearne. The fragm^{ts} were at that time not numbered, but you will know the volume by its containing fragments of Caxton's Troybook and St. Wenefryde and a leaf of Rastell's edition of Chaucer's Assembly of Fowls. It also contained a fragment of the Life of St. Margaret, certainly printed by Pynson in the type which he used before the close of the xvth century.

30 Maria (S.) Virgo Deipara.

    492   1 lamentation of oure lady. 1^d.

Our copy of W. de Worde's edition has the appearance of having been printed between 1502 and 1510, nearer 1502 than 1510. It consists of 6 leaves in 4°.

31 Maria (S.) Virgo Deipara.

> 257   1 the myracke of our lady ypsiiwise [?]. 2^d.
>
> 1193   1 the mirack[l]es of oree lady (with another). 4^d.
>
> The second book in this latter entry, as also in the entry of St. Margaret (675), is the life of St. Katherine, which must therefore have cost 2^d, leaving 2^d as the price of the <u>Miracles of our Lady</u> in both the entries 257 and 1193. Hazlitt mentions two editions printed by W. de Worde, one at Westminster about 1498 in 4° and another in Fleet Street in 1514, 24 leaves in 4°. Of the latter a copy is in the British Museum (Case 21. c.), from which it could easily be seen whether your conjecture is confirmed, by finding in a prominent position some narrative of miracles connected with Our Lady of Ipswich.

32 <u>Maria (S.) Virgo Deipara.</u>

> 1793   1 rosarium beate marie in latino. 3½^d.
> 1807   2 rosaria beate marie. 4^d.
> 1836   1 rosarium beate marie virginis. 1^d.
>
> There is a Rosary bound up with a Sarum Horae printed by Pynson in small narrow 12° in 1514, in Clare College library.

33 <u>Maria (S.) Magdalena.</u>

> 1176   1 the complant of sant magda[lene]. 1^d.
>
> Hazlitt gives an edition printed by W. de Worde in 4° without date, from Caldecott's sale in 1883.

34 <u>Medulla grammaticae.</u>

> 1132   1 medulla grammatice in quaternis. 5^d.
>
> The book known by this name is the English-Latin Dictionary more commonly called the Promptorium Parvulorum, printed by Pynson in 1499 in small folio. You have a copy in your Auctarium, QQ. sup. 2.10 (the last number is probably not correct now). It is called

the Promptorium Parvulorum in the author's preface and Medulla Grammatice in the imprint; but the price here mentioned (5^d) seems to preclude the possibility of Dorne's book being the same as Pynson's.

35 Mundus.

1530   1 mundus a play.   2^d.
  Surely this must be the "Proper new interlude of the World and the Child (Mundus et Infans)," of which a reprint, taken from W. de Worde's edition dated July 17, 1522 (18 leaves in 4°), was presented to the Roxburghe Club by Lord Althorp in 1817. There is nothing to show that there may not have been earlier editions, and the price is not against this identification. With a good deal of careful comparison it would not be difficult after a time to infer from Dorne's prices the actual size of a book.

36 Nobilitas.

1649   1 opusculum de vera nobi[litate].   5^d.
  I was at first tempted to think that this might be Poggio's Liber de nobilitate, which was printed at Antwerp by Gerard Leeu in 1489, 14 leaves in 4°. (CA. 1427). But the price is too high for such a small book, and I think the word vera must have been in the title of Dorne's book.

37 Pamphilus Saxus.

624 1 pamphulus de amore.   3^d.
771 1 pamphulus de amore (with another). 5^d.
  There are several editions with this title. We have one printed by Ger. Leempt at Utrecht about 1476 in folio (CA. 1352) bound in the same volume with an Ovid De arte amandi and De remedio amoris from the same press. There is also an edition of Pamphilus from the

same press in 4°., of which copies are at Dresden and Wolfenbüttel (CA. 1351). And there is still another edition printed at Cologne in the type of the Augustinus de Fide of 1473, containing 16 leaves in 4°., which I saw in 1875 in the University library at Freiburg in Breisgau. Though headed "Querimonia pamphili," at the end is "Explicit panphilus de amore."

38 Petrus Blesensis.

1897 Epistole petri blesensis. 1. 3^s.
The edition printed at Brussels about 1480-81 (CA. 1403) consists of 208 leaves in small folio, and can hardly fail to be the one offered for sale by Hunt in 1483.

39 Prognostica.

175 1 pron̄osticon in en[glis?] bigls [?]. 2^d.
Can this pronosticon ī en bigls be merely=pronosticon in englis? I am inclined to think it is not impossible. The price is that of the ordinary pronostica in englis (8, 79, 125, 130, 134, 144, 171, 237, 245, 284, 324), though many are sold for a penny, others for 1½^d (called pronosticata in englis, see 24, 45, 234), others again as high as 3½^d (65, 241, 292, 304, 329, 371). The whole class has no doubt perished, as literature; but many of them are yet to be recovered, with care and patience, from contemporary bindings.

40 Restitutiones.

1921 De Restitutionibus [   ].
This is probably the "Opus restitutionum usurarum et excommunicationum" of Franciscus de Platea, of which Hain gives (13034-13040) seven editions, any one of which might have been offered for sale at Oxford in 1483.

41 Roche.

1032   1 sermones quintini ligati in corio ⎫
1039   1 the lyf of sant rocke   ⎭ . 11^d.

As we find four copies of the "Sermones Quintini ligati in corio" (164, 217, 424, 1613) priced 10^d, and one in parchment at the same price (41), as against 632 charged 8^d and 198 sold for 11^d, it is fair to suppose that the Lyf of sant Rocke was a penny book, one of the "Penny Godlinesses" of which Samuel Pepys made such a collection. The cultus of St. Rock was so widely spread at this time, all the recent breviaries and missals having special offices and votive masses connected with him, that the only wonder is that some fragment of an English Life of the saint has not yet been publicly noticed. Here again contemporary bindings are sure to yield the necessary evidence, when the time comes.

42   Sermones tredecim.

179   1 sermones xiii ligati in corio.   8^d.
232   1 sermones xiii ligati in corio ⎫
233   1 bene fundatum   ⎭ . 9^d.
837   1 sermones xiii parue li' in pergameno. 8^d.
876   1 sermones xiii li' in corio   ⎫
877   1 sermones quintini li' in percomeno ⎭ . 1^s 4^d.
1886   sermones xiii 3 quilibet 1^s 4^d.

These seem to be the <u>Sermones tredecim universales</u> of Michael de Hungaria, which were very popular at one time; so much so that seven editions are mentioned printed by John de Westfalia alone at Louvain (CA. 1244-45-47-48-49-50-51). The one in Hunt's list (1886), being double the price of Dorne's, may point to the fact of its being an old book which brought a higher price when in fuller run of popularity.

43   Speculum.

1899   Quinque specula 2 quilibet 3^s 4^d.

Two editions of the five Specula printed at Louvain by Joh. de Westfalia are described by Campbell (CA. 391 and 392), but unfortunately, from want of proper discrimination, both are described as printed about 1483; whereas one of them (392) cannot be later than 1483, and the other, placed first (391), cannot possibly be earlier than 1483. CA. 392 then is almost certainly the book referred to in Hunt's list of 1483. The book consists of five separable parts, though the signatures run through the whole. The five parts are as follows:

(1) Speculum de confessione, with printer's name (sig. a-d).

(2) Speculum aureum anime peccatricis, with printer's name (sig. e-f).

(3) Tractatus artis bene moriendi and Speculum ecclesie (sig. g and h). The Speculum sacerdotum is merely a few paragraphs at the end of the Speculum ecclesie in most of the editions; whence the Speculum ecclesie itself sometimes gets erroneously the name of Speculum sacerdotum, as for instance in CA. 1007.

(4) Speculum humane vite, with printer's name (sig. i-u).

(5) Speculum conversionis peccatorum, with printer's name (sig. x-y).

You have one of the editions in your Auctarium, marked IQ.4.12, but I took no note at the time when I saw it, which of the two editions it was. The earlier one has no hyphens dividing the words at the end of a line, the other has.

44 Sphaera.

1626   1 Spera parua   ⎫ non recepi a mocke⎫
1627   1 Spera heginy [?] ⎭ [these 4 words   ⎬ . 1^s.
                                    erased]

The second book can hardly fail to be a copy of the Poeticon Astronomicon of Hyginus (see Hain 9061-9067). Of these editions n° 9063 (Venice, E. Ratdolt, Jan. 22, 1485, 56 leaves, 4°.) contains the title "Scemmus sphaeraecina secundum Hyginii descriptionem"; and n° 9065

(Venice, Th. de Blavis de Alexandria, June 7, 1488, 56 leaves, 4°.) has the title "Scemma sphericum secundum Hyginij descriptionem."

45   Summa angelica.

    768   1 Suma angelica rowan ligata. 1^s 8^d.
  1488   1 Suma angelica rowan ligata. 1^s 8^d.
  1683   1 Suma angelica lion ligata. 2^s.

This is the great Summa de casibus conscientiae, known as the Summa Angelica long before the death of the author (in 1495), Angelus à Clavasio, a well know Franciscan. Hain mentions 21 editions of the book, though some of them are apparently doubtful. The one printed at Alost by Thierry Martens (CA. 448) consists of 334 leaves of close print in double columns. That its popularity extended/ well into the sixteenth century, so that editions may well have appeared at Lyons and Rouen as above, may be inferred from the fact that Wadding mentions an Italian version of the work published in 1593 (Scriptores Ord. Min. p. 22).

46   Theologia naturalis.

  729   1 textus sententiarum li' in 2^{bus} li' in asse[ribus]
  730   1 theologia naturalis li' in ass[eribus?]   .3^s.
  829   1 theologia naturalis li[gata]. 1^s 4^d.

Theologia naturalis is the entire title as printed on the last page of the Theologia naturalis of Raimundus de Sabunde printed at Deventer by Ric. Paffroed about 1480, F°. 256 leaves. Hain gives two other editions, and from the price I should infer that there may have been others more compressed. You have two copies of the Deventer edition, one among Mr. Douce's xvth century books (n° 158), and one in the Auctarium, marked IQ.3.15.

47   Theorica.

1729   1 theorica planetarum. 1ˢ 6ᵈ.
        Hain gives a Theorica Planetarum under
Gerardus Cremonensis (5824-25) and a Theoricae
Planetarum under Georgius Purbachius (13595-
97). The latter were published with the Sphaericum Opusculum of Joannes de Sacro Busto by
Joannes Regiomontanus or de Monte Regio as
antidotes to the "deliramenta" of Gerardus Cremonensis. There was an ever increasing vital-
ity in this class of literature for a long time,
and it ought not to be difficult, with a little
research, to go far towards identifying the
book which appears in Dorne's list.

48 Thomas Wallensis.

1893   Walensis super psalterium. 1. 5ˢ 4ᵈ.
        There can be little doubt that this is
the book which was printed in London by John
Lettou in 1481, F°. You have a copy in your
Auctarium, marked IQ.4.12, to which Herbert
refers under its old mark before the creation
of the Auctarium. It is printed from an incomplete copy, and from the words of the imprint
"Reuerendissimi domini Valēcii," the final s̄
having been misread as an ī, the work has been
confounded with the commentary of Jacobus
Perez de Valencia (in Spain), which was printed
at that place in 1484 and 1493 (12597-98) according to Hain, who also includes Thomas Wallensis by mistake under the same heading
(12596). The V for W and the absence of the
Christian name would also serve to create the
confusion or at any rate to perpetuate it.

49 Virgilius Maro (Publius).

1078   1 virgilius in englis van 4 quaterni. 2ᵈ.
        You will readily withdraw your identifi-
cation of this with Caxton's edition of the Eney-
dos, which consists of 11 (not 4) quires, and
could not well have been sold for 2ᵈ. The actual
book is no doubt the "Virgilius" printed at Ant-

werp by John Doesborcke in 4°., which does in fact consist of 30 leaves, and therefore (I presume) of 4 quires (van 4 quaterni). You have a copy in the Douce collection; which is placed by mistake among his xvth century books (n° 40), so that you can see and judge for yourself. We have a fragment of it, which I rescued from the binding of an old medical book. The date generally assigned to it is about 1520.
The price is quite suitable when compared with Dorne's prices generally. Hazlitt, who refers to the Douce copy, gives the title thus: "This boke treateth of the lyfe of Virgilius and of his deth, and many maruayles that he dyd in hys lyfe tyme by whychrafte and nygramancye thorough the helpe of the deuyls of Hell."

50 Miscellaneous titles:

Tractatus sacer de^{ls}[?].
817   1 parochiale cura[torum] ⎫
818   1 tractatus sacer de^{ls} ⎬ . 1^s 2^d.
                                ⎭

 This latter entry (818) looks as if it ought to be read Tractatus sacerdotalis; and, though I cannot advance the matter very far, it is as well to refer to CA. 1679, where a "Tractatus sacerdotalis de sacramentis deque divinis officiis" is cited from the Lammens Catalogue, Vol. I, n° 39 (2), as bound up with a copy of Boethius printed at Louvain by Joh. de Westfalia (1486?).

ADDITIONS TO INDEX I (AUTHORS & BOOKS) RENDERED NECESSARY BY THE PRECEDING NOTES

[The numbers refer to my Notes]

Aesopus.
    Esopus grecus, see Valla (Laurentius), Facecie morales alias Esopus grecus, 1.

Angelus à Clavasio.
    Summa Angelica de casibus conscientiae, 45.

Annius (Johannes).
    See Johannes [Annius or Nannis] Viterbiensis.

Antonius de Butrio.
    Speculum de confessione, followed by the Speculum aureum animae peccatricis, the Tractatus artis bene moriendi and the Speculum ecclesiae, the Speculum humanae vitae, and the Speculum conversionis peccatorum, 43.

Augustine (St.), Abp. of Canterbury.
    Miraculum sancti Augustini, 2.

Augustinus (S. Aurelius), Bp of Hippo.
    Miraculum, see Augustine (St.), Abp of Canterbury, Miraculum, 2.

Barclay (Alexander).
    7 Quaterni, 3.

Bassolis (Johannes de).
    See Johannes de Bassoliis.

Bernardus (S.) Clarae-vallensis.
    Modus vivendi, see Gerson (Johannes), De modo vivendi omnium fidelium, 4.

Breviarium.
    Breviarium Praemonstratensium. See Jesus Christ, Festum Nominis Jesu, 21.
    Breviarium Romanum pro fratribus Augustinianis, 5.

Butrio (Antonius de).
    See Antonius de Butrio.

Carmen juvenile.
    See Sulpitius (Johannes) Verulanus, Carmen juvenile, 6.
Cerasinus (St.).
    See Erasmus (St.).
Chronica Angliae.
    Chronica Angliae, 8.
Clavasio (Angelus à).
    See Angelus à Clavasio.
Complot....
    Complot..., 9.
Cookery.
    The book of cookery, 10.
Cremonensis (Gerardus).
    See Gerardus Cremonensis.
Cyclus.
    Cyclus, 11.
Digestum Vetus.
    See Justinianus, Digestum Vetus, 15.
Dionysius Carthusianus.
    See Dionysius de Leeuwis alias Rykel Carthusianus.
Dionysius de Leeuwis alias Rykel Carthusianus.
    Speculum aureum animae peccatricis, see Antonius de Butrio, Speculum de confessione, 43.
    Speculum conversionis peccatorum, see Antonius de Butrio, Speculum de confessione, 43.
Dionysius de Rykel.
    See Dionysius de Leeuwis alias Rykel Carthusianus.
Diurnale.
    Diurnale Sarum, 12.
Erasmus (Desiderius).
    Colloquia, printed by Theodericus Alostensis at Louvain, 13.
    De constructione, 14.
    The life of St. Erasmus, see Erasmus (St.), The life of St. E., 7.
Erasmus (St.).
    The life of St. Erasmus, 7.
Ff.
    Ff Vetus (= Digestum Vetus), see Justinianus, Digestum Vetus, 15.
Franciscus de Platea.
    See Platea (Franciscus de).

French and English.
    French and English, 16.
Gerardus Cremonensis.
    Theorica Planetarum. See Theorica, Theorica planetarum, 47.
Gerson (Johannes).
    De modo vivendi omnium fidelium, 4.
Godeschalcus (Johannes).
    Praeceptorium. See Hollen (Gotteschalcus), Praeceptorium, 17.
Groshede (Master).
    See Grosseteste (Robert), Bp of Lincoln.
Grosseteste (Robert), Bp of Lincoln.
    Husbandry. See Husbandry, The book of Husbandry, 19.
Hackum and Hontigle.
    See Hawking, The book of hawking, 18.
Hawking.
    The book of hawking, 18.
Heginy.
    See Hyginus (C. Julius).
Hollen (Gotteschalcus).
    Praeceptorium divinae legis, 17.
Hugo de sancto Caro.
    Speculum ecclesiae (with the Speculum sacerdotum subjoined), see Antonius de Butrio, Speculum de Confessione, 43.
Hungaria (Michael de).
    See Michael de Hungaria.
Hunting.
    The book of Hunting. See Hawking, The book of Hawking, 18.
Husbandry.
    The book of Husbandry translated by master Groshede (Robert Grosseteste, Bp of Lincoln), 19.
Hyginus (C. Julius).
    Poeticon astronomicon (schema sphaericum), 44.
Hymni.
    Hymni cum notis, 20.
Jacobus Perez de Valencia.
    Commentaria in Psalmos. See Thomas Wallensis, Expositiones super Psalterium, 48.

Jesus Christ.
    Festum Nominis Jesu, 21.
Johannes (S.) Evangelista.
    Glosa super Apocalipsim. See Johannes [Annius or Nannis] Viterbiensis, Glosa super Apocalipsim, 22.
    Saint John Evangelist, an interlude (?), 23.
Johannes [Annius or Nannis] Viterbiensis.
    Glosa super Apocalipsim, 22.
Johannes de Bassoliis.
    Super quarto libro Sententiarum, 24.
Johannes de Bassolis.
    See Johannes de Bassoliis.
Johannes de sancto Laurentio.
    Postillae Evangeliorum dominicalium et aliquorum festorum, 25.
Johannes de Vassolis.
    See Johannes de Bassoliis.
Ipswich (Our Lady of).
    See Maria (S.) Virgo Deipara, The miracles of Our Lady (of Ipswich?), 31.
Justinianus.
    Digestum Vetus, 15.
Laurentius (S.)
    See Johannes de sancto Laurentio.
Leeuwis (Dionysius de).
    See Dionysius de Leeuwis alias Rykel Carthusianus.
Lidgate (John).
    Stans puer ad mensam. See Sulpitius (Johannes) Verulanus, Carmen juvenile (Stans puer ad mensam), translated into English by John Lidgate, 6.
Logica.
    Insolubilia Oxoniae, 26.
Lydgate (John).
    See Lidgate (John).
Lyndewode (Gulielmus).
    Constitutiones provinciales, 27.
Maneken (Carolus).
    Epistolae, 28.
Margaret (St.)
    The life of St. Margaret, 29.
Maria (S.) Virgo Deipara.

The Lamentation of Our Lady, 30.
The Miracles of Our Lady (of Ipswich?), 31.
Rosarium Beatae Mariae Virginis, 32.
Maria (S.) Magdalena.
The Complaint of St. (Mary) Magdalene, 33.
Medulla Grammaticae.
Medulla Grammaticae, 34.
Michael de Hungaria.
Sermones tredecim universales, 42.
Mundus et Infans.
Mundus et Infans, the World and the Child, an interlude, 35.
Nannis (Johannes).
See Johannes [Annius or Nannis] Viterbiensis.
Nobilitas.
Opusculum de vera nobilitate, 36.
Pamphilus Saxus.
De Amore, 37.
Perez (Jacobus) de Valencia.
See Jacobus Perez de Valencia.
Petrus Blesensis.
Epistolae, 38.
Platea (Franciscus de).
Opus restitutionum usurarum ex excommunicationum, 40.
Poggius (Franciscus).
Liber de nobilitate. See Nobilitas, Opusculum de vera nobilitate, 36.
Primarium.
Primarium Praemonstratensium. See Breviarium, Breviarium Praemonstratensium, 21.
Prognostica.
Pronosticon in English, 39.
Promptorium Parvulorum.
See Medulla Grammaticae, 34.
Purbachius (Georgius).
Theoricae Planetarum. See Theorica, Theorica planetarum, 47.
Raimundus de Sabunde.
Theologia naturalis, 46.
Raymundus.
See Raimundus.
Restitutiones.

See Platea (Franciscus de). Opus restitutionum
usurarum et excommunicationum, 40.
Rikel.
See Rykel.
Roch (St.)
The life of St. Roch, 41.
Roche.
See Roch (St.)
Rodericus Zamorensis Episcopus.
Speculum humanae vitae. See Antonius de Butrio,
speculum de confessione, 43.
Rykel (Dionysius de).
See Dionysius de Leeuwis alias Rykel Carthusianus.
Sabunde (Raimundus de).
See Raimundus de Sabunde.
Sermones.
Sermones tredecim. See Michael de Hungaria, Sermones tredecim universales, 42.
Speculum.
Quinque specula, see Antonius de Butrio, Speculum
de confessione, 43.
Speculum aureum animae peccatricis, see Dionysius
de Leeuwis alias Rykel Carthusianus, 43.
Speculum conversionis peccatorum, see Dionysius
de Leeuwis alias Rykel Carthusianus, 43.
Speculum de confessione, see Antonius de Butrio,
Speculum de confessione, 43.
Speculum ecclesiae, see Hugo de sancto Caro, Speculum ecclesiae, 43.
Speculum humanae vitae, see Rodericus Zamorensis episcopus, Speculum humanae vitae, 43.
Speculum sacerdotum, see Hugo de sancto Caro,
Speculum ecclesiae, 43.
Sphaera.
See Hyginus (C. Julius). Poeticon Astronomicon
(Schema sphaericum), 44.
Stans puer ad mensam.
See Sulpitius (Johannes) Verulanus, Carmen juvenile (Stans puer ad mensam), 6.
Sulpitius (Johannes) Verulanus.
Carmen juvenile de moribus puerorum in mensa servandis (Stans puer ad mensam), 6.
--translated into English by John Lidgate, 6.

Summa Angelica.
    See Angelus à Clavasio, Summa Angelica de casibus conscientiae, 45.
Theologia naturalis.
    See Raimundus de Sabunde. Theologia naturalis, 46.
Theorica.
    Theorica Planetarum, 47.
Thomas Wallensis.
    Expositiones super Psalterium, 48.
Tractatus artis bene moriendi.
    See Antonius de Butrio, Speculum de confessione, 43.
Tractatus sacer de1s (?).
    See Tractatus sacerdotalis, 50.
Tractatus sacerdotalis.
    Tractatus sacerdotalis de sacramentis deque divinis officiis, 50.
Valencia (Jacobus Perez de).
    See Jacobus Perez de Valencia.
Valencius.
    See Thomas Wallensis.
Valla (Laurentius).
    Facetiae morales alias Aesopus Graecus, 1.
Virgilius.
    The life of Virgilius, 49.
Virgilius (Publius Maro).
    See Virgilius Maro (Publius).
Virgilius Maro (Publius).
    Virgilius in English. See Virgilius, The life of Virgilius, 49.

INDEX

ABC 53

Alexandrinus, Codex 22

Allix, Peter, History of the Churches of Piedmont 80

Aragon, Catherine of 50

ATHENAE Cantabrigiensis 72

Augustine, Saint, of Canterbury 239

Augustinian Friars used the Roman breviary 240

Barbour, John 47

BARNETT, HOARE & CO. 1

Bede, the Venerable 52

BIBLES, Early 59

Blades, William 23, 24, 26, 48, 56

BLOCK printing 42

Book of Deer 19

BOOKS, how to distinguish and describe their sizes and forms 208-212

Bradshaw, Joseph Hoare 1

Bullock, Henry 60, 62

Bunyan, John 45

CAMBRIDGE University Library 41, 42, 55, 56, 57, 59

CAMBRIDGE University Printers 57

Campbell, M.F.A.G. 24, 25, 26, 73

CANONES. Collectio Canonum Hibernensis:
    Dr. Wasserschleben's edition 221-225
    The Lyons MS. a myth 226
    Existing MSS. 226-229
    Compiled at the beginning of the eighth century 228-229
    Suggested identification of Gildas cited in it 229

Caxton, William 23, 24, 48, 53, 164-173

Chaucer, Geoffrey 4, 13-16, 42-45, 47, 51-53, 160-163

Clark, J.W. 33, 72, 99

Codex Alexandrinus 22

Codex Sinaiticus 21, 42, 95-98

COLLATION of books which have no printed signatures 108

COLOGNE 50

CONTRACTIONS in early printed books 110

Conway, W.M. 32

Cooper, Charles Henry 72

Cooper, Thompson 72

Cox, J. Charles 55, 182

De Deguilleville 45, 49

De Meyer, M.J. 50

Deer, Book of 19

DERBY, Collegiate Church 7, 55

DIURNALE sold In Oxford 244

Dorne, John, bookseller in Oxford 59, 234-266

DUTCH type 132-159

DUTCH woodcuts 132-159

Earle, Professor 19, 42
Ellis, R. 54
Erasmus, St., his life sold by John Dorne 241

Finn, Edmund 46
FORM notation 208-212
Furnivall, F.J. 30, 49, 53, 160

Gaselee, Sir Stephen 30
Gilly, Dr. 93
Gotz, Nicholaus 50
GREEK manuscript 49, 127-131
Greg, Sir Walter 13

Haeghen, Ferdinand Vander 73
Hellinger, Wytze & Lotte 73
HENRY BRADSHAW SOCIETY 11
Henry VIII 50
HERMATHENA, The 60-63
HISPERICA FAMINA 70-71
Historia Ecclesiastica of Bede 52
Holtrop, J.W. 24-26, 31, 73-74
Hope, W.H. St. John 55, 182

Ipswich, Our Lady of Ipswich 252
IRISH books 3, 71-72
Irish Literary Enquirer 46
IRISH missal 174-179

James, Montague Rhodes 2, 11, 18
Jenkinson, F. 19, 31, 61, 62, 70, 72, 75
Johannes de Bassoliis 249

Kingsley, G.H. 53

LAMBETH library 48, 103-105
Lawley, Stephen W. 55
LINCOLN Cathedral 54, 66-68
LITURGICAL works 6-11

McKitterick, David 73-74
Machiels, J. 73
Madan, F. 59, 234-237
MAZARINE Bible 55
MEDIAEVAL SERVICE BOOKS 182-187
Moore, William 20, 93
Morris, R. 47

NOTATION 208-212

ORIENTAL manuscripts 48, 99-102
Ovid 54, 180-181

Palmer, Edward H. 48, 99-102
PANZER, the one true naturalist among bibliographers 206
Pearson, C.H. 25
Pollard, A.W. 13, 70
Proctor, Francis 64

Prothero, G.W.   4, 30, 34, 52, 67

Quiller-Couch, Sir Arthur   10

St. Abbanus   53
St. Abel   53
St. Abranus   53
St. Achea   53
St. Albans   48, 59, 106-126, 216-220
St. Columba's college   5
St. Erasmus   54
SARUM breviary   64
Shirley, Walter W.   47
Siberch, John   60, 62
SIGNATURES in books, their great antiquity   123
Simonides, Constantine   21-22, 95-98
<u>Sinaiticus, Codex</u>   21, 42, 95-98
SIZE notation   208-212
Skeat, W.W.   17, 52
Smith, William   53
SOCIETY OF FRIENDS   1
Stewart, Catherine   1
Stewart, H.F.   72
Stokes, Whitley   34
Stowasser, J.M.   71

Tew, Edmund   127-131
Thackeray, Francis St. J.   55
Thynne, Francis   53, 160-163
Tindale, William   188-207

Tischendorf, Lobegott Friedrich Constantin von   21, 97
Todd, James Henthorn   41, 92
Toyes of an Idle Head, The   58, 213-215
Tuckwell, William   30
Tuke, Sir Bryan   53
Tyrwhitt, Thomas   13-14

Van Der Haghen, Godfried   56, 60, 188-207

Wace, Henry   53
WALDENSIAN manuscripts   19-21, 41, 77-94
Warren, F.E.   174
Wasserschleben, F.W.H.   59, 70, 221-223
WELSH language   51
Wordsworth, Christopher   11, 64, 66
Wright, A. Aldis   19, 42, 49

YORK breviary   55

Zel, Ulrich   3
ZWOLLE, its connection with block books   136